KAMIKAZE

Japan's Suicide Samurai

神風

As we are born aloft as *Samurai* of the Skies.
    Our eyes ever-searching for signs of battle,
See how our outstretched arms carry us forward
    Like divine wings.

Here we are – comrades of the Sacred Land of the Rising Sun!
    Enemy ships are sighted – loud alerts are sounded.
Let us drive them beneath the waves!

Men of the Cherry Blossom Squadrons – rally to the charge!
    As we look down at our base spread below us,
Through the flow of tears that fills up our hearts,
    We can see a fading glimpse of hands waving farewell!

Now is the time for our final, plunging blow.
    We're ready to spill our blood, oh so red.
See how we dive towards the ships in the Seas of the South!

The cool waves will console our departed spirits
    And some day we'll be reborn as cherry blossoms
In the garden of the *Yasukuni-jinja*.

Song: Kamikaze Divine Thunderbolt Corps.
(*Hagoromo-kai* Collection, 1952).

KAMIKAZE
Japan's Suicide Samurai

Raymond Lamont-Brown

ARMS AND
ARMOUR

Arms and Armour Press
An Imprint of the Cassell Group
Wellington House, 125 Strand, London WC2R 0BB

Distributed in the USA by Sterling Publishing Co. Inc.,
387 Park Avenue South, New York, NY 10016-8810.

British Library Cataloguing-in-Publication Data:
a catalogue record for this book is available from
the British Library

ISBN 1-85409-367-3

Designed and edited by DAG Publications Ltd.
Designed by David Gibbons; edited by Michael Boxall;
printed and bound in Great Britain by
Creative Print and Design Wales, Ebbw Vale.

22.46

CONTENTS

ACKNOWLEDGEMENTS

All quotes in the text are acknowledged as they occur, but to the following go the author's special thanks. To Robert Laffant, Paris, for the short line quotes from B. Millot's *L'Epopée Kamikaze* and Calmann-Levy, for the sequence of psychological interpretations concerning kamikaze from Jean Baechler's *Les Suicides*. To the *Hagoromo-kai* for the 'Song of the Kamikaze Divine Thunderbolt Corps'.

Grateful thanks are also extended to Ichiro Ohmi and Naro Naemura for a sight of the research work they carried out in the personal documentation of kamikaze pilots (i.e., letters and diaries). In terms of research too, the author is appreciative for the permission given by Jonathan Stamp, producer, to use the research background contributed to the BBC TV *Timewatch* programme on the kamikaze by Miss Reiko Sakuma and Professors Ikuhiku Hata and Haesuho Naito.

One work, *Japanese Naval Aces and Fighter Units of World War II* by Ikuhiku Hata and Yasuho Izawa is cited for special mention as a basis for individual biographical portraits of kamikaze pilots. The UK and US publishers are Airlife Publishing Ltd., and Naval Institute Press, and the author's grateful thanks go to Airlife Chairman and Managing Director, Alastair Simpson, and Permissions Editor, Patrica A. Seppington of Naval Institute Press, for permission to quote the relevant kamikaze pilot names and career details. Again special mention must be made of the text of *Japan's Longest Day* prepared by the Pacific War Research Society and publishers Burgei Shurju and Kodansha for their 1968 data on the sequence of events leading up to Japan's surrender.

The assistance with source material given by Professor Brian Bond, Department of Military History, King's College, University of London, is gratefully acknowledged; and the author's thanks go to the staff of St Andrews University Library; W. J. R, Gardner, Honorary Secretary, The Society for Nautical Research, London; Chris Heather of the Public Record Office, Kew, Richmond; and Satomi Shinjo, of the Information Section of the British Embassy, Tokyo.

All photographs are individually acknowledged. The author gives grateful thanks to the following for help with compiling the photographic record: P. J. V. Elliott, Keeper of Research and Information Services, Royal Air Force Museum; Mrs M. Bracegirdle, Office Manager, the Aerospace Museum, RAF Museum Hendon; Photographic Department, Imperial War Museum, London; R. C. Sturtivant, Military Aviation Historian; M. D. Richardson, Research Officer, Fleet Air Arm Museum, RNAS Yeovilton; Japan Research Projects.

THE SUICIDE ATTACK PHENOMENON

'I would attack any squadron blockading a port. Nothing could prevent
me from dropping out of the clear blue sky on to a battleship with 400
kilos of explosives in the cockpit. Of course it is true that the pilot would
be killed, but everything would blow up, and that's what counts'.
— *Jules Védrines, French aviation pioneer, pre-1914*

On 23 October 1983 world-wide newspaper headlines announced the story
of the truck-load of explosives, driven by a suicidal Muslim, which crashed
through flimsy defences around the US Marine barracks in Beirut. In the
ensuing explosion 237 US Marines died and 80 were wounded. It was the
first multi-casualty suicide attack US forces had suffered since WWII. Simultaneously another explosion took place at the French military HQ, killing 58
and injuring fifteen, and on 4 November a similar attack was made on the
Israeli HQ at Tyre.

Responsibility was claimed by a pro-Iranian Shiite Muslim group which
called themselves 'The Islamic Holy War', and the human race once again
was confronted by the concept of a fanaticism taken to the extreme of self-
destruction as being a logical extension of terrorism. The motivation of the
WWII kamikaze pilots was deemed to be still alive, and indeed a Japanese
terrorist group known as the Japanese Red Army and based in the Middle
East, had already won their own kamikaze headlines on 31 May 1972 when
they murdered 26 passengers and wounded about 80 others at Tel Aviv
airport. So commentators spoke again of the concept of 'suicide missions'
that had long been forgotten and used the term 'kamikaze'. The description
was quite accurate and a reminder to the world of a suicide phenomenon
that had been considered essentially Japanese. Here at Tel Aviv were three
fanatical Japanese terrorists, with little thought of self-preservation (two of
them died), engaged in horrendous combat from which there was no way
out, completely willing to make the ultimate sacrifice for their political aims.

The kamikaze of WWII were an example *par excellence* of what
psychology theorists such as the French hypothesiser Jean Baechler (*Les
Suicides*, 1975 / *Suicides*, Blackwell, 1979) called practitioners of the 'institute

of sacrifice within the context of war'. Baechler saw the kamikaze of WWII not as suicides for 'patriotic or romantic exultation' but purely as conducting a military technique: 'The search for efficiency and not for gratuitous glory was the overriding aim of the kamikaze phenomenon.' In his book *L'Epopée Kamikaze* (Laffont, 1970), B. Millot quotes a kamikaze instructor who appears to support Baechler: 'The code of the samurai demands that we must always be ready to die, but that does not mean we must commit suicide on the slightest pretext. Our tradition desires that we should live and fight as best we can so as to experience neither regret nor remorse at the moment of death.'

When we look at the development of the kamikaze as a military rank (and divine status), we can see that Baechler was only reflecting part of the truth for the recruitment patterns reveal a multitude of motivations for self-sacrifice. Recruitment began as a strictly voluntary sacrifice, to become an almost obligatory act through the intense enlistment propaganda carried out by the Japanese government. We shall see too, that the kamikaze pilots evolved from four main sources of recruitment.

First came the 'patriotic crusaders' who were all volunteers, usually from *daimyo* or samurai families; they were motivated by nationalistic fervour, military ideals and the concept of chivalry upon which their ancestors had based personal sacrifice to fulfil perceived duties to the state. From this group evolved the ritualisation of the kamikaze before suicide flights (i.e., the wearing of samurai symbols, singing patriotic songs, writing poetry glorifying kamikaze action, composing testamentary last letters home, distributing personal effects and so on).

Next came the 'nation's face savers'. These were recruits who did volunteer, but often for negative reasons, to avoid personal shame in not emulating the deaths of the patriotic crusaders, or to espouse military heroism in order to save the *Kami* land of Japan from humiliating defeat. Like the patriotic crusaders, they too were conformists to the traditions of Japanese society. As the kamikaze Susumu Kitjitsu (1923–45) was to write to his parents: 'I live a quite normal life. Death does not frighten me; my only care is to know if I am going to be able to sink an aircraft carrier by crashing into it.'

By the last few months of the war the third category of recruits emerged: these were the 'young rationalists'. They came mostly straight from higher education, went through hurried training and died to sustain the war effort and to keep Japan free from foreign taint. As B. Millot wrote: 'With a few very rare exceptions, they were the most affectionate, well-educated, least troublesome sons who gave their parents the greatest satisfaction.'

The last group of recruits were also mostly young, the 'appointed dare-devils', who emerged right at the end of the war. It may be noted that among their number were do-or-die delinquents, hell-raisers and those of shady moral reputation and social deviation who, through the drastic measure of suicide, were escaping the legal, civic and social consequences of their behaviour.

And what of the 'kamikaze' of the 1990s? Does the spirit of the self-sacrificing Japanese of WWII live on? The answer is probably yes; that spirit is still to be found among the world's terrorists.

Civil war in Sri Lanka has produced a terrorist violence that incorporates kamikaze tactics. Since 1983 the guerrilla group Liberation Tigers of Tamil Eelam (LTTE) have been fighting Sri Lankan government forces for control of the Tamil majority areas of the NE province from Jaffna in the north to south of Trincomalee in the east. Within the ranks of the Tigers are the Black Tigers, an élite group that includes women who fight as equals of the men.

When bent on suicide missions the Tigers are indistinguishable from peaceable Tamils, and they have become increasingly effective. On 1 May 1993 a Tamil kamikaze assassinated President Ranasinghe Premadasa, and on 4 July 1996 a female Tiger attacked a government motorcade, killing an army commander and 21 others with her torso-strapped bomb.

The Black Tigers are all volunteers, motivated by a resentment of their country's being 'occupied' by the Indian Army and Sri Lankan government forces. Their aim is an independent Tamil homeland within Sri Lanka. The female Tamil Tigers are also fighting for self-liberation from subserviency to men. The Tigers have glamour and prestige, but they are unpaid (most are fed and clothed by sympathisers), and the females in particular have to forswear family life.

The Sri Lankan government dismisses them as 'drugged fanatics', but most Tamil kamikaze are motivated by personal experiences of oppression and army violence. They carry cyanide capsules in case they are captured, but unlike the WWII kamikaze there is no promise of the spiritual reward of a swift passage to paradise after death. Recently they have begun to adopt techniques of Japanese seaborne kamikaze of WWII by ramming government vessels with explosive-crammed boats.

While mentioning the survival of the kamikaze spirit, this book endeavours only to show how and why the Japanese WWII suicide missions came into being. It is open to anyone who studies the history of the kamikaze to form a personal opinion as to whether they were romantic, mysterious, patriotic, insane or just plain desperate in the face of a relentless enemy. In doing so something may be learned about the state of mind of would-be terrorist suicides in the years to come.

CHAPTER ONE

KAMIKAZE: THE FEARSOME AND FASCINATING CONCEPT

'Kamikaze attacks ... were carried out with no possible hope of return. It is clear evidence of our fear of inevitable defeat that no other chance of turning the tide of war was visualised.' — *Taisho Danshaku*, Kantaro Suzuki (1867–1948), *Sori-daijin*, 23 July 1944–16 August 1945, in his *The Phases of Terminating the War.*

Not far from the *Eikoku Taishikan* (British embassy) and the *Kyujo* (Imperial Palace) in Tokyo, is the *Yasukuni-jinja* on Kudan hill, a place of tranquillity and intense national devotion usually overlooked by *gaijin* (foreign) tourists. Its name means 'Shrine for Establishing Peace in the Empire', and it is dedicated to Japan's war dead. In the shrine is the *Yushukan*, which contains an exhibition of emotive wartime artefacts.

During WWII the 4-day 'Extraordinary Grand Festival' beginning on 24 April at the *Yasukuni*, was an important national emotional outpouring at which the 20,005 souls of the war dead were deified. The *Yasukuni-jinja* is a controversial place for here are enshrined personal remembrances and memorials of *all* Japan's war dead including the *Sori-daijin* (prime minister) Hideki 'Kamisori' ('the razor') Tojo (1884–1948) and many other executed war criminals. Even today any Japanese government minister who makes an official visit to the shrine would be technically liable to be stripped of office.

The shrine began as a small memorial hall – the *Shokonsha* ('Shrine for Inviting the Spirits') erected in 1869 to honour the dead of various conflicts since 1853. Its name was changed to *Yasukuni-jinja* in 1879. With the wars against China (1894–5), Russia (1904–5), and WWI (when the Japanese fought on the side of the Allies against Germany), the hall expanded. Since 29 June 1896 the shrine has been officially dedicated to the repose of the spirits of all Japan's war dead. It was destroyed in the *Kanto Dai-Shinsai* (Great Earthquake Disaster of the Kanto Plain) of 1 September 1923, but was rebuilt in 1934. And in this complex today the displays of the dead of the *Dai Toa Sen* (Great East Asian War, as the Japanese call WWII) include relics of the kamikaze suicide pilots, from an *Ohka* suicide attack bomber to a *kaiten* 'dare-to-die' human torpedo. A memorial to the *Ohka* dead is to be found at the Kenchoji Temple, a headquarters of the Buddhist religion at Kamakura.

For decades since the passing of the 1947 Fundamental Law of education, the *Mombusho* (Ministry of Education) has outrageously distorted history textbooks in order to place Japan always in a favourable light. Even the courts have backed the *Mombusho* with rulings that such outrages as the '1937 Rape of Nanking' where, on 13 December 1937, *Taisho* (General) Iwane Matsui, Commander-in-Chief of the Central China Area Army, unleashed his forces to slaughter and maim about 300,000 Chinese, must be softened in Japan's favour.

Since the beginning of the 1990s, though, the *Mombusho* has permitted new textbooks to give more detailed accounts of WWII. This has prompted a nation-wide examination of wartime activities concerning Japan, and has spawned a new interest in the various kamikaze attempts.

Present at the *Yasukuni-jinja* on a regular basis are groups of war veterans and representatives of such as the *Nihon Isokukai* (Bereaved Families Association), petitioning the public to sign requests for the shrine to be re-instated as the official war memorial. It was proscribed as a war shrine – *ergo* a focal point for the fanatical Japanese militarism of the 1930s – after the Japanese surrendered to the Allies on 14 August 1945, and was reduced to a simple shrine by the *Nihon Koku Kempo*, the New Constitution, of 3 May 1947. As time passes, according to some sections of the Japanese press, the spirits of the dead kamikaze 'cry out' for honourable, official recognition through the members of the 'Thunder Gods Association' who meet annually at the *Yasukuni-jinja* on 21 March (the day on which the first *Ohka* suicide attack was made).

Japan never had a self-governing Air Service, the Naval Air Service being organised as a synthesised section of the Navy, and the Japanese Army Air Service as an integral part of the Army. Both developed their own aircraft and training programmes. Within the Japanese High Command System, the Emperor as Commander-in-Chief of the Army and Navy controlled the Air Services through the various Imperial Headquarters Agencies. The Japanese Naval Air Organisation is shown in the diagram.

During the period of the development of the kamikaze there were sixteen *daitai* (squadrons); eight *chutai* (divisions); four *shotai* (sections), and two *buntai* (pairs) in naval service. Purists might like to note in passing that Japanese air groups were not numbered or read in sequence. So for example it is correct Japanese practice to write *Kokutai-Ichi-San-Ichi* for 'Air Group

131'; although it is Western practice among historians to refer to '131st Air Group'.

The Navy Air Service was directed by the *Gunreibu* (Navy General Staff Office), the *Kaigun Sho* (Navy Ministry) and the *Koku Hombu* (Naval Aviation Headquarters). Likewise the Army Air Service was organised through the *Sambo Hombu* (Army General Staff Office), the *Rikugunsho* (War Ministry) and the *Rikugun Koku Sokambu* (Inspector-General of Aviation). There were five *Kokugun* (Air Armies), each with its own area. It is important to note that the *Dai Nippon Teikoku Kaigun* (Imperial Japanese Navy) was autonomous from the *Dai Nippon Teikoku Rikugun* (Imperial Japanese Army) and there was serious rivalry between them; their mutual jealousy deprived each other access to arsenals, strategy experience and combat discipline.

It was not until the evolving Allied attack on the *Nansei Shoto* (main island *Okinawa Gunto*) that there were any official orders for co-operation between the Army and Navy. On 20 March 1945 the Japanese Imperial General Staff issued this directive: 'The Navy will have the Army's careful co-operation ... Each service is directed to concentrate its full strength to attack and crush the American Navy ...' No one had considered this before. For six years the Army and Navy had paid lip service to each other's needs, and even up to as late as February 1944, when the Allies surrounded the Japanese in the

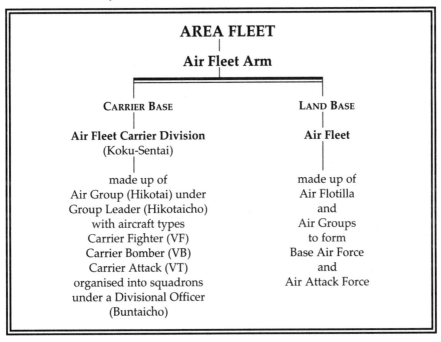

AREA FLEET
|
Air Fleet Arm

CARRIER BASE	LAND BASE
Air Fleet Carrier Division (Koku-Sentai)	**Air Fleet**
made up of Air Group (Hikotai) under Group Leader (Hikotaicho) with aircraft types Carrier Fighter (VF) Carrier Bomber (VB) Carrier Attack (VT) organised into squadrons under a Divisional Officer (Buntaicho)	made up of Air Flotilla and Air Groups to form Base Air Force and Air Attack Force

Solomon Islands, the two services ignored each other. And even when they were to co-operate at Okinawa the chain of command was complicated. For instance, the naval bases in the *Nansei Shoto* were under the command of *Chujo* (Lieutenant-General) Mitsuru Ushijima, Commander, 32nd Army, while all the attack forces were under *Chujo* (Vice-Admiral) Soemu Toyoda.

Five key senior naval officers were to stand out as promoters of kamikaze attacks with ultimate enthusiasm and diligence when all was thought lost; and their names are forever associated with the history of the kamikaze:

Chujo Soemu Toyoda, Commander-in-Chief, Combined Fleet.
Chujo Koshiro Oikawa, Chief of the Naval General Staff (after initial reluctance).
Chujo Takijiro Onishi, Commander, 1st Naval Air Fleet (fanatical 'Father of the kamikaze')
Chujo Matome Ugaki, Commander, 5th Naval Air Fleet.
Chujo Ryunosuke Kusaka, Commander-in-Chief, 5th Naval Air Fleet (another late convert to suicide attacks).

No Army commander was to be their equal in kamikaze organisation, although several were to be greatly involved.

The Japanese Air Armies were developed into *hikoshidan* (air divisions), *hikodan* (air brigades), and three *hikosentai* (air regiments) of three *hikojo chutai* (air companies). The *Koku Chiku* or *Shireibu* (Air Sector Control) had direction of three *hikojo daitai* (air battalions) of three *shotai* (platoons). A back-up network of construction units, repair depots and navigational regiments completed the Army Air Service which also sported its own *Koku Tsushin Rentai* (Air Signal Regiment). The Navy had its own command structure of a Base Air Force, Air Flotillas and an Air Group leading from the Air Fleet under the command of an Area Fleet.

By the outbreak of WWII Japanese schoolboys (*shonen hikohei*) from the age of fourteen were receiving *koku* (aviation) training (with an emphasis on the use of gliders) as an extension of the normal Japanese military training within the education system from the age of eight. Indeed elementary instruction in air mechanics was given from primary level. Those destined for an aviation career were sent on a 3-year course. After a primary year at a general aviation school at Tokyo or Otsu, all students were graded into pilots, signalmen or mechanics and sent to specific training establishments. The *tokuso* (cadet pilots), for instance, were sent to the garrison town of

Utsunomiya, or to Kumagai. There they spent two years, the last year as youth soldiers in the Army. Candidates with special aptitude would omit the first year and go directly to the flying school at Tachiarai. Here they would train on the 480hp biplanes, the Model 95 Ki–9 trainers known colloquially as *akatombo* (red dragonflies).

Pilots for the Army Air Service were sent to one of eight training schools; six in mainland Japan, one in Chosen (the Japanese colonial territory of Korea) and one in Manchuquo (Japan's puppet kingdom of Manchuria, ruled for them by the ex-Emperor of China, Pu Yi). After basic training candidates were graded to bomber, fighter or reconnaissance pilots, gunners and technicians. Advanced training was given to the most able.

Before the war Army Air Service training took three and a half years from enlistment to graduation as a pilot; as the needs of war escalated, the training course was gradually reduced to ten months and then to three months, with emphasis on theoretical training rather than actual flying. This meant that no set training in navigation and dead reckoning, combat techniques or even simple aerobatics was given. So by the time of the Battle of Rabaul in 1943, poorly trained teenage pilots were being thrown at the enemy with high casualties.

At the outbreak of the war, in contrast to their European and US counterparts, Japanese air commanders favoured various light aircraft with low wing-load and good manoeuvrability; the ability to execute steep turns being highly rated. And these characteristics were largely responsible for the initial victories scored by the Army and Navy Air Services. Japan of course lacked the large strategic bombers such as the US Boeing B–17 Fortress and B–29 Superfortress.

During WWII Western observers found the Japanese system of numbering and naming aircraft very complicated and confusing, and the Allies evolved a nickname code. For instance the *Aichi Tokei Denki KK Aichi D3A2* became 'Val'. Functional letters A–S appear alongside the manufacturer's letter. So an A6M2 might indicate that the Zero aircraft was a fighter (A), the sixth (6) to go into Imperial Japanese Navy service, built by Mitsubishi Jukyogo KK (M), of which it was the second version.

Representative aircraft in the Navy Air Services included: Model *Zeroshiki Kanjo Sentoki* (shortened to *Zerosen* 'Zero' fighter, Mitsubishi, 1940, with a range of 420 nautical miles); Model 96 (Mitsubishi, 1936); *Shiden* (modified, Kawasaki, 1941); *Hayate* (Nakajima Ki 84, 1944); *Saiun* (Nakajima, 1944); and flying-boats 97 and 2 (Kawasaki of 1937 and 1942).

The Army Air Service had a long-range aircraft whose streamlined fuselage gave it a high speed. Of limited firepower, it was mostly used for reconnaissance and photographic sorties over a wide area. Representative aircraft of the Army Air Service were the Models 97 and 100 (Mitsubishi 1937 and 1940).

Japanese pilots and their aircraft were not taken very seriously by the Western powers in the 1930s and the early war years, largely because of racial prejudice; Western strategists averred that the Japanese were short-sighted, suffered from night blindness and disequilibrium. They also dismissed Japanese equipment as third rate. This arrogance helped the Japanese to make rapid progress in the initial stages of the war.

'Kamikaze', when used as an absorbed English word, has a much more extensive meaning than when it was originally applied in Japanese to suicide crash-dive pilots only. Thus kamikaze can be dealt with historically to cover every element of the Japanese fighting man's willing eagerness to volunteer for certain death. But from October 1944 to August 1945 the kamikaze spirit embodied in systematic suicide was to be a phenomenon unprecedented in history. Its philosophy permeated the nation; as the war drew to an end, Japan's propaganda machine was calling all Japanese nationals *Tokko Gunjin* (Special Attack Services).

For days after Japan's surrender, the imperial plaza outside the *Kyujo* was stained with the blood of many non-combatant suicides who killed themselves as an apology to the Emperor for losing the war and humiliating the *Kodo* – his sacred reign. In February 1941 the *Naimu Daijin Danshaku* Kiichiro Hiranuma had made a speech to three thousand primary school teachers at Hibuya Hall in Tokyo, to celebrate the '2601st Anniversary of the Founding of the Japanese Empire'. His words now rang in the memories of the Japanese, exacerbating their shame:

'Japan's national polity is unique in the world. Heaven sent down Niningi-no-Mikoto [grandson of Sun Goddess Amaterasu-o-Mikami] to Kishihara in Yamato Province with a message that their posterity should reign over and govern Japan for ages eternal. It was on this happy day, 2601 years ago, that our first Emperor, Jimmu, ascended the Throne. Dynasties in foreign countries were created by men. Foreign kings, emperors and presidents are all created by men, but Japan has a Sacred Throne inherited from the Imperial Ancestors, Japanese Imperial Rule, therefore, is an extension of Heaven. Dynasties created by men may collapse, but the Heaven-created Throne is beyond men's power.'

And more than a thousand Japanese army and navy senior officers propelled their souls to the *Yasukuni-jinja* rather than give up the fight. For many it was the ultimate act of protest for denying Japanese defence of the concept of *Hakko Ichiu* (Eight Corners of the Whole World Under one Rule, i.e., Japanese domination), and the extended empire that they had forged into the *Dai Toa Kyozonken* (Great East Asia Co-Existence Sphere – the Japanese euphemism for occupied territories).

What exactly was it that made the Japanese fighting man – and, for that matter, the ordinary Japanese citizen – volunteer with such ardent intent for certain death in defence of their country? The answer lies in the Japanese concept of suicide in the face of humiliation and family shame – and *Bushido*.

CHAPTER TWO

BUSHIDO AND THE SPLENDID DEATH

'What is the duty today? It is to fight.
What is the duty tomorrow? It is to win.
What is the daily duty? It is to die.'

— Last diary entry of Chu-i Heiichi Okabe (1923–45) of the
Shichisho Butai Kamikaze Unit No 2.

With the Meiji Restoration of 1868, Japan was set on the road of transformation from an introspective feudal state to an outward-looking nation. On 13 February 1867 Mutsuhito – who took the reign-name of Meiji (Enlightened Rule) – son of Emperor Komei, succeeded to the *Takamikura* (Imperial Throne of Japan) and personally took the reins of government from the hands of the *Shogun* (generalissimos) who for centuries had ruled Japan with unlimited powers through puppet emperors. Among the new political changes enacted under the new reign, Meiji's government endorsed the age-old twin virtues of loyalty and filial piety. Again at this time the medieval notion of *chu* (total loyalty), to one's feudal lord was transformed into loyalty to the *tenno* (emperor) who, as a *kami* (living god), became an integral element of the state religion of *Shinto*. This loyalty was formally articulated into the *Gunjin Chokuyu* of 1882, known as the 'Imperial Rescript to Soldiers and Sailors'.

On 3 January 1941 Tojo (then Army Minister) gave the spirit of the *Gunjin Chokuyu* a more immediately relevant boost by instructing that a new official code of ethics be published and given to every member of the armed forces. It was called the *Senjin Kun* (Ethics of Battle) and included this exhortation:

'Do not think of death as you use up every ounce of your strength to fulfil your duties. Make it your joy to use every last bit of your physical and spiritual strength in what you do. Do not fear to die for the cause of everlasting justice. Do not stay alive in dishonour. Do not die in such a way as to leave a bad name behind you.'

So every Japanese soldier, sailor and airman believed that he had a sacred mission. This was to die for their Emperor (all wars in his name were holy), and for this sacrifice they had the ultimate reward of *Senshi* (death in battle). Consequently it was never necessary to command a Japanese fighting man to fight to the last round, then perish; for to turn one's back on the enemy and flee brought dishonour to the name and to *Dai Nippon Teikoku* (Empire of Great Japan).

Military training was harsh and all were taught that death was destiny. The suicide charge was an everyday Japanese wartime weapon. Families were exhorted to do nothing to dissuade combatants to thwart an honourable death, and many officers had their funeral rites performed before leaving home for the front. And among servicemen about to engage the enemy the catch phrase was 'See you in *Yasukuni-jinja*'.

It is well known that the Japanese have a strongly ritualised and stylised tradition of self-disembowelment known as *seppuku* (they regard the term *hara-kiri* as being vulgar). For centuries it had been a badge of courage and honour reserved for the third level of Japanese social class, the *samurai*. With the coming of Emperor Meiji and his revitalising of Japan as a foreign power, the increased amount of stress in Japanese society – from loss of face abroad to letting down the emperor at home – there was a marked increase in suicides. Today suicide is still the inspiration of dramas, novels, plays and films, and newspapers monitor such incidences for their news value. Perhaps the most famous suicide in recent times was that of the fanatical kamikaze devotee, the writer Yukio Mishima, who killed himself on 25 November 1970 after exhorting soldiers of the Japanese Self-Defence Force to rise with him against the post-war democracy that had denied Japan her military/kamikaze spirit.

Compared to other countries and cultures Japan has always had a rather high suicide rate; a fact proved when suicides were first reported in the *Japanese Empire Statistical Year Book, 1882*. Again, unlike the West, the rate of suicides among individuals below 30 and above 60 is considerably higher than among those of middle years. This was to be reflected during WWII; most of the kamikaze were under 30 and those who suffered most loss of face by defeat were over 60. The year 1936 was marked by the *coup d'état* known as the *Niniroku Jiken* (26th February Incident) which pushed Japan into the role of militarism. Suicides thereafter declined as Japan's international confidence/arrogance increased so that the incidence of kamikaze suicides was given a greater prominence.

Premeditated suicide then has long been an institution in Japan. The motivation for it and its ecstasy of enactment is without world parallel. In

WWII Japan suicide was linked not only to imperial devotion, but with national and family pride and duty.

To engender national pride, all Japanese were indoctrinated with a medieval emotionalism that Japan was superior and that it was a divine mission to liberate the Orient from Western influence. Suicide brought expiation for any perceived surrender to that aim. Each Japanese had a personal slant on when that atonement should occur. For instance, following the London Naval Conference of 1930, the Japanese staff officer Chu-i Kusukara, who considered that Japan had been humiliated by Britain and the USA at the conference by the agreed limits on submarines and auxiliary surface craft, redeemed himself by committing ritual suicide with his officer's sword while kneeling in his pyjamas in the narrow berth of a railway sleeping-compartment.

The religious and philosophical base of this obsession can be simply stated. *Shinto* ('The Way of the Gods'), the state religion, melded nature worship and ancestor veneration with devotion to the Emperor as the direct descendant of Amaterasu-o-Mikami, the Goddess of the Sun and the Great Ancestress of the Japanese. This was interlarded with Buddhism (which found its way to Japan in 552) whose principles included a quartet of thoughts which were fundamental to the military mind of 1930s Japan: Liberation of mankind from earthly ties, linked with an Attainment of Truth through insensitivity to suffering, with the renunciation of attachment to physical things and an impassive attitude to death.

All this merged with *Bushido* (*do* the way of the *bushi* 'warriors'), a perceived code of honour upon which every *samurai* (alternative to *bushi*) was expected to base his conduct. Martial spirit, skill in weaponry, absolute loyalty, personal honour, devotion to duty, the courage to sacrifice one's life in battle were all fundamentals of *Bushido*. But all of these had been encapsulated in the Japanese philosophy of *kokutai* (fame and honour for one's country) during the Edo Period (1600–1868). As A. Morgan Young pointed out in *The Rise of the Pagan State* (1939): '*Bushido* was probably invented mainly for foreign consumption.' The word found its way into the dictionary in the early 1900s following the seminal work on the subject by the Imperial Nipponese Army apologist Dr Inazo Nitobe, author of *Bushido. The Soul of Japan* (1905). Nitobe used *Bushido* to romanticise the *samurai* tradition.

Bushido had become somewhat old fashioned by the turn of the 19th century, but was still practised by the old *samurai* class families. For instance, when the Sino–Japanese and Russo–Japanese War hero, *Taisho* Moresuki

Nogi (*b*.1849) heard of the death of Emperor Meiji in 1912, he and his wife Shizuko decided to commit *goi shinju* (a family suicide by mutual consent) on the morning of the imperial funeral; and they did it according to their *Bushido* beliefs.

Thus *Bushido* was a code of honour, but when it was revived in the 1930s as part of the ideological equipment of the military regime, its ethics were seen as perverted by the West. This opinion was underlined with the publication of such books as *Bamboo and Bushido* (1955) by A. G. Allbury – recounting Japanese WWII atrocities – and *The Knights of the Bushido* (1958) by Lord Russell of Liverpool who averred that because *Bushido* said that 'it was ignominious to surrender to the enemy ... the Geneva Prisoner of War Convention of 1929 was never ratified by Japan'. Yet although Lord Russell linked *Bushido* with the bestialities of the Japanese POW camps, the kamikaze upheld *Bushido* as precepts of great honour.

Out of the traditions of *Bushido* the kamikaze forged their own code. Here, for instance, is *The First Order of the Kamikaze*:

'Do not be in too much of a hurry to die. If you cannot find your target, turn back; next time you may find a more favourable opportunity. Choose a death which brings the maximum result.'

If nothing else, it was a convenient interpretation of the age-old code. Japan's kamikaze were not motivated by hatred of the enemy nor by the avenging of dead comrades. It is clear from such surviving personal testimonies as Ichiro Omi's anthology *Kike Wadatsumi no Koe* ('Harken to the Ocean Voices'; Tokyo 1952) that they drew from *Bushido* ethics a duty to protect motherland Japan from foreign pollution and to screen their families from danger. The kamikaze express a debt of *on* (gratitude) for having been born Japanese and to the Emperor as the embodiment of *kokutai*. Here is testimony of this from the letter of *Chu-i* Teruo Yamaguchi (1923–45), who graduated from the Amakusa Air Group to the 12th Air Flotilla, to his *chichiui* (revered father) before he flew to his death:

'... it is of no avail to express it now, but in my twenty-three years of life I have worked out my own philosophy.

'It leaves a bad taste in my mouth when I think of the deceits being played on innocent citizens by some of our wily politicians. But I am willing to take orders from the high command, and even from the politicians, because I believe in the polity [*kokutai*] of Japan.

'The Japanese way of life is indeed beautiful, and I am proud of it, as I am of Japanese history and mythology which reflect the purity of our ancestors

21

and their belief in the past ... That way of life is the product of all the best things which our ancestors have handed down to us. And the living embodiment of all wonderful things out of our past is the Imperial Family which, too, is the crystallisation of the splendour and beauty of Japan and its people. It is an honour to be able to give my life in defence of these beautiful and lofty things.'

The philosophy of *Bushido* brought a mental calm to the kamikaze. From their bases in the Philippines, Taiwan and Kyushu men went to their deaths with no apparent morbid anxiety. In the days leading up to their final attacks, the pilots went about their duties with conscientious devotion. And during rest periods they read, sang, played cards and listened to gramophone records, all apparently with a strange detachment. Their last personal acts were performed in a ritualistic calm; belongings distributed among friends and comrades; a final toast drunk together; last letters written home, many inscribed on scrolls or cloth in the traditional calligraphy they had learned as children. Kamikaze pilots always retained copper coins in their pocket to make up 3 *sen* (100 *sen* = 1 *yen*), the mythologically purported fare to take their souls across *Sanzu-no-kawa* (the Buddhist Styx).

Throughout the personal documentation of the kamikaze, from letters home to diary entries, et cetera, there is a strong mix of traditional *Shinto* and *Buddhist* philosophy, and the medieval tales that emerged in parallel. One source of inspiration to go out to the 'Splendid Death' of the kamikaze came from the *Shi-ju-shichi Shi no Hanashi* ('The Story of the Forty-Seven Samurai').

These warriors, without a master (so they were called *ronin*), were vassals of Asano Naganori, Lord of the Castle of Ako in the province of Harima. In the spring of 1701 Asano and another *daimyo* (feudal lord) named Date Munehara, were delegated to entertain an Imperial Envoy. Because they were young and inexperienced in the ways of the court, the *Shogun* appointed another high official, Kira Yoshinaka, to assist them. Kira, a greedy, conceited old man, berated the unfortunate Asano for his lack of knowledge. One day, unable to control his anger any longer, Asano challenged Kira, and wounded him in a scuffle. Asano was ordered by the Shogunate to commit *seppuku*. To cut a rambling story short, the House of Asano was humiliated and sequestrated, and handed over by the chief councillor of the Asano household, Yoshio Oishi.

In the meantime, Oshio and a band of forty-six *ronin* had attacked Kira's mansion in retribution and succeeded in killing him on 14 December 1702. In true *samurai* style Oishi reported what they had done to the magistrate and they retired to the Sengakuji Temple at Takanawa. They were condemned to commit *seppuku* in penance and were all buried beside the grave of their lord at Sengakuji.

Tales of the ancient *samurai* became very popular in Japan as the desperation of their war plight worsened, and among the kamikaze there was a certain fascination with the *Hagakure* (lit. 'Hidden among the Leaves'), an 18th-century collection of writings on 'The Way of the Samurai' compiled by the warrior-turned-priest, Jocho Yamamoto (1659–1719). The work appealed to them because the best known quote from the *Hagakure* (recited still today by those who have never read the book) is: 'I have discovered that the way of the Samurai is death.' Yamamoto went on to say:

'In a fifty-fifty life or death crisis, simply settle it by choosing immediate death. There is nothing complicated about it. Just brace yourself and proceed ...

'One who chooses to go on living having failed in his mission will be despised as a coward and a bungler ...

'In order to be a perfect *samurai*, it is necessary to prepare oneself for death morning and evening, day in and day out.'

Following the tenets of the *Hagakure* and inspired by Yamamoto's line 'Men must be the colour of cherry blossom, even in death', the kamikaze when preparing for death dressed themselves as immaculately as possible. Some even inscribed a quote from the *Hagakure* on their *hachimaki* (headbands). (After the war, incidentally, many copies of the *Hagakure* were destroyed so that they would not be read by the Occupation authorities; families with kamikaze sons believed that possession of the book would label them as 'dangerous and subversive'.)

Some kamikaze made themselves mascots depicting the *gunshin* (war gods) of old. The army kamikaze chose the war god Hachiman, the posthumous title of the Emperor Ojin (370–310 BC), son of the warrior Empress Jingu Kogo, who had been deified for his exploits; families sent their pilot relatives *nosatsu* (votive cards) from Hachiman's chief shrines such as that at Kamakura. Army *kamikaze* also favoured the military hero Saito Takamori (1827–77) who had been Commander-in-Chief of the Imperial Bodyguard. Minatogawa was the war god of the Navy, but the navy kamikaze particularly favoured as their patron Saint Masashige Kusunoki (1294–1336) the paradigm of the Japanese loyalist hero. On being defeated in battle, Masashige committed *seppuku*. In 1872 his shrine was erected at Minatogawa on the site of the farmhouse where he died.

As the time drew near for the final take-off the kamikaze would be summoned for a final briefing. They would chat nonchalantly as to how best strike the enemy. As one commander said: 'Such talk, always seemed more like a discussion of a good fishing place than an analysis of a rendezvous with death.'

Historians aver that the spirit of *Bushido* was a great Japanese strength. In it though, there were the seeds of weakness. The belief that Japan's fighting men were the reincarnation of *samurai* and that the holy spirit of *Bushido* would overcome military shortcomings, led the Japanese high command sorely to under-estimate the potential effectiveness and extent of the US military might.

CHAPTER THREE

PREPARING FOR JAPAN'S LAST THROW

'Everyone talks about fighting to the last man, but only the Japanese actually do it.' — *Field Marshal William Slim (1891–1970), Supreme Allied Commander SE India*

At dawn on 18 April 1942, some 668 miles to the east of Tokyo, two US carriers and a cruiser of Task Force 16 were discovered by the Japanese picket boat *Nitto Maru No 23*. Less than half an hour later the Japanese vessel had sunk, and Vice Admiral William 'Bull' Halsey, aboard the carrier *Enterprise* set in motion what was to be a shattering blow to the national belief that Japan's homeland was invulnerable to air attack.

Presuming that the picket boat would have alerted the headquarters of the *Teikoku Kaigun Ringo Kantai* (Imperial Japanese Navy Combined Fleet), Halsey ordered a flight of sixteen US Army B–25B Mitchell bombers to take off from the 20,000-ton carrier *Hornet*. This was to be the famous Doolittle Raid organised by Halsey in conjunction with Lieutenant Colonel (later General) James H. Doolittle, the distinguished ex-Shell Oil Company aviator and aeronautical engineer. The centre of Tokyo was bombed as were the city's docklands and peripheral steel plants and oil refineries. Other targets were hit at Osaka, Yokohama, Nagoya and Kobe, but although extensive damage was done to the Kawasaki aircraft factory, the raid had little material effect and would be the last on Japan for many months. All sixteen aircraft crash-landed in China and their crews were rescued by the Chinese.

The shock of the raids was soon to be compounded for the Japanese High Command when, during 4–6 June 1942, *Chujo* Chuichi Nagumo, Commander, lst Air Fleet (First Carrier Striking Force), was defeated at *Middoue Kaizen* (Battle of Midway), losing four aircraft-carriers: his flag ship the *Akagi* (36,500 tons), *Soryu* (18,800 tons), *Akaga* (33,693 tons) and *Hiryu* (20,250 tons). This was the turning-point of the war in the Allies' favour, but so tight was the censorship that the Japanese people did not learn of the defeat until 1951 when Nagumo's Air Unit Commander, Mitsuo Fuchida, and Aviation Officer Masatake Okumiya wrote a book on the subject.

By 1944 many in the Japanese High Command were realising that victory over the Allies was unlikely. Great psychological blows had been added to the Doolittle raids by the deaths of two *Taisho*. Grand Admiral Isoroku Yamamoto (*b*.1884), the Harvard-educated Commander-in-Chief of the Combined Fleet, had been targeted by P–38s of Major John Mitchell's 339th Squadron and shot down at Buin, Bougainville, Solomon Islands on 18 April 1943 while on an inspection tour. And his successor, Admiral Mineichi Koga, was killed in an air crash, off Cebu, Philippines, on 31 March 1944 while transferring his headquarters to Davao to counter an expected US attack on the Palau Islands.

During 18–20 June 1944 at the Battle of the Philippine Sea (usually referred to by the Japanese as the Marianas Sea Battle), *Taisho* Jisaburo Osawa's 1st Mobile Fleet had faced Vice Admiral Marc A. Mitscher's Task Force 58, and the outcome rendered the Imperial Japanese Navy's Combined Fleet incapable of carrying out any future offensive programmes. Japan's merchant fleet was also virtually destroyed, and the casualty rate among navy pilots had been so high that there were not enough to crew the remaining aircraft. But in any case, the Japanese were hopelessly outnumbered in aircraft, and by September 1944 all air bases in the Marianas, Carolinas and the north-east of New Guinea were in US hands. There was a need of desperate measures, but although the kamikaze were a last reckless throw by a desperate enemy, this Special Attack Force was not formed on the spur of the moment.

From the time of the earliest air encounters some Japanese and American pilots had deliberately crashed their disabled aircraft into enemy targets. For instance, on 5 June 1942, Captain Richard E. Fleming of the Marine Corps rammed his aircraft into the 11,200-ton Mogami Class heavy cruiser *Mikuma* at the Battle of Midway; the vessel sank next day. By August 1942, when the Japanese were getting into difficulties with the US Invasion of Guadalcanal and the Solomon Islands, the psychological background to Japanese defensive fighting changed. There was an escalation of the fanatical and self-destructive military attacks wherein the Japanese soldiers screamed *banzai!*

Following his appointment as Senior Deputy Chief of Army General Staff (second to *Sori-daijin* Hideki Tojo), *Taisho* Jun Ushiroku put forward the idea that hard-pressed soldiers in the New Guinea and Bougainville theatres should carry primed charges on their backs and act as *nikudan* ('flesh bullets'); the idea being that they should throw themselves under enemy tanks. The Imperial General Staff agreed to the tactic, but it produced so much criticism among the *Shokan* (Generals and Flag Officers) that Ushiroku was promoted to *Rikugun Koku Sokambu* (Inspector-General of Military Aviation) to get him away from the direction of any strategic decisions in the Pacific islands. But Fleming's example and Ushiroku's sentiments had taken seed.

The deliberate crashing into enemy targets and *kesshi* ('dare-to-die') tactics began to escalate from 1942. On 26 October 1942 the US carrier *Hornet* was attacked by Aichi 99 dive-bombers, and later pilots of Nakajima 97 torpedo-bombers took their aircraft to total destruction against *Hornet* to hasten her end. During March 1943, too, the Inspector-General of Army Aviation and Chief of the Army Aeronautical Department, Takeo Yasuda, clandestinely commended a *Tokkotai* (Special Attack Corps – a term used from as early as 18 December 1941) training programme. And on 8 May 1943 *Gunso* (Flight-Sergeant) Oda of the 2nd Squadron, from a base in New Guinea, crashed his Ki–43 *Hayabusa* ('Falcon') into a B–17, while protecting a convoy making for Madan. The 'Strategy of Suicide' steadily grew in direct proportion to the desperation of Japan's plight.

Two other forms of attack were discussed and tried out at this time by the Japanese, namely skip bombing and ramming. Zero fighters were fitted with 250kg bombs which were released 200 to 300 yards away from an enemy ship. There was a great risk of damage to the fighter either from the bombs bouncing back or from an explosion on the target, but a successful training programme was carried out in the Bohol Strait, near the Cebu base, under the eye of *Taisho* Kimpei Teraoka, Commander of 1st Air Fleet. The programme was abandoned when the US attack on Davao on 9–10 September 1944 wiped out 50 per cent of the participating 201st Air Group.

The tactic of ramming was successfully used by *Chu-i* Tadashi Minobe's night-fighter squadron. On 5 September 1944 *Junshikan* (warrant officer) Yoshimasa Nakagawa and Senior *Junshikan* Isamu Osumi rammed a B–24 with their Gekko ('Irving') aircraft. But the Japanese were losing impetus. Protective armour had been sacrificed in the interests of increased speed and manoeuvrability, but their aircraft were not a patch on the Grumman F6F–5 Hellcat fighters. And the Japanese were unable to produce enough aircraft to make up for their enormous losses, and things were worsened by a shortage of gasoline and inadequate training.

All this led to informal discussions concerning *jibaku* (suicide attacks) to counter these overwhelming obstacles. Suggestions came from various quarters. *Shosho* (Rear-Admiral) Kameto Kuroshima advocated suicide attacks at the War Preparation Examination Conference of July 1943, but his plan, which he called 'Invisible War Preparation', was spurned. A few unit commanders had already discreetly, but officially, put forward ideas for *jibaku* to the High Command in Tokyo, but their suggestions likewise were rejected or rebuffed. This, of course, was not surprising. In Japan's armed forces the upward expression of opinion or suggestions (as opposed to the 'downward' receiving of orders) was an extreme form of *fujujun* (disobedience) which earlier in the war would have been punished.

By 1944 *Shosho* Sueo Obayashi, Commander of 3rd Carrier Division in 1st Mobile Fleet, and *Taisa* Eiichiro Iyo, of the carrier *Chiyoda*, were openly discussing the idea of a Special Attack Force with *Taisho* Jisaburo Ozawa, Commander of 1st Mobile Fleet. The suggestion of a properly organised *jibaku* force was taken to *Taisho* Soemu Toyoda, Commander-in-Chief of the Imperial Navy's Combined Command. During initial discussions *Chujo* Kimpei Teraoka, then Commander of 1st Air Fleet (formed July 1944), scorned the idea of a Special Attack Force, but jotted down these thoughts at a specially convened strategy meeting:

'Ordinary tactics are ineffective.

'We must be superhuman in order to win the war.

'Volunteers for suicide missions will have to be reported to Imperial Headquarters before their take-off, so that they will feel secure and composed.

'Should we speak directly to the young fliers or through their group commanders?

'It would be better for future actions to have their group commanders present the proposition.

'If the first suicide unit is organised by fighter pilot volunteers, other units will follow their example. If all air units do it, surface units will also be inclined to take part. And if there is a unanimous response the Navy and Army will follow.

Despite his rebuttal of the idea, in his last paragraph Teraoka had presciently realised what would happen. Yet it was the colleague on whom he had poured the most scorn who was to produce a catalyst to effect *Taisho* Toyoda's ultimate decision about the Special Attack Forces.

The Commander of 26th Air Flotilla, under 1st Air Fleet, the English public school educated and Royal Navy trained *Shosho* Masafumi Arima was an early supporter of *jibaku,* and after his rebuttal by Teraoka he deliberately set out on his own suicide mission. On 15 October 1944 the US Task Force

Group 38–4, commanded by Rear Admiral Ralph E. Davison, was sighted off Luzon. Arima, stripped of his rank insignia, boarded the lead aircraft (whose mascot name was *naifu* (knife)) of 26th Air Flotilla at Nichols Field, Manila. His was one of the second wave of thirteen Type 1 Suisei bombers, sixteen Navy Zeros and seventy Army fighters. Arima deliberately crash-dived on the carrier USS *Franklin*, Admiral Davison's flagship.

Toyoda was much moved by Arima's suicide mission, and reviewed again the pros and cons of the mooted *jibaku*. There were three main stumbling-blocks – which were to be summarised by *Shosho* Toshiyuki Yokoi, later Chief of Staff of 5th Air Fleet, in an essay republished for the US Navy Institute's *Proceedings* of 1969. In essence the difficulties were:

1. The expenditure of personnel, aircraft and equipment would be likely to be great. It took a long time to train a good pilot, and on a successful *jibaku* mission the pilot and his aircraft could be lost after just one sortie. The whole idea ran counter to Toyoda's operational training.

2. His advisers estimated that the velocity of an aircraft at the point of impact would be insufficient for it to penetrate the decks, say, of a fleet carrier or battleship, so the resultant damage would be insignificant. Effective success would only be likely if the decks were full of equipment. [In fact the wooden decks of the US vessels made them highly vulnerable.]

3. Operational command of *jibaku* raids would be very difficult because results would be hard to evaluate accurately.

Toyoda, however, was won over by the 'vanity of heroism' as Yokoi called it, and now consented to the creation of the kamikaze, and orders were sent for implementation to the man who was to be nicknamed *Otosama no kamikaze* ('Father of the Divine Wind'), *Chujo* Takijiro Onishi.

CHAPTER FOUR

BIRTH OF THE KAMIKAZE

'Put forth everything that you have. All of you come back dead.'
— *Briefing by Shosho Sadaichi Matsunaga, 11th Air Fleet.*

On 17 October 1944, *Chujo* Takijiro Onishi, co-creator with *Taisho* Isoroku Yamamoto of the Imperial Japanese Navy's Air Arm, and Commander of 1st Air Fleet, arrived at HQ Manila, Philippines, to replace his old classmate at the Japanese Naval Academy, *Chujo* Kempei Teraoka. Teraoka had been in authority for less than two months after taking over from *Shosho* Kakaji Kakuta, the defender of Tinian Island; Kakuta lost it to the US forces and his name went missing from Japanese records, his suicide is a presumption. The Commander-in-Chief Combined Fleet *Taisho* Toyoda believed that Teraoka had lost the will to win at all costs so he had replaced him. On the ground, a new commander so soon caused consternation, but Onishi brought orders that would rock the whole of the Philippines Command.

On 19 October the 54-year-old Onishi reached Mabalacat airfield, which formed a part of the sprawling Clark Base Complex, almost fifty miles north of Manila, on the island of Luzon. He initially instructed his aide *Taisa* Chikanori Moji to call for an immediate meeting with the executive officer of 201st Air Group *Chusa* (Commander) Asaichi Tamai and the senior Staff Officer of lst Air Fleet *Taisa* Rikihei Inoguchi, adviser to the 201st.

Onishi, Japan's most prominent authority on naval aviation, was a controversial, outspoken career officer. His appearance always underlined his personality. Short, and solidly built, his close-cropped hair, distinctive features and stern eyes bespoke a brave, intelligent and aggressive character. He was known to be ruthless towards those he deemed inefficient. No respecter of persons, he earned the nickname *gusho* ('the foolish admiral') from *Shosho* Sokichi Takagi of the Imperial Naval General Staff, and it stuck throughout the war. With him there were no half-measures – you either worshipped him or loathed him.

Since the fall of Saipan and the drawing back of the Japanese lines of defence, Onishi had been pressuring the High Command to change tactics, and had even made a special journey to Tokyo to seek an audience with the

Emperor. When Emperor Hirohito learned from the duty courtier of the *Kunaicho* (Imperial Household Agency) why Onishi wanted the audience it was refused. What Onishi wanted to say was this:

'The country's salvation depends on the appearance of the soldiers of the gods. Nothing but the sacrifice of our young men's lives to stab at the enemy's carriers can annihilate the enemy fleet and put us on the road to victory.' Undaunted by the Imperial snub, Onishi now proclaimed his belief to his colleagues in the words quoted in Daizo Kusanayagi's *Tokko no Shiso*:

'Japan must be realistic, the battleship is no longer the prime line of defence. It costs as much to keep a single battleship in fighting trim as it does to operate a hundred aircraft and provide for casualties. Therefore Japan must now abandon all her concern for major capital ships and concentrate on air power for national defence.'

Although an instinctive leader, Onishi was a somewhat quarrelsome, undisciplined product of the prestigious Kaibara Junior High School and the *Kaigun Heigakko* (Naval Academy) at Etajima, Hiroshima Bay. His contemporaries remembered him as a keen gambler and a regular attender at the brothel and the *okiya* (*geisha* house), and in fact his slapping of one of these skilled entertainers and witty conversation artists led to a charge of conduct unbecoming an officer and he was disbarred from taking his final examinations. He spent two years studying in Britain and then served aboard Japan's first 4-seaplane tender, the 7,600-ton *Wakamiya Maru*, built in 1901. When Onishi was a young *Chu-i* in 1915, *Wakamiya Maru* was basking in her glorious reputation of having sent her seaplanes over the German-held fortress of Tsingtao to sink a German minelayer, thereby establishing the first recorded use of an aircraft carrier. Onishi also achieved renown as an air ace flying the first aircraft produced by the Nakajima Aircraft Co (which he helped to set up in 1916), and under his own auspices he trained as a paratrooper.

By the outbreak of WWII Onishi was serving as Chief of Staff, 11th Air Fleet at Takao (Kaoshuing), Formosa, and was considered the leading authority on naval aviation. As he rose in rank his opinions were less and less tempered with diplomacy. He castigated the building of the great battleships *Yamato* (1941, 72,809 tons, 27 knots) and her sister ship *Musashi* (1942); for him the developing conflict would be won – or lost – by air power. Onishi was a founder member of the 1938 'Society for the Study of Aerial Might' and with fellow-member *Chusa* Minoru Genda and *Shosho* Shigeru Fukudome he helped prepare the pre-attack study for the *Shinjuwan Kogeki* (the attack on Pearl Harbor). While *Taisho* Chuichi Nagumo's task force was attacking Pearl

Harbor as from 7 December (8 December Japanese time) 1941, Onishi was attacking Luzon, and soon the Philippines were in Japanese hands.

Onishi's present mission to Mabalacat was against his own inclinations, although he was a supporter of *Hito Shogo Sakusen* (Operation 'Victory'); this was the national offensive–defensive plan completed in July 1944 by Imperial HQ at Tokyo, after Japan's main lines of defence had been severed by US forces in New Guinea and the Marianas. *SHO-GO* had been activated before Onishi arrived at Mabalacat, in response to the US invasion of Leyte; the Philippines therefore were identified as a 'theatre of decisive battle'. Despite the necessity of *SHO-GO*, Onishi was acting on orders from combined Fleet Commander *Taisho* Soemu Toyoda, so he was to give the mission his best efforts.

Chujo Onishi called an immediate meeting at the requisitioned Filipino/Western-style house which served as the HQ of 201st Air Group. He was well aware of the reputation of the 201st who vaunted their 'overwhelming strength of martial spirit'. The 201st had been formed at Roi Island in the Marshalls on 1 December 1942, from the Chitose Air Group Fighter Squadron which had had a great deal of experience as a training unit for young pilots. The Chitose (in Hokkaido) were combined with 752nd Air Group Fighter Squadron and 11th Bombardment Squadron to form 201st Air Group under *Chusa* Ryutaro Yamanaka, to operate from Roi and Wake Islands in various *buntai* (Air Divisions) as trainers.

They flew their first offensive in the raid on Rendova as an element of 21st Air Flotilla (11th Air Fleet) during July 1943, and were to fight on as the last defensive unit in the Buin area before falling back on Rabaul. After logging 450 enemy aircraft shot down, the 201st withdrew to Saipan, to be transferred to Peleliu, via Guam. Decimated by enemy raids, they were reorganised on 4 March 1944 from two 48-aircraft units, the Fighters *Hikotai* 305 (under *Tai-i* Kawai) and *Hikotai* 306 (under *Tai-i* Tarajiro Haruta).

At first the 201st (II) were active against mountain guerrillas, and were then under consideration for deployment in *chohi bakugeki* (skip bombing) of enemy targets. Training for this had been carried out at bases in the Bohol Strait, off Cebu, under the guidance of carrier bomber instructors from the Yokosuka Air Group, but several enemy bombings of Cebu meant that the 201st were never actively used for this tactic.

On 12 December 1943 forty-one fighters of the 201st took off from Cebu to attack US aircraft. Huge losses were incurred, and these continued on the 13th when the US carrier fleet raided Manila. On 22 December ten *Suisei* bombers accompanied by a volunteer force of fifteen Zeros fitted with bombs attacked the US fleet east of Lamon Bay. Five bombs found their target and daring strafing attacks were reported. Despite the large losses morale was high among the 201st's pilots as *Chujo* Onishi prepared for their finest hour.

Chusa Tamai and *Taisa* Inoguchi were joined at HQ by the 26th Air Flotilla staff officer Chuichi Yoshioka, and two squadron leaders of the 305th and 306th Squadrons, naval *Tai-i* Isusuki and Yokoyama.

In his book on the 'Thunder Gods', technical *Tai-i* Hatsuho Naito of the Imperial Japanese Navy Aeronautical Research Laboratory confirms that at the meeting Onishi was lying when he told the assembled officers that he had already apprised the 201st overall commander, *Taisa* Sakae Yamamoto, of his mission. Indeed the *Taisa* was then in hospital in Manila with a broken ankle after an aircraft crash. Onishi further averred that Yamamoto had indicated his full support of the plan Onishi was about to develop. The six were to discuss one of the most important plans that Japan ever mooted.

Onishi's opening gambit to the assembled officers was to the point:

'As you know, the war situation is grave. The appearance of strong American forces in Leyte Gulf has been confirmed. The fate of the Empire depends upon the outcome of the *Shogo* operation, which Imperial General Headquarters has activated to hurl back the enemy assault on the Philippines. Our surface forces are already in motion. *Chujo* Kurita's 2nd Fleet, containing our main battle strength, will advance to the Leyte area and annihilate the enemy invasion force. The mission of the 1st Air Fleet is to provide land-based air cover for *Chujo* Kurita's advance and make sure that enemy air attacks do not prevent him from reaching Leyte Gulf. To do this we must hit the enemy's carriers and keep them neutralised for at least one week.'

Chujo Takeo Kurita was commander of 5th Fleet in Operation *Sho Ichi* (SHO-1, Philippines). His fleet comprised the super battleships *Yamato* and *Musashi*, five battleships, eleven heavy cruisers, five light cruisers and nineteen destroyers, but no aircraft carriers. So it was important to provide air cover if he was to get through to Leyte Gulf.

By this time 201st Air Group were down to thirty aircraft. Onishi informed the assembled officers that the best use of these would be to organise them into *Kamikaze Tokubetsu Kogekitai*, or *Tokkotai* (Suicide Attack Units) armed with 250kg bombs, each aircraft to target an enemy carrier in a *tai-atari* ('body-crashing') tactic. After consultations the 201st Air Group commanders agreed and Onishi acquiesced in their request that they themselves organise the affair.

The word kamikaze was not unknown to literate officers who heard Onishi's address, it having appeared often in Japan's histories as the epithet *kamukaze*; a passage in the *Nihon Shoki* (first official Chronicle of Japan of AD 720) contained this poem by Japan's founding Emperor Jimmu:

'Kamukaze no Ise no umi no Oishi ya' (On the great rock of the Divine Wind, Sea of Ise ...)

At the Great Ise Shrine in the Mie Prefecture priests had offered prayers to save the country from the Mongol invasions, and a great wind had come to their succour. The story went like this:

Kublai Khan (1214–94), that great conqueror and first Mongol Emperor of China, whose hordes had overrun Central Asia and advanced almost to the walls of Vienna and Moscow, was not a man to cross. But the freebooters of Japan had long ravaged the coasts of China and Korea, and he now demanded of the Japanese *Shikken* (regent) Hojo Tokimune (1256–84) that the freebooters be leashed. There was more to it than that, of course. The Khan wanted to build up his suzerainty of the waters east of China and control more strictly the provinces of south China; a pliant Japan would make that easier. So he also demanded that Japan acknowledge herself a tributary state to China and do homage to him. To pave the way for peaceful submission he sent six embassies to the Japanese court. Each time his ambassadors were sent back with the regent's scornful replies. Sterner measures were needed.

In early November 1274, Kublai Khan sent an invading force of nine hundred vessels and 40,000 troops. The islands of Tsushima and Iki – guarding the straits between Japan and Korea – were captured after a desperate struggle, during which the Japanese defenders immolated themselves on the Mongol lances. Although a landing was made at Hakata Bay, in north-west Kyushu, the Khan's commanders withdrew when their ships were threatened by a great storm. The Japanese were elated that their *kami* (the generic term for the nation's *Shinto* gods) had stirred the forces of nature to defend the sacred island of *Nihon* which had been created in the Eastern Sea when the Divinities Izanagi and Izanami-no-Mikoto had dipped their jewelled spears into the salt water. But Kublai Khan was only temporarily thwarted.

The Mongol conqueror sent embassies again in 1275 and 1279. This time *Shikken* Hojo Tokimune executed the ambassadors and their staff. In angry response the Khan prepared an armada of some 4,350 vessels and 140,000 men and launched a great invasion. For seven months in 1281 a coastal battle raged and the Japanese defenders were losing heavily. The *kami* were petitioned again and this time, according to the chroniclers, Amaterasu-o-Mikami, the Goddess of the Sun, herself, and Susano-o-no, the Storm God, answered their prayers by sending a *Kami Kaze* to shatter the Mongol fleet to perdition.

The historical and political significance of the Divine Wind was filed away for centuries in the Japanese psyche and was called upon again in the propaganda of the 19th-century wars against China and Russia and again in the early 1940s. A pro-Axis publication (i.e, promoting the alliance of powers, as if forming together an axis of rotation; first Germany and Italy in 1936, then to include Japan) called *Hochi* – usually regarded as subsidised by Hitler's National Socialists and directed by the Imperial Japanese Army's cadres – wrote in 1941 of the international situation blowing 'two kinds of *Kami Kaze* to the country of the gods'. The new Divine Winds had now first removed the Russian Menace stemming from the Russo–Japanese conflict along the Manchuquo–Outer Mongolian Border, by the Germans launching Operation 'Barbarossa', on 22 June 1941, along a front from the Baltic to the Black Sea. And *Hochi* was supporting what they saw as another Divine Wind, the prospect of a German–American war. 'Use this gods-sent opportunity', the paper told the Japanese Government, 'to implement Japan's lordship over Asia.'

As the Pacific War loomed ever closer, more and more the words of the *Gaimu Daijin* Yosuku Matsuoka in his recently published book were thought relevant: 'I firmly believe that the great mission that the *Kami Kaze* has given to Japan is to save humanity in conformity with the great spirit in which Emperor Jimmu founded the Empire.'

So some six and a half centuries after the coming of the great Mongol fleet, the same tempestuous forces were to be summoned again to Japan's defence, but this time man took on the role of the *kami*. It has often been propounded that the use of the word kamikaze for Onishi's suicide pilots was the suggestion of one of those assembled for the *Chujo*'s initial briefing on 19 October 1944, namely *Taisa* Rikihei Inoguchi. If so it was hardly an original thought. Purists might note, too, that kamikaze had appeared as the name of an aircraft a few years before. Owned by the newspaper *Asahi Shimbun*, this was a Mitsubishi-built high-speed liaison aircraft which, piloted by Iinuma Masaaki and Tsukakoshi Kenji, set up the first Japanese world speed record in April 1937. They had clocked-up the 9,537 miles from Tokyo to London in 94 hours, 17 minutes and 56 seconds with fuel stops. *Kamikaze* was also the name of a 1905 destroyer and a 1921–2 class of destroyers.

In any study of the history of the kamikaze, two names occur regularly: Inoguchi and Nakajima. And at this stage a simple biography will suffice.

Taisa Rikihei Inoguchi graduated from the *Kaigun Heigakko* in 1921, lectured at this academy and before WWII had served in the naval *kyoku* (bureau) of personnel. By February 1944 he was commander of 153rd Air Group, campaigning in New Guinea, Timor and Peleliu. In July of that year he was transferred as naval *sambo* for 23rd Air Flotilla at Kendari. In August he joined 1st Air Flotilla as senior staff officer to Onishi.

Chusa Tadashi Nakajima graduated from the *Kaigun Heigakko* in 1927 and went to flight training school in 1933. He was in charge of an aircraft unit in the 33,693-ton carrier *Kaga* the year after its conversion at Sasebo yard in 1935. Nakajima served as commander of an air unit in China during the late 1930s incursions and was transferred to command of the Tainan Air Group in 1942, serving at Bali, Rabaul, New Guinea, the Solomons and Guadalcanal. During 1943 he commanded the Yokosuka Air Group at Iwo Jima. In 1944 he became flight operations officer of 201st Air Group.

Recruited into Onishi's Special Suicide Attack Units were those pilots of *Chusa* Tamai's 263rd Air Group who had had experience of combat from the Mariana Islands to Yap in Micronesia. They had been moved from the air base at Matsuyama in Shikoku, to the southern Philippines to be incorporated into the late *Taisho* Kakuji Kakuta's 1st Naval Air Fleet, as 201st Air Group. They were young, and keenly motivated to serve their Emperor and country. When *Chusa* Tamai put to them Onishi's proposals they volunteered to a man to fly to certain death. There was no compulsion.

After the war Ichiro Ohmi collected letters and diary entries of kamikaze pilots about to die. The comments, for instance of *Kashikan* (Western equivalent Flying Petty Officer First Class) Isao Matsuo of 701st Air Group, were to sum up the feelings of the newly born kamikaze recruits, and those that followed:

[28 October 1944]

'*Watashi no ryoshin* (Beloved parents)

'Please congratulate me. I have been given a splendid opportunity to die. This is my last day. The destiny of our homeland hinges on the decisive battle in the Southern Seas, where I shall fall like a blossom from a radiant cherry tree.

'I shall be a shield for [the] *Tenno* and die cleanly along with my squadron leader and other friends. I wish that I could be born seven times, each time to smite the enemy. [Japanese classics teach that there are Seven Evils which will assail Japan.]

'How I appreciate this chance to die like a man. I am grateful from the depths of my heart to the parents who have reared me with their constant prayers and tender love. And I am grateful as well to my squadron leader and superior officers who have looked after me as if I were their own son and given me such careful training.

'Thank you, my parents, for the twenty-three years during which you have cared for me and inspired me. I hope that my present deed will in some small way repay what you have done for me. Think well of me and know that your Isao died for our country. This is my last wish, and there is nothing else that I desire.

'I shall return in spirit and look forward to your visit at the *Yasukuni-jinja*. Please take good care of yourselves.

'How glorious is the *Giretsu Tai* (Special Task Force Unit 'Heroic') whose *Suisei* [-Kai] (Aichi–Yokosuka D4Y–4 Model 43) bombers will attack the enemy. Our goal is to dive against the aircraft carriers of the enemy. Movie camera-men have been here to take our pictures. It is possible that you may see us in newsreels at the theatre.

'We are sixteen warriors manning the bombers. May our death be as sudden and clean as the shattering of crystal.

'Written at Manila on the eve of our sortie. Isao.'

Isao Matsu added this last romantic flourish: 'Soaring into the sky of the Southern Seas, it is our glorious mission to die as the shields of [the] *Tenno*. Cherry blossoms glisten as they open and fall.'

Throughout the personal documentation of the kamikaze the *sakura* (cherry blossom) motif is much mentioned, and in his *Zen in the art of Archery* (1971), Eugene Herrigel summed up the sentiment: '... the samurai have chosen for their truest symbol the fragile cherry blossom. Like a petal dropping in the morning sunlight and floating serenely to earth, so must the fearless detach himself from life, silently and inwardly unmoved.'

Yet were the Mabalacat kamikaze fighters really volunteers? Or were they – as Westerners usually aver – 'brainwashed' into joining the suicide sorties? When dealing with Japanese emotions no answer is ever simple. Even so it seems likely that during the early kamikaze missions in the Philippines (and in Taiwan) the pilots were volunteers in the dictionary definition of 'entering by free choice'. As the typical kamikaze pilot was a young conscript university student with an interrupted education, there must have been many a diffident young man who ultimately was persuaded to die through psychological pressure exerted by his peers in that feverish combat milieu. Indeed it is recorded that young pilots who thought that they might not be chosen importuned their superior officers with impassioned requests written in their own blood, just as had the samurai of old.

In the Imperial Japanese Navy records there is no evidence of coercion by recruitment boards or superior officers, though in the Imperial Japanese Army coercion was a daily occurrence. As time went by the 'informal system of spontaneous volunteering' as historian Ivan Morris called it in his *The Nobility of Failure* (1975) changed slightly to a new type of enlistment. *Chusa* Nakajima was to comment about this in the 1950s:

'Many of the new arrivals seemed at first not only to lack enthusiasm, but, indeed, to be disturbed by their situation. With some this condition lasted only a few hours, with others for several days. It was a period of melancholy that passed with time and eventually gave way to a spiritual awakening. Then, like an attainment of wisdom, care vanished and tranquillity of spirit appeared as life came to terms with death, mortality with immortality.

'An example of the achievement of this spiritual calm was seen in the case of *Sho-i* Kuno, who was extremely perturbed upon arrival at the base. Then suddenly, after several days of sulking about, he came with jaunty step and a spark in his eye, asking permission to divest his plane of all unneeded equipment, saying that it was inconsiderate to homeland workers to take nonessentials along on a kamikaze mission.'

Back at Mabalacat base they were asking the question: Who was to lead the new Special Attack Force? *Chusa* Tamai immediately thought of the daredevil pilot *Tai-i* Naoshi Kanno of 306th Fighter Squadron. He was the most spectacular aerial performer of 201st Air Group, indeed he had already undertaken his own version of a 'suicide mission' and survived. This had occurred at Yap in the Pulau Islands (which had been attacked by General Douglas MacArthur's bombers) where he and other 201st pilots had taken on the Allied B–24s, those heavy bombers that were difficult to shoot down. Kanno had read the reports about the pilots who rammed the enemy head-on and felt that he could better the technique, and maybe live. His method was to make a head-on approach and then sheer away so that he would be able to cut up a B–24's stabiliser with the propeller of his Zero. He had done this and had passed out. To his surprise when he awoke he was still flying, but in a spin. He centred the controls and pulled out in time to see the B–24 crash into the sea, after which he returned to Yap. Tamai wanted him but there was a snag – Kanno had been sent back to Japan by *Taisho* Teraoka.

A recent transfer from *Taisho* Shigeru Fukudome's 2nd Air Fleet on Taiwan was *Tai-i* Yukio Seki. Although he had been trained to fly carrier bombers, not fighters, there was no more enthusiastic a devotee to the task. Tamai spelled out what was required and the recently married Seki agreed.

On 20 October a notice of intention signed by Onishi, and naming Seki, was posted up at Mabalacat base:

'The 201st Air Group will organise a Special Attack Corps and will destroy or disable, if possible by 25 October, the enemy carrier forces in the waters east of the Philippines.

'The corps will be called *Shimpu* Attack Unit. It will consist of twenty-six fighter planes, of which half will be assigned to crash-diving missions, and the remainder to escort, and will be divided into four sections, designated as follows: *Shikishima, Yamato, Asahi* and *Yamazakura*.

Shimpu (or *Shin-fu* 'God' and 'Wind') was simply another reading/pronunciation of the Sino–Japanese calligraphic ideographs for kamikaze in a more solemn and dignified manner. In his book *I was a Kamikaze*, Ryuji Nagatsuka avers that the use of kamikaze for *shimpu* was because the *nisei* (second-generation Japanese) serving in US forces (i.e., the 442nd Regimental Combat Team, and the 100th Battalion) 'pronounced the two Japanese characters for "Divine Wind" in the same vernacular way'. The

KAMI——KAZE
Shin——Fu'

Imperial Japanese Army, by the by, employed the description *Shimbu Tokubetsu-Kogekitai* for their Special Attack Corps, *Shimbu* meaning 'Gathering of Courageous Forces'.

The designations set out in Onishi's notice were derived as follows: *Yamato* was the name of the province by which Japan was known in ancient times; the name of the country was not changed to *Nippon* until the 6th century. *Shikishima* was the poetic name for *Yamato*, derived from the site of the ancient capital of the province. *Asahi* means 'dawn', i.e., 'the rising sun', and *Yamazakura* is the mountain cherry blossom. All these names were culled from the *waka* (Japanese indigenous poem) by the classical scholar Norinaga Motoori (1730–1801):

> *'Shikishima no Yamatogokoro o*
> *hito towaba Asahi ni niu*
> *Yamazakura-hana.'*

(The Japanese spirit to a man is like the wild mountain cherry blossoms, radiant in the morning sun.)

Soon after the concept of the suicide missions had become official at Mabalacat, Onishi was to send to his fledgling kamikaze a poem in his own calligraphy:

'*Kijo sakite, osu chiru*
Hana no wagami ka na
Ikade sono ka wo
Kiyoku todomen.'

(Blossoming today, tomorrow scattered/ Life is like a delicate flower/ Can one expect the fragrance to last forever?)

He signed it *Onishi Kamikaze Tokkotai Ei* – not only was he their father, he was an *ei* (member) of the group.

It may be noted in passing, that although most histories credit Onishi with being the originator of the first 'officially planned' suicide attacks, *Tai-i* Hatsuho Naito in his book *Thunder Gods* declares that: 'The first officially planned suicide attack against an American ship occurred on 25 May 1944, when a plane crash-dived into the Subchaser 699 off the coast of West New Guinea'.

On 20 October 1944 the twenty-six fighter pilot volunteers who were to make up the *Shimpu* Force were given a pep-talk by Onishi. His words were to be some of the most emotive of the war and remain much quoted in the Japanese hagiographies of the kamikaze. He began:

'My sons, who can raise our country from the desperate situation in which she finds herself?

'Japan is in grave danger. The salvation of our country is now beyond the power of the Ministers of State, the General Staff, and lowly commanders like myself. It can come only from spirited young men such as you. Thus on behalf of your hundred million countrymen, I ask you this sacrifice, and pray for your success. You are already gods, without earthly desires. But one thing you want to know is that your own crash-dive is not in vain. Regrettably, we will not be able to tell you the results. But I shall watch your efforts to the end and report your deeds to the Throne. You may all rest assured on this point. I ask you to do your best.'

Whereas historians have suggested that the kamikaze gave their lives for Emperor and Country, *Tai-i* Yukio Seki, the newly designated leader of Onishi's Special Attack Unit, was to express a less altruistic motive according to the testimony of Masashi Onoda, a war correspondent for the Japanese news agency *Domei*. Onoda had interviewed Seki as they walked along the banks of the River Bamban at Mabalacat:

'Japan must be in very bad shape if it has to kill an experienced pilot like me. If they would let me, I could drop a 500-kilogram bomb on the flight deck of a carrier without going in for body-crashing and still make my way back. I am not going out tomorrow for the Japanese Emperor, but for my beloved *ka* [a colloquial term used by naval officers for their wives, '*ka*' being a burden carried on a pole across the shoulders]. If Japan were defeated, who knows what the Americans would do to my wife [*Mariko*]. I am going to die to protect her.'

Onoda added a *haiku* (a traditional Japanese short poem of seventeen syllables in the arrangement, 5,7,5) to his filed report, written by Seki which more selflessly remembered his trainee pilots who were to die:

> 'Fall my pupils
> My cherry blossoms
> Just as I will fall
> In the service of our land.'

From the earliest days of the kamikaze, the pilots were to become easily identified. They wore a white scarf loosely knotted around the neck. Under their leather helmet they wore the *hachimaki*, the replica of the headband worn by the medieval *samurai*. Most of them also wore a *sennin-bari* (lit. 'a thousand stitches worked by a thousand people'), a cloth or silk band stitched with red threads, or hair from the heads of a thousand women. The band was deemed to have the talismanic powers of a bullet-proof vest; the practice of wearing such an occult vestment was begun by military personnel during the Sino–Japanese War (1894). It was not an unusual sight in the streets of Japan's main cities to see women respectfully accosting others to contribute a lock of hair for *sennin-bari* embroidery.

Many kamikaze carried a personal patriotic flag, usually a square of white cloth with a *hinomaru* ('round of the sun' Japanese flag emblem) in the centre, surrounded by calligraphy exhorting the suicide spirit. The kamikaze and their families received the title *homare no ie* ('very honourable') and were given special privileges; families were allotted extra food rations, privileged seats at ceremonies and had their pictures in the newspapers. Distinguishing features on a kamikaze's uniform were seven buttons decorated with three petals of *sakura* on the tunic, and an anchor of the Navy, or relevant military insignia for the Army kamikaze.

Soon after Onishi's pep-talk, the 4-Zero strong *Yamato* Unit was sent with four escort planes to Cebu Island, one of the Central Philippines Visayan Islands, for training under the leadership of the flight officer of 201st Air Group *Chusa* Tadashi Nakajima. His brief included the setting up of a further unit at Cebu. Immediately on arrival Nakajima addressed the pilots:

41

'I have come to Cebu to organise another Special Attack Unit. Others will want to follow in the footsteps of the first pilots charged with this mission. Any non-commissioned officer or enlisted flyer who wishes to volunteer will so signify by writing his name and rate [naval rank] on a piece of paper. Each piece of paper is to be placed in an envelope which will be delivered to me by 2100 hrs today.

'It is not expected, however, that everyone should volunteer. We know that you are all willing to die in defence of your country. We also realise that some of you, because of your family situation, cannot be expected to offer your life in this way. You should understand also that the number of volunteers required is limited by the small number of planes available. Whether a man volunteers or not will be known only to me. I ask that each man, within the next three hours, come to a decision based entirely upon his own situation. Special attack operations will be ready to start tomorrow. Because secrecy in this operation is of utmost importance, there must be no discussion about it.'

Just before 2100 hrs a petty officer entered Nakajima's room. Later the *Chusa* remembered:

'I stared for some moments at the envelopes, hesitating to open them. I had not urged the non-coms to volunteer, but had left the decision entirely up to them. I had even offered a sincere excuse for those who could not volunteer. What if they all declined?'

Nakajima opened the envelopes; two contained blank pieces of paper submitted by pilots then too ill to reply formally. All the pilots had volunteered. Nakajima reflected: 'The Special Attack Corps had spread to Cebu'.

It should be noted here too that kamikaze tactics were actively being promoted within the Army Air Service from March 1943 by *Chujo* Takeo Yasuda. As *Rikugun Koku Sokambu* and Chief of the Army Aeronautical Department, he was a proponent of the *tai-atari* tactic, which was used in his command but only as 'secret operations'. The tactic was frowned on by the Army High Command, so Yasuda reshuffled his senior officers until he had around him those sympathetic to his views. He now issued orders that the trainees learning *tai-atari* attacks should not be informed that they were to be part of an operational fighting force.

But by 20 October 1944 the Army had formed the 1st Special Attack Unit to be known as the *Banda* ('10,000 petals'). This was made up of a group of sixteen army pilots under *Tai-i* Masuomi Iwamoto from Hokota Air Training Division, Itaragi Prefecture, north-east of Tokyo. This unit was followed by that named *Fugaru* (Mount Fuji).

CHAPTER FIVE

KOKUKI – CHARIOTS FOR THE GODS

'We do not wish the kamikaze tactics to be described by the term "suicide-attacks". Right up until the end, we believed we could outweigh your material and scientific superiority by the force of our moral and spiritual convictions.' — *Taisho* Masakazu Kawabe, Commander-in-Chief of the Air General Army, at a US Commission of Inquiry in 1945.

It was under the second cabinet of *Sori-daijin Miya-sama Taisho* (Prime Minister Prince General) Taro Katsura that in 1909 Japanese service aviation began. By 1911 separate air arms were evolving for the Army and Navy in this the year when Narahara Sanjo successfully flew the first Japanese-built aircraft. Until WWI army aviation made greater progress than that of the navy, but by 1914 both elements were still small and their participation in the war extremely limited. Japan declared war on Germany on 23 August 1914 and began to bombard the Chinese port of Tsingtao (where the Germans had a concession). Although appearing to honour its 1902 alliance with Britain, Japan was fighting its own agenda (to control China's Shantung Province) and wanted to gain air experience in a theatre of war.

In 1917 an interest in aviation was being developed by the triumvirate of industrial giants: Mitsubishi Jukogyo KK; Nakajima Hikoki KK; and Kawasaki Kokuku KK, the latter two working under licence (or influence) of Fokker and Douglas, and Blohm & Voss of Hamburg, respectively. Further guided by advice from a French Air Mission of 1919 and a British Mission of 1921, this trio were to dominate the emergent Japanese aircraft industry. Construction then was mostly under foreign licence, but by 1922–3 Mitsubishi had produced some basic home-designed combat aircraft (i.e., the Type 10 Mitsubishi), and the Imperial Japanese Navy was completing its first aircraft carrier, the 7,470-ton *Hosho* ('Flying Phoenix') at the Yokosuka Naval Arsenal for launching on 27 December 1922 (the world's first purpose-built aircraft carrier). By 1923, of course, the first graduates of the Department of Aeronautics at the University of Tokyo were emerging to form the nucleus of the future Japanese aviation industry.

Although small by international standards, both Japan's air arms were firmly enough established to cut their teeth during the Japanese invasion of Manchuquo (Manchuria) in 1931–2. During this period the Imperial Japanese Navy had just outpaced the army in development, but home-produced aircraft were poor. But the Mitsubishi Model 13 (1924) and the Kawasaki Model 88 reconnaissance aircraft of 1928 were adopted as standard. By the mid-1930s, though, such aircraft as the Mitsubishi A5M and the G3M bomber were showing comparability with foreign designs, and on the drawing-boards was a new generation of Japanese military aircraft including the A6M Zero fighter which was soon to be encountered by the Allies.

In 1937 the Japanese campaign against China recommenced and by 1938–9 there were clashes with Russia concerning the borders with Manchuria and Mongolia. A consequence was a new tranche of battle experienced aircrew who were to catch the Allies napping.

As the war initiative slipped from the Japanese grasp into that of the Allies, the air war shifted from carrier- to shore-based aircraft. Replacements now appeared that had been under study before the war. Allied observers now monitored the Kawanishi H8K flying-boat, the Yokosuka D4Y *Suisei* dive-bombers, the Mitsubishi G4M medium bomber and improved Zeros. The army also brought into service new types such as the Mitsubishi Ki–45 and Ki–84 fighters, and Ki–49 and Ki–67 *Hiryu* bombers. As Japan's situation deteriorated any serviceable aircraft was considered fit for kamikaze action. This was certainly the case in Taiwan.

Pre-eminent among the kamikaze aircraft, and the first to be deployed in this way, was the single-seat Mitsubishi A[ichi] 6M[itsubishi] *Reisen* (Zero *Sen* Fighter), code-named 'Zeke' by the Allies. Produced by Mitsubishi Jukogyo Kabushiki Kaisha, this was the Imperial Japanese Navy's standard fighter throughout WWII, although it had been listed as 'obsolescent' by the end of 1943. The Zero was designed by a team led by Jiro Horikoshi, a young graduate from the Department of Aeronautical Engineering at Tokyo Imperial University, and derived from an Imperial Japanese Navy specification that Horikoshi had seen on 5 October 1937. The specification was so demanding that only the Mitsubishi company was willing to tackle it as a replacement for the A5M4.

In 1939, while the supply of *matériel* from the Allies was hardening the resolve of Chiang Kai-shek, leader of the Kuomintang Army fighting the Japanese on mainland China, the development of the carrierborne fighter 12Si – which was to evolve into the Zero – was nearing completion. The first ground tests took place at the Nagoya Aircraft Works of Mitsubishi Heavy Industries on 18 March 1939, and the first test flight of the duralumin constructed aircraft powered by a lightweight 780hp Mitsubishi *Suisei* 13 radial engine took place on 1 April at the Kagamigahara airfield in Gifu Prefecture, piloted by chief test pilot Katsuzo Shima. Tests were carried out on two prototypes – designated A6M1 – but the navy ordered a third prototype – A6M2 – to be tested, this time with a 925hp Nakajima *Sakae* 12 radial engine. Tests on 18–19 January 1940 by pilot *Tai-i* Seiichi Maki led to the Imperial Japanese Navy's adoption of the prototype.

In China the Japanese air forces were clamouring for machines to counter the Chinese Air Force's fast recovery after the fall of cities in Wuhan, and news of the Zero's performance led to pressure for it to be used there. A programme of testing was accelerated, but was thwarted by the sudden disintegration of Prototype 2 while being flown by test pilot Masumi Okuyama at Oppama airfield. The cause of the fatal accident was traced to 'flutter' (aerodynamic forces causing violent vibration of plane surfaces), adjustments were made, the Zero was accepted by the Navy and production began at Nagoya Aircraft Works.

On 18 June 1940 *Tai-i* Tamotsu Yokoyama, squadron leader of the Omura Naval Air Corps, Nagasaki District, was transferred to Yokosuka Naval Air Corps with orders to take his squadron and the Zeros to China. It was, of course unheard of for an aircraft to be taken into the front line while still being operationally tested, but the Navy were confident in their new fighter and Yokoyama's group were given an intensive drill/practice programme. The groups left for China in July 1940 with a batch of six Zeros from an as yet total production of 64 aircraft, now designated A6M2s Model 11. The long-range possibilities of the Zero were tested immediately with a long hop from Omura (as refuelling base) to Shanghai – a record distance for a Japanese fighter.

On landing at Hankow airfield the Zeros were met by a group including *Chujo* Takijiro Onishi, then commander of 2nd United Air Corps; thus the future 'Father of the Kamikaze' was one of the first to assess the combat capabilities of the aircraft that was to be the first chariot of his pilot *kami*. And with the arrival of four more A6M2s, the official name of *Rei* (Zero-Sen) was given to the aircraft. The first operational sortie took place on 19 August 1940 against Chungking. The raid proved successful against the outdated Soviet-built Polikarpov I–15s and I–16s being flown by the Chinese. The returning Zero pilots were met by *Chujo* Onishi who praised them for their efforts and shared a cup of *sake* with them – a ceremony he was to perform several times with his kamikaze. The triumphs of the Zero pilots were recorded in Japanese newspapers, although the censors deleted references to the aircraft's name and technical data. At Nagoya Aircraft Works there was jubilation; their new aircraft was to achieve the reputation in the Far East that the Vickers-Armstrong Supermarine Spitfire P.37/34 was to have in Europe.

Chujo Onishi had in mind to test the reconnaissance capabilities of the Zero and sent *Tai-i* Yokoyama on a highly risky aerial photographic sortie over western China's commercial centre (to assess bomb damage). Yokoyama was able to test low-level flying (altitude 100 metres) over Chungking and reported great damage. Onishi filed the Zero's performance in his memory and began plans to attack the Chinese air bases at Chengtu, Szechwan Province. During the period 19 August–22 December 1940 the Zeros flew twenty-two sorties (59 kills and damage to 101 aircraft) with no Japanese losses. The Zero had proved itself in dogfights and reconnaissance, and now showed potential in strafing attacks. The Imperial Japanese Navy were ecstatic, and as 1940 closed took delivery of 120 Zeros from the Nagoya Aircraft Works.

During January 1941 the frequently held contest between Navy and Army fighters took place, wherein an overall comparison was made of the performances of Japanese aircraft against the known particulars of Britain's Spitfire and Hurricane and the US Curtiss P–36 and P–40 fighters. The Army put forward Nakajima Ki–44 *Shoki*, Ki–43 *Hayabusa* and Ki–27s against the Navy's sole entry of the Zero. Pilots of the Aeronautical Technology Institute and the Akeno Flying School took off for the Army and pilots from the Yokosuka Naval Air Corps for the Navy. Once again the superiority of the Zeros was confirmed.

They continued to be deployed in the Chinese theatres of war. Russian and US advisers to the Chinese began to monitor the Zero's capabilities, and Chiang Kai-shek's Director of the Chinese Air Force, the retired flight captain of the USAAF, Claire Lee Chennault, produced a report on the Zero which was read by US and British air strategists. They dismissed it as inaccurate and declared that Chinese losses were not caused by a superior Japanese aircraft but by Chinese aircraft inadequacies and pilots' lack of skill. So the Japanese were able to war test Zeros in all China's battle zones without foreign powers paying any attention. With the vanquishing of the Chinese Air Force, Zeros were withdrawn from the Sino–Japanese conflict on 31 August 1941, the battle score totalling 264 Chinese aircraft destroyed to the loss of two Zeros.

The A6M2 Model II was now modified to feature wing tips that could be folded ninety degrees upward to fit the storage areas of aircraft carriers. This new version was called A6M2 Model 21, and after the sixty-first of these had been produced, tabs were fitted to the rear edges of the ailerons, ostensibly to enable slow rolls to be achieved without difficulty, but the tabs produced 'flutter' and were removed.

The Germans invaded Russia on 22 June 1941, and by 29 July the Japanese had moved into southern French Indo-China. The war escalated with the attack on Pearl Harbor. At the outbreak of the Pacific War, Japan had a total air strength of 3,202 aircraft, and by 1941 740 Model 21s were available; most of the fighters were Zeros which were to spearhead the Imperial Japanese Navy's challenge to the US, British and Netherlands fleets.

The Imperial Japanese Navy had great confidence in the Zero although it had not been tested against the Allied navies. Strike waves of Zeros attacked Pearl Harbor with great success and the aircraft's astounding range took it into Formosa and thence to the Philippines. As Japan began to secure complete air superiority over a huge area of the Far East, the retreating Allies began to study the Zero and re-assess their naïve and arrogant under-estimation of Japanese air power capability. Since Pearl Harbor the Zero had emerged as the main battle aircraft of the Naval Air Corps, and in the first sixteen weeks of war (up to the Dutch surrender in Indonesia on 9 March 1942, the Naval Air Corps had destroyed 565 British, US and Dutch aircraft, of which the Zeros claimed 83 per cent. So Japanese successes at Pearl Harbor, the Philippines and the East Indies was down to the Zero's capabilities and good tactical planning. And in Malaya the Imperial Japanese Army were using the Nakajima Ki–43 *Hayabusa* to deadly effect.

The Nagoya Aircraft Works was now greatly expanded in area and workforce, and was to be run in parallel with new works at Kumamoto and Mizushima under the Mitsubishi umbrella. Horikoshi and his design team were now working on a range of aircraft, but improvements were also being made to the Zero. By 1942, 508 examples of a two-seater training variant had been produced as the A6M2–K, manufactured by the factories at Hitachi and Sasebo. Then the A6M3 Zero, powered by a 1139hp *Sakae* 21 engine appeared. In this year too 342 A6M3 Model 32 with slightly clipped wings were produced, and twenty-two more A6M3 Model 22.

By the end of the war the Zero was to have gone through many model changes. In 1943 the improved performance A6M5 Model 52 appeared with an engine boosted to 358hp, and various refinements were added from firepower to armour on the models M6M5a/5b/5c, so the Allies were recording these as brief technical details for the A6M5b:

Maximum speed: 273mph at 9,480ft

Maximum range: 746 miles

Service ceiling: 32,150ft

Weight: 2,681lb; 3,684lb (operational load)

Wing span: 36ft 1in

Length: 24ft 9.5in

Height:10ft 6in

Engine: one 710hp Nakajima *Kotobuki* 41 radial

Armament: two 7.7mm machine-guns; two 66lb bombs (optional)

Crew: one

Historians also note the Zero models 52–*Ko*, 52–*Otsu*, 52–*Hei* and 54–*Hei*.

The A6M6, powered by a *Sakae* 32 engine proved a disappointment, but work went ahead on the A6M5 to adapt it into the A6M7, and this entered production in a dive-bomber role when the last German shots were being fired in Europe on 11 May 1945. Because of difficulties in obtaining a regular supply of *Sakeo* engines, late in 1944 Mitsubishi started producing their own 1560hp *Kinsei* 62 engine for what history notes as the last of the Zero variants, the A6M8. Only two prototypes of the latter were flown. The total tally for Zero production (not taking into account the 327 Mitsubishi A6M2–N, Nakajima *Sakae* 12 radial-engined fighter/reconnaissance floatplane) was 10,611; 3,879 constructed by Mitsubishi and 6,215 by Nakajima.

More than any other weapon, the Zero was to have a consistently stringent security blanket throughout its production variations. The Nagoya Aircraft Works, for instance, had a Zero factory consisting of a huge, closed room where approved mockup designs were turned into working proto-types. All employees were subjected to a body search on entering and leaving any 'Zero' area, and individual identification badges (different from any other) had to be worn, and employees' personal files had to be cleared by the military police. No other employees were allowed near the Zero production section.

There were to be five famous bombers used in suicide missions. The Mitsubishi [*Hiko*] Ki–67–1 KAI was the Imperial Japanese Army's version of the Ki–67 *Hiryu* (Flying Dragon), code-named by the Allies 'Peggy', which had been converted by the Tachikawa Dai Ichi Rikugun Kokusho Company. The conversion consisted of removing the turrets and fairing over the spaces left, and reducing the crew seats from eight to three. Their place was taken by a 6,383lb explosive charge (or two 1,764lb bombs) which was detonated on impact by a rod projecting from the aircraft's nose. On a wing span of 73ft 9in, the power plant consisted of two 1810hp Army Type 4, Mitsubishi Ha–104 radial engines, giving a speed of 334mph at 19,980ft. Maximum range was 2,360 miles at a ceiling of 31,070ft. Although it was the Army's best bomber, it was only used during the last eleven months or so of the war.

The Navy's most celebrated bomber of the war was the Mitsubishi G4M, code-named 'Betty', but its lack of protective armour, particularly to the fuel tanks, made it extremely vulnerable. The 63ft 1in wing span carried two 1825hp Mitsubishi MK4T–D *Kasei* 25b radial engines which produced a speed of 292mph at 16,895ft. Service ceiling was 30,250ft and it had a range of 2,694 miles. (NB. The G4N2e was specially modified to carry the *Ohka* suicide aircraft, but in this mode the weight and slow speed made it easy prey for Allied fighters.)

The Nakajima B6N2 *Tenzan* ('Heavenly Mountain'), code-named 'Jill', was a single-engined, three-seat carrier-borne torpedo-bomber, built by the Nakajima Hikoki Kabushiki Kaisha Company. With a wing span of 48ft 10in, and powered by one 1850hp Mitsubishi MK4T Kasei 25 radial engine, it was capable of 299mph at 16,075ft. Service ceiling was 29,660ft and maximum range 1,644 miles. After the Imperial Japanese Navy's carriers were decimated the *Tenzan* flew from land bases and performed within an aggressive kamikaze programme at Okinawa.

The Navy's standard fast medium bomber of the declining period of the war was the Yokosuka P1Y1 *Ginga* ('Milky Way'), code-named 'Frances'. Despite its irritatingly troublesome engines (the Japanese mechanics' heartstop machinery) and temperamental hydraulic system, it was an easily manoeuvrable and speedy aircraft. With a wing span of 65ft 7in, its two 1820hp Nakajima NK9B Homara 11 radial engines produced a speed of 340mph at 19,335ft. Maximum range was 2,900 miles and service ceiling 30,840ft. The *Ginga* began life in 1940 at the 1st Naval Air Technical Arsenal at Yokosuka Naval Air Depot, but its 1943 service production was carried out at the Nakajima Company

The Yokosuka D4Y1 *Suisei* ('Comet'), code-named 'Judy', was designed as a carrier-borne dive-bomber, and appeared as a kamikaze weapon in the Philippines as the D4Y2. A 1,764lb bomb was installed in the aircraft's belly, and three Rocket Assisted Take-Off Gear Units were fixed to the fuselage (to assist take-off from short runways and accelerate diving speed). With a wing span of 37ft 8in, it was powered by one Aichi AE1P *Atsuta* 32 1400hp inline engine which gave it a speed of 360mph at 17,225ft. Service ceiling was 35,105ft and maximum range 2,239 miles.

It may be noted that the Japanese also manufactured the Nakajima Ki–115 *Tsurugi* ('Sword' or 'Sabre') specifically for kamikaze attacks, and to make use of a variety of surplus engines; a crutch under the central fuselage could accommodate a 1,764lb bomb. Flight trials were completed in June 1945 and the design incorporated a Nakajima Ha–35 14-cylinder radial 1130hp engine which could produce a maximum speed of 340mph at 9,185ft. Wing span was 28ft 2in and range was 745 miles. Estimates show that some 105 of these aircraft had been completed by the time of the surrender, but none was ever operational.

Japanese historical aviation records show that the design of an aircraft called *Kawanishi Baika* ('Plum Blossom') was on the drawing-board when Japan surrendered. It was to have been fitted with a 560lb warhead, and it was intended that the pilot jettison the undercarriage after take-off. The proposed power for this aircraft, whose wing span was 21ft 7in, was to be one Maru Xa–10 pulse jet which would give a maximum speed of 460mph.

CHAPTER SIX

THE GREAT DAY COMES

'Shichisei hokoku' ('Would that I had seven lives to give to my country').
— *Shugo* (Constable) Masashige Kusunoki (*d.* by suicide 1336),
military leader.

On the fall of the Marianas, Japan's high command evolved a new plan for a push towards a 'decisive battle'. They named it *SHO-GO* (Operation 'Victory'), but in fact it consisted of four offensives that would embrace all parts of their contracting empire. The Japanese believed that the Allies would first attack the Philippines so this area was covered by *SHO-1*; *SHO2* concerned Formosa and the Ryukyu Islands; *SHO-3*, the Japanese main islands of Honshu, Kyushu and Shikoku; *SHO-4*, the northernmost main island of Hokkaido and the Kurile Islands farther north astride the Pacific and the Sea of Okhotsk.

SHO-1 would combine a quartet of efforts with the basic objectives of attacking the US landing-craft assembled in Leyte Gulf for the invasion of Leyte Island. For the anchorage at Lingga, Japan's 1st Striking Force, with *Chujo* Takeo Kurita's 5th Fleet as the main body, were to sail through the San Bernadino Strait in the Philippines and hit the US amphibious forces from a northerly point on 25 October 1944. The second offensive called for *Chujo* Kiyohide Shima's 2nd Division Attack Force to be moved from its base in the Ryukyus to the Pescadores off Formosa.

The 2nd Division Attack Force was to be directed by the flagship, the 5,570-ton light cruiser *Abukama*. They would be joined by a third prong of vessels advancing through the Surigao Strait from Kurita's main body under the command of *Choji* Nishimura aboard the elderly superdreadnought, the 31,785-ton *Yamashiro*.

Commander-in-Chief of the Combined Fleet, *Taisho* Toyoda, knew that his remnant of the Imperial Japanese Fleet was not a match for the US Fleet. He prepared to use as the fourth prong an offensive decoy fleet – ironically called the Main Force – made up of the remaining carrier, light carriers, and the converted battleships the 35,800-ton *Ise* and the 38,676-ton *Hyuga*, commanded by *Chujo* Jisaburo Ozawa, to try to lure the US Fleet away from

Leyte's landing areas. Kurita believed that this would give the large guns of the *Yamato* and *Musashi* a chance to pound the unprotected US transports and amphibious forces.

The ultimate Japanese strategy was now clearly set out: their forces would join at Leyte Gulf to crush the US transports and fall upon Admiral William F. 'Bull' Halsey's Third Fleet. The *SHO* plans began to disintegrate when the Third Fleet struck Luzon, the Ryukyus and Formosa. The Japanese jumped to the conclusion that the Americans would invade Formosa, and prematurely launched *SHO-2* with the consequent loss of 600 aircraft.

The Battle of Leyte opened on 23 October. As *SHO-1* got under way *Chujo* Shigeru Fukudome moved the whole of 2nd Air Fleet and 6th Base Air Force to the Philippines; these were the cream of Japan's naval aviators who were prepared to strike the enemy with some 450 fighters and bombers.

This was the situation as *Chujo* Onishi was preparing his kamikaze offensive. Although the enemy was sighted on 20 October they were too far away for the Mabalacat and Cebu kamikaze to be effective, but next day a US task force was sighted east of Leyte and the kamikaze of the *Shikishima* unit were alerted.

Assembled with *Tai-i* Seki, the pilots fell in to take a ritual farewell drink of *mizu* (water) from the container left by Onishi. It was an old *samurai* custom in which a leader offered his comrades a traditional libation of water from a sacred spring. They drank and sang the ancient warriors' song:

'*Umi yukaba*
Mizutsuku kabane
Yama yukaba
Kusa musu kabane
Ogimi no he mi koso shiname
Nodo niwa shinaji'

(If I go away to sea/ I shall return a corpse awash/ If duty calls me to the mountain/ A verdant sward shall be my pall/ Thus for the sake of the Emperor/ I will not die peacefully at home)

At last orders for the sortie were received and *Tai-i* Seki handed over to *Chusa* Tamai the last souvenir that he wished to be sent to his family. In *samurai* style he had prepared a few strands of his hair in a folded paper, as all medieval warriors had done as they prepared for battle. In the event Seki's final gesture was premature. The aircraft searched the area where the enemy fleet was supposed to be but finding nothing returned to base.

At Cebu Island in the meantime, the *Yamato* unit was ready for an initial sortie, having been informed on the 21st that an enemy task force had been sighted some sixty miles east of Suluan Island. Before the *Yamato* unit could get aloft a group of US carrier-borne fighters – Grumman F6F–5 Hellcats – appeared and strafed the airfield. The fighters gave way to bombers which inflicted severe damage on the waiting Zeros.

As soon as the attackers had left, *Tai-i* Nakajima ordered a flight of three aircraft to follow the bombers. Two bomb-laden Zeros with an escort, led by *Tai-i* Yoshiyasu Kuno took off. Two aircraft returned to report that bad weather had prevented them from finding the enemy. It is not surprising that the *Yamato* and *Shikishima* units had not made contact with the enemy because they had no radar. *Tai-i* Kuno was reported missing; he had told Nakajima that if he did not engage the enemy along the target route he would fly to Leyte to take out a US vessel in a kamikaze dive. No suicide attack was reported for 21 October, so Kuno's fate remains unknown.

All this time *Chujo* Kurita's fleet was approaching San Bernadino Strait, now well within the range of US fighters. On 23 October the kamikaze unit leaders heard the news that US submarines (*Dace* and *Dasher*), patrolling Philippine waters unchallenged, had sunk two heavy cruisers of Kurita's main force, the 15,781-ton flagship cruiser *Atago*, and the emergency flagship, the 14,838-ton *Maya*; the heavy cruiser *Takao* was disabled but was able to return to Brunei Bay. Frustration for the Japanese was now rising to a high pitch. In this spirit *Chujo* Onishi addressed *Chujo* Fukudome:

'The 1st Air Fleet has been terribly shot up during the past month. It has fewer than fifty aircraft actually available for combat. There are about thirty fighters and only a few Mitsubishi G4M ['Betty' bombers], Nakajima B6N2 *Tenzan* ['Jill' torpedo-bombers] and Yokosuka D4Y *Suisei* ['Judy' dive-bombers].

'With so few planes it is impossible for us to continue fighting by conventional tactics. To do so would just wipe out our remaining strength. In view of this situation, and after a full examination and investigation of the various possibilities, lst Air Fleet has decided upon Special Attacks as offering the only chance of success. It is my hope that 2nd Air Fleet will join us in these attacks.'

Fukudome was not enthusiastic and it took Onishi a few days to persuade him of the value of the strategy:

'The evidence is quite conclusive that Special Attacks are our only chance. In this critical situation we must not lose precious time. It is imperative that the 2nd Air Fleet agree to Special Attacks.'

Day after day kamikaze sorties were attempted but all returned without making contact with assigned targets because of the frequently changing weather; sudden rain squalls allowing the US vessels to dodge the Zeros. The 350 aircraft of *Chujo* Fukudome's 2nd Air Fleet were also unsuccessful as they flew south to the Philippines, but their arrival boosted aircraft strength for a planned sortie on 24 October.

A 250-strong raid by Fukudome's 2nd Air Fleet – in bad weather – damaged the US vessels *Princeton* (CVL-23), *Leutze* (DD481), *Ashtabula* (AO-51) and *LST-552* on 24 October. A flight of fourteen Zeros attempted to give air cover to Kurita's vessels in the Sibuyan Sea, but soon the 10,000-ton heavy cruiser *Myoko* and the super-battleship *Musashi* were fleeing out of action. Then came a great psychological blow, *Musashi* was sunk, and Kurita was complaining of poor or non-existent air support. The kamikaze had had no successes.

On 24 October, too, hundreds of Imperial Japanese Army aircraft attacked the Americans in Leyte Gulf, but with little success. The lone Army kamikaze group (4th Army's 1st Air Group), formed after the Army had heard of Onishi's plans, did little damage. Records show that the US fleet tug *Sonoma* (Lieutenant W. R. Zursler) of Admiral Daniel E. Barbey's Northern Attack Force (TF 78) off Tacloban was struck by an Army kamikaze. It may be noted that on 28 November 1944, in *Imperial Ordinances* 649 and 650, a provision was set out giving posthumous promotion to any Army pilot who died in action after 15 October.

In the history of the Pacific War, 25 October 1944 marks the date of the core battle which the Japanese called *Reito Oki Kaisen* (Battle of Leyte Gulf, or the Battle off the Philippines). And it was the day when the kamikaze units noched up their first official personalised strikes and entered air history. And it was the day when the Japanese realised that their *taikan-kyoho-shugi* ('great warships, great guns') strategy had failed and that they could not drive the Americans from the beachheads on Leyte. Nothing remained but to try to discourage the enemy from moving closer to the mainland of Japan.

It was also a momentous day for the 'Father' of the kamikaze *Chujo* Onichi. Modern historians believe that Onichi only considered the use of the kamikaze as a temporary effort designed for a specific strategic purpose (the defence of the Philippines). He gave the impression that once this had been achieved through *Yamato damashii* (Japanese spirit), operational tactics could return to normal. The kamikaze units would thus be few, they would target specific enemy vessels, while other pilots carried out their regular duties.

Because of this impression Onishi managed to recruit a large number of volunteer pilots. Japan's perceived danger would inflame these pilots with a sense of patriotic duty and self-sacrifice – albeit in the short term. This potential Onishi intended to use to return the Japanese Navy to an advantageous position and ensure the success of *SHO-1*.

Today, too, historians speculate as to whether Onishi intended the kamikaze to attack on one day only (25 October) and with such devastating results that he would be able to disband them immediately. Certainly members of the Japanese Naval Staff interpreted his motives in this way, although he himself never clarified them. Purists also note that on 25 October the 2nd Air Fleet launched the unsuccessful conventional mass formation raid against the US Fleet which finally convinced *Chujo* Fukudome that the formation of 2nd Air Fleet kamikaze units was necessary. The 1st and 2nd Air Fleets were unified under Fukudome, with Onishi as Chief-of-Staff.

At sunrise on 25 October six aircraft of the *Yamato* unit took off from Cebu and turned eastwards. At 0735 hrs contact was made with the US force code-named 'Taffy 1' (77-4-1). This consisted of Rear Admiral Thomas L. Sprague's one *Kaiser* Class and three *Sangamon* Class escort carriers, three destroyers and five DEs, and they were steaming north of Mindanao, some forty miles from Surigao Island. The element of surprise was perfect. A lead Zero of the *Yamato* unit plunged into Captain R. E. Blick's 12,000-ton Fleet Aircraft Carrier *Santee* (CVE-29), striking the forward elevator of the flight deck, blasting a 15ft x 30ft hole and killing sixteen men; the vessel was able to remain in formation. A second Zero attacked the similar sized carrier *Sangamon* (CVE-26), but the aircraft was struck by a 5-inch shell fired from the nearby carrier *Suwannee* (CVE-27).

The Zero that attacked the 10,200-ton *Casablanca* class escort carrier *Petrof Bay* (CVE-80) was also destroyed, while the gunners of *Suwannee* downed another and crippled a third; the latter pilot rallied his machine and, aiming it at the US vessel, struck the flight deck forward of the stern elevator, inflicting a 25ft hole. The sixth aircraft of the *Yamato* unit disappeared. *Suwannee* was operational some two hours later.

At 0725 hrs the *Shikishima* unit, led by *Tai-i* Yukio Seki, took off from Mabalacat and some three hours later, about ninety miles east of Tacloban, made contact with Rear Admiral Sprague's 'Taffy 3' (77-4-3), a force that had been reduced at the Battle of Samar. Flying under the American radar, the *Shikishima* aircraft also achieved complete surprise, and the first Zero to be spotted was confronting the Escort Aircraft Carrier *Kitun Bay* (CVE-71), flagship of Rear Admiral R. A. Ofstie. Although the Zero's wing struck the superstructure above the flight deck which tipped the aircraft into the sea, its bomb did considerable damage. At the same time the carrier *Kalinin Bay* (CVE-68) was badly damaged when a Zero plunged into the flight deck. The carrier *Fanshaw Bay* (CVE70) shot down two Zeros, and two more attacked the carrier *White Plains* (CVE-66) but were driven off. The burning vessels, planes and exploding bombs created so much smoke that the gun crews were unable to spot the Zeros' line of approach and gunfire was erratic. Captain F. J. MacKenna's escort carrier *St Lo* (CVE-63) was sunk and it was claimed for unit leader *Tai-i* Seki. The 2nd Air Fleet were only able to log one instance of damage on 25 October when the *Rudderow* Class *Richard M. Rowell* (DE-403) was strafed.

At 1110 hrs *Kitun Bay* was under way when the bridge was informed that fifteen Yokosuka D4Y *Suisei* ('Judy') aircraft were approaching from astern. Captain J. P. Whitney ordered two Grumman F4F Wildcats to be catapulted off, but it was too late and the ship was left without a screen; one of a group of three kamikaze made a dive for the vessel from astern. The aircraft's wings were shot off, its bomb hit the water and some of its fuselage hit the forecastle. *Kalinin Bay* also received a hit on the flight deck, and a second aircraft crashed into her after deck. Much damage was caused, but the fires were quickly put out.

Instead of heading back to Mabalacat, the *Shikishimas'* escort Zeros made for Cebu. Here one of the pilots, air ace (Chief Warrant Officer) Hiroyoshi Nishizawa filed a totally misleading report of spurious successes. It was clear to all who read the report that Onishi's ideas were vindicated, and the pilots with whom Nishizawa now had contact were eager to get some last minute tips before they took their aircraft to destruction.

But *SHO-1* had failed and the Japanese forces had been utterly routed. Hailed as 'the greatest battle in naval history', the Japanese had lost twenty-six vessels grossing some 305,710 tons in the main encounters and several others in peripheral skirmishes. The loss of the super-battleship *Musashi*, ripped apart by twenty torpedoes and seventeen bombs, was a stunning psychological blow. The propagandists at Imperial Headquarters used NHK (*Nihon Hoso Kyokai*), the state broadcasting system, to describe in honorific terms the divine vengeance of the kamikaze. The excited commentator enthused:

'The *Shikishima* Unit of the *Shimpu Tokubetsu Kogekitai* made a successful surprise attack on an enemy task force containing four aircraft carriers at a point thirty miles north-east of Suluan Island at 1045 hrs. Two aircraft hit one carrier, which was definitely sunk. A third hit another carrier, setting it aflame. A fourth hit a cruiser, which sank instantly.'

The resulting euphoria had three further consequences. *Chujo* Fukudome was now totally won over to the suicide strategy; kamikaze volunteers came forward enabling Onishi to form more units; Japanese confidence that they could demoralise the Americans was strengthened. These first experimental kamikaze had had little success, but the Japanese believed that relentless waves of suicide pilots could win through.

Not long after these kamikaze attacks had taken place, Emperor Hirohito was informed of the *seifuku suru* (overwhelming defeat) of enemy forces by the *Shikishima* units. The Emperor had already commented to Marquis Koichi Kido (Lord Keeper of the Privy Seal):

'It is really regrettable, it's a shame, but I've given orders to the Chiefs-of-Staff to be careful not to lose our sense of combativity, not to become passive as far as operations are concerned.'

This was taken as being the Emperor's blanket approval of the kamikaze raids, although no order was issued directly by him. The *Kunaicho* now agreed a wording of a message to be sent to the kamikaze pilots and the Imperial General Staff sent it as a cablegram. Onishi passed it on in his own words:

'When told of the *Tokkotai*, *Sumeragi* said: "Was it necessary to go to this extreme?" *Sumeragi*'s words suggest that *Sumeragi* is greatly concerned. We must redouble our efforts to relieve *Sumeragi* of this concern. I have pledged our every effort toward that end.'

Off the record, Onishi himself was not pleased by the Emperor's words. Later Tadashi Nakajima was to remember: 'I think that the *Chujo* interpreted *Sumeragi*'s comments as criticism of the commander responsible for these tactics.' Historians aver that the words of the cablegram were to be bitterly remembered by Onishi when he took his own life.

On 28 October NHK stepped up the propaganda with news that Japan had used a secret weapon against the Americans:

'The *Shimpu Tokubetsu Kogekitai* guards the *Taikoku Nippon Kokumu* (Imperial Japanese Nation) and has admirably demonstrated the pure heart of the Japanese that was about to scatter like the petals of the cherry blossoms of [Mount] Shikishima. When thinking of them who behave like true Japanese, is there any amongst the hundred million nationals who will not raise his sleeve to his eyes?'

Such sentiments interlarded with misinformation were to follow from *Taisho* Toyoda:

'By deliberately self-blasting against enemy objectives, they achieved brilliant war results of one aircraft carrier sunk, another set on fire, and one cruiser instantly sunk. The memory of these gallant officers and men who died heroic deaths for the cause of their country will forever live in the minds of the nation.'

Propaganda films began to appear in Japanese cinemas showing exuberant kamikaze singing as they marched to their aircraft, the voice-overs lauding their courage. Teachers at schools, colleges and universities were instructed to praise the kamikaze to their pupils, many of whom would be conscripted and ultimately serve as kamikaze. And all the propaganda was wrapped up in sentiments of Japan's unrivalled moral and virtuous fibre when compared to occidentals. As the Chancellor of Osaka University said: 'We are far superior to America and Britain in our spiritual strength.'

Yet while NHK was prating there was immediate disquiet among Japanese intellectuals as to the morality and sense of the kamikaze attacks. One opponent was the distinguished disciple of Buddhism, Dr Daisetsu Teitaro Suzuki (1870–1966), who was highly regarded in the West. He believed that the kamikaze attacks were an exploitation of a Japanese 'mental defect' by the military. His views about the kamikaze had to wait a while before being given a public airing, for a tight censorship on intellectual thought was exerted by such agencies as the dreaded *Kempeitai* (Military Police). In March 1946 the magazine *Sekai* published this:

'The recent war must be considered from many angles. Certain characteristics peculiar to the Japanese deserve our special consideration. One manifestation of these peculiarities is the *Shimpu Tokubetsu Kogekitai* ...

'The *Dai Nippon Teikoku Rikugun* was imbued with certain German ideologies [after 1872 the Japanese Army's organisation was influenced by Prussian militarism] including the thought that war is destruction. The war potential of the enemy, whatever it be, must be destroyed ... War is the collision of two physical forces. The opposing force must be destroyed as quickly as possible. Soldiers, therefore, should not be thought of as human beings, but merely as a means of destruction. In this concept there is no distinction between the opposing forces.

'The kamikaze was born of such thinking. Shrink from nothing that may serve to destroy the war potential of the enemy. There were uttered such specious phrases as "the highest cause of our country", but thoughtful visions of the utterers never went beyond the physical realities of war. They were totally blind to the spiritual side of things.

'These war professionals strove endlessly to preserve from the *Tokkotai* the members of their own group who were best trained to fight. They first threw into the maw of battle the non-members of their clique – the civilian non-professionals fresh from colleges and universities.

'It is most regrettable that Japanese military men have consistently been so irreligious in their outlook. Army and Navy men reiterate endlessly such Shinto ideas as "the Divine Glory of *Sumeragi*", "the Divine Nation", "the Holy War", "the Imperial Host", and similar phrases. But they neglect or ignore such truly universal ideas as love, humanity, and mercy.

'*Shinto* is replete with gods of war, but there are no gods or goddesses of love. These war gods, as a consequence of Japan's insularity, are totally lacking in universality. They do not give life; they only take it.

'Deeming destruction the only way of war, the goal was to kill the enemy by any means at all. And the eternal thought was, "The essence of life is to die like a true *samurai*". Kamikaze attacks, the product of these two feudalistic concepts, provided a maximum of efficiency from man and material. And professional militarists cunningly took advantage of the situation.'

The Americans, though, back in October 1945, were assessing their own responses to the kamikaze attacks.

CHAPTER SEVEN

INITIAL AMERICAN RESPONSE

The psychology behind [the kamikaze attacks] was too alien to us. Americans who fight to live, find it hard to realise that another people will fight to die. — Admiral William Frederick Halsey (1884–1959), Commander of US Third Fleet, after the attack on USS *Intrepid*, 25 October 1944.

In 1995 a group of American ex-servicemen was gathered together for a programme on the kamikaze attacks which was given prime time by the British Broadcasting Corporation. The men were to speak about what they had experienced and witnessed during such raids. After fifty years they still remembered their initial reactions of bewilderment and terror as the kamikaze screamed their machines at them.

US naval photographer Robert Fentriss, who took the first film ever of a kamikaze dive, recalled how he and his comrades could not believe what was happening. That Japanese pilots were deliberately crashing their planes left them dumbstruck. Gunner's mate John Mitchell said that he was "scared stiff", and all were to experience a new type of war fear. Aviation metallurgist Dr Bill Simmons said, 'Suddenly we were not the great navy we thought we were.' The war had indeed entered a new phase.

The Japanese had expected that the suicide attacks would demoralise the American forces and panic the senior command into a hurried change of tactics away from the Japanese homeland, but, not for the first time, they had under-estimated American coolheadedness and a public attitude that almost suggested indifference.

Yet undoubtedly there was an emotion close to panic among the Allied forces in the Pacific when they had their first experience of the inhuman, premeditated death dive. Admirals Chester W. Nimitz and W. F. Halsey were genuinely worried, and Nimitz ordered a complete blackout on the kamikaze, as did the Australians. Indeed news of the kamikaze was concealed from the American public until April 1945. And because this, one of the greatest news stories of the war, was revealed in the press on the day (12 April) of the death at the age of sixty-three, of President Franklin Delano Roosevelt, while vacationing at Warm Springs, Georgia, little attention was given to the story. The British Admiralty also recommended silence, but the journals and log books of serving officers recorded the new horrific phenomenon. One such entry was written in his diary on 25 October by Captain Ray Tarbuck, senior naval representative on the staff of the Supreme Commander of the Allied Powers, General MacArthur:

'An innovation of this battle is the suicide dive. If [the Japanese Navy] has a hundred planes, which will be shot down tomorrow, [they] might as well "suidive" them today and burn out a hundred ships. A countermeasure must be found soon.'

In his *Le Survivant du Pacifique*, George Blond set out a standard example of how a suicide attack first appeared. Jean Larteguy edited it into his edition of *The Sun Goes Down* (1956):

'On 14 May, at 6.50 a.m., the radar plotter reported an isolated "blip", bearing 200° at 8,000 feet, range about 20 miles. The rear guns were pointed in that direction, ready to fire as soon as the "phantom" should appear. At 6.54 it came into sight, flying straight for the carrier. It disappeared for a moment in the clouds; then, after approximately three and a half miles, it emerged again, losing altitude. It was a Zero. The five-inch guns opened fire. The Japanese aircraft retreated into the clouds. The batteries continued to fire. The crew had been at action stations since four in the morning. All the aircraft that were not in the air had been de-fuelled and parked below decks.

'The Japanese machine approached from the rear. It was still not to be seen, as it was hidden by the clouds. Guided by radar, the five-inch guns continued to fire at it, and soon the 40-mm machine-guns began to fire as well. It was very strange to see all these guns firing relentlessly at an invisible enemy.

'The Japanese aircraft emerged from the clouds and began to dive. His angle of incidence was not more than 30 degrees, his speed approximately 250 knots. There could be no doubt – it was a suicide plane. [NB. It was to be several months before kamikaze became 'official', but other cases had been recorded.] It was approaching quite slowly and deliberately, and manoeuvring just enough not to be hit too soon.

'The pilot knew his job thoroughly and all those who watched him make his approach felt their mouths go dry. In less than a minute he would have attained his goal; there could be little doubt that this was to crash his machine on the deck [of the 19,800-ton carrier *Enterprise* (CV-6)].

'All the batteries were firing: the five-inch guns, the 40mm and the 20mm, even the rifles. The Japanese aircraft dived through a rain of steel. It had been hit in several places and seemed to be trailing a banner of flame and smoke, but it came on, clearly visible, hardly moving, the line of its wings as straight as a sword.

'The deck was deserted; every man, with the exception of the gunners, was lying flat on his face. Flaming and roaring, the fireball passed in front of the "island" [the single superstructure housing funnels, bridges, etc.] and crashed with a terrible impact just behind the for'ard lift.

'The entire vessel was shaken, some forty yards of the flight deck folded up like a banana-skin: an enormous piece of the lift, at least a third of the platform, was thrown over three hundred feet into the air. The explosion killed fourteen men; those boys would never laugh and joke again. The last earthly impression they took with them was the picture of the kamikaze trailing his banner of flame and increasing in size with lightning rapidity.

'The mortal remains of the pilot had not disappeared. They had been laid out in a corner of the deck, next to the blackened debris of the machine. The entire crew marched past the corpse of the volunteer of death. The men were less interested in his finely modelled features, his wide-open eyes which were now glazed over, than in the buttons on his tunic, which were to become wonderful souvenirs of the war for a few privileged officers of high rank. These buttons, now black, were stamped in relief with the insignia of the kamikaze corps; a cherry blossom with three petals.'

Initial countermeasures by the Americans included the restructuring of Task Force 38 (Vice Admiral Marc A. Mitscher) from four task groups to three; each group made up of a large number of carriers supported by a heavy screen, all under command of Vice Admiral John S. McCain aboard *Hornet* (CV-12). With his Staff Officers, Rear Admiral Wilder D. Baker and Captain J. S. Thatch, McCain planned certain tactical innovations to thwart the kamikaze.

First, by intensive training they increased the density and accuracy of anti-aircraft fire, and AA defences were strengthened on ships (and land bases). A consensus held that the best defence would be concentrated, precise and rapid fire. It was soon realised that the Zeros (slowed by their heavy bomb load) could easily be shot down. Secondly the number of dive-bombers on carriers was reduced and more fighters were added. Thirdly fighters were kept continually in the air above Japanese airfields in an endeavour to prevent the Japanese mounting any large-scale kamikaze attacks. Fighter patrols were also increased from carriers to intercept approaching kamikaze.

In due course returning Japanese pilots were reporting to their superiors the various American changes in tactics. For instance Ryuji Nagatsuka mentions in his *I Was a Kamikaze* (1972) that *Tai-i* Uehara reported that the Americans had 'invented a new tactic'. They were exploding shells around fleet vessels to create water spouts; as the kamikaze approached they were blinded by these and were caught in the AA fire.

Eventually Nimitz and Halsey reckoned that one in four kamikaze were making strikes, and one in thirty-three were sinking a vessel. The USSBS Report No 6. for the Philippines campaign officially reported to Washington that 26.8 per cent of the kamikaze were hitting a ship and 2.9 per cent were achieving a sinking.

In simple summary, the overall American reaction was to deal with the kamikaze with methodical efficiency, yet be fuelled by apprehension. The men slowly became unfazed by the somewhat creepy ideological and philosophical intentions of the suicide pilots and became more bothered about concrete results.

CHAPTER EIGHT

SUICIDE GROUPS EXPAND

'Weapons exhausted, our blood will bathe the earth, but the spirit will survive. Our spirits will return to protect the motherland.' — Poem by *Chujo* Mitsuru Ushijima (*d.* by suicide, 1945)

On 26 October *Chujo* Fukudome officially agreed to undertake suicide attacks. The great defeat of the Imperial Japanese Navy at Leyte Gulf had been such that no future co-ordinated action was possible. The only offensive weapon left to Japan was the air force. So an immediate follow-up was made. Quite early on the morning of the 26th, a Japanese reconnaissance pilot reported US vessels off Surigao. This was the formation that had been attacked by the *Yamato* unit the previous day. At 0815 hrs a kamikaze attack group took off, but disappeared without trace. Another group took off at 1030 hrs and sighted the enemy ships east of Surigao. With great skill they penetrated the cover being operated by some three-score Grumman F6F Hellcats and dived on the carriers *Sangamon* and *Petrof Bay*. They missed and plunged into the sea.

By this time a third group of kamikaze was in position and dived on the escort carrier *Suwannee*. One struck a Grumman TBF Avenger parked near the carrier's elevator; both aircraft exploded and set fire to a flight of nine Avengers. The attack killed 85 men, wounded 102, and fifty-eight men were missing. *Suwannee* left the formation to make for a repair base.

Kamikaze attacks were beginning to engender specific acts of bravery. *Suwannee*'s Executive Officer, Commander S. Van Mater, reported in the Action Report of 26 October 1944:

'After several calls to have medical supplies brought to the forecastle for those seriously injured were unproductive of results, an enlisted man informed Chief Aviation Electrician's Mate C. N. Barr that he would try to get through the flames to get medical supplies because he could no longer stand the sufferings of the wounded. Despite Barr's efforts to stop him, the man climbed to the 20mm mounts just forward of the flight deck. A second later a torpedo-bomber directly in his path exploded and the man was seen holding on to the starboard side of the flight deck with one leg blown off. A moment later he fell into the water and was not seen again. Every effort to ascertain his name has proved unavailing.'

Both extant Japanese Air Fleets were now given a common policy and Fukudome became overall commander with Onishi as Chief-of-Staff. The operations officer was to be *Taisa* Bunxo Shibata of 2nd Air Fleet, and *Tai-i* Rikihei Inoguchi became responsible for the suicide attacks. Thus Southwest Area Fleet (under the overall command of *Chujo* Guinichi Mikawa out of Manila) instituted a Combined Land Based Air Force.

Meanwhile *Chujo* [Army] Kyoji Tominaga, erstwhile Vice-Minister for War, was engaged in the air defence of the Philippines. He was soon to authorise the use of Army aircraft in his 4th Air Army for kamikaze *banda* (innumerable branches) missions; these Special Units trained by *Shosho* Imanishi and led by *Tai-i* [Army] Iwamoto became a part of the official war machine during November 1944, and the renamed *Manda Sakura* Unit rammed US bombers on 5 November. Initially Fukudome planned to use the former twelve Air Fleet fighters, from Chishima, the Japanese name for the northern Kurile bases, as kamikaze, and the remainder of the 2nd Air Fleet as conventional attackers. But the keenness to volunteer was such that by 27 October the 701st Air Group alone had formed four kamikaze units under *Taisa* Tatsuhiko Kida. They were to be called *Chuyu* (the Chinese literary sentiment of 'Fidelity and Courage'), *Seichu* (Chinese 'True Loyalty and Patriotism'), *Juncho* ('True Faith') and *Giretsu* ('Gallantry and Chivalry').

Determination and new tactics were also to make up for the serious shortage of new aircraft, fuel and limited pilot training facilities. The constant bombing of Japanese air bases by the Americans had reduced the effectiveness of the Japanese air forces who since 1943 had been unable to match the enemy's air power.

A new set of formations and procedures was set up for the kamikaze attacks. A standard 'best ratio' sortie of five kamikaze was formulated: three to attack and two escort aircraft. It was decided that small groups would be the most effective, giving maximum mobility and a better chance to get to targets unnoticed. Small groups were also relevant for another reason. The US attacks were so frequent that kamikaze aircraft had to be hidden at Philippine airfields under trees (often a long way from the runways and set among dummy decoy aircraft); small groups were easier to get into position.

Overall though, group sizes would vary to suit circumstances. The two escorts would fly one above and one below the attack aircraft to ward off enemy fighters. As *Tai-i* Tadashi Nakajima was to comment:

'Escort pilots had to be able to dodge adroitly and bluff the enemy, rather than just shoot him down. An escort pilot's first duty was to shield the suicide planes in his mission, even if it meant the sacrifice of his own life.'

As it took great skill to fly escort effectively, the best pilots were detailed for the job. A procedural pattern was formulated. First a search plane would radio sightings of enemy targets to base. This would be relayed to an airstrip operations room. Then an alert would be relayed to the airstrip operations room. The position of the enemy force would be pinpointed and the alert would be sounded. Ground crews would be mustered to wheel out the hidden aircraft to their runway. The enemy's course, strength and perceived tactical objective would be assessed and flying conditions to and from the target evaluated. By now the aircraft would have been bombed up and fuelled, and engines warmed up. Finally the number of kamikaze groups to launch would be assessed; pilots would get a final briefing and be dispatched. Usually it took about four hours from the sighting of an enemy task force to get the kamikaze away.

Kamikaze pilots flying from Clark Field in the Philippines might follow this kind of scenario from take-off to target:

The Yokosuka D4Y *Suisei*, Aichi D3A2 or Mitsubishi A6M *Zero-Sen* would head out to sea. The final view of land would be the lush greenery of the coconut forests along the margins of white beaches as depicted on the 5-centavos stamp issued by the Japanese postal authorities on the spot for the Filipino puppet government. On oxygen, the pilots would climb steadily, there being less chance of interception at high altitude. When the black dots that were enemy ships appeared on the horizon, the flight would go down, increasing speed, the escort fighters in close attendance to thwart interception. On this last leg the bomb's fuse safety-pin would be removed. From their carriers the Hellcats would take off to intercept. On the leader's signal, each of the pilots would dive on his chosen target (a carrier for preference), aiming at the flight deck elevator, and cutting through the barrage of gunfire, pray that his life would not be extinguished before the hit was made – 'See you at *Yasukuni!*' A strike would set off huge sheets of flame with thick spirals of carbon-black smoke, and another kamikaze soul would be deemed to have soared to the realms of the *kami*.

From 27 October, while Japanese airfields were being continually strafed and bombed, kamikaze attacks were being launched against the US combat fleet at sea and the vessels of the amphibious force in Leyte Gulf. As many aircraft as possible (mostly Zeros) were sent to the airfields at Cebu and

Luzon, via Kyushu and Formosa, to supplement losses. For instance, seventeen Zeros were transferred from Mabalacat to the increasingly important operational base at Cebu to reinforce the *Yamato* unit. On its way the flight, led by *Tai-i* Kanno, encountered Grumman F6F Hellcats; the Japanese pilots downed a dozen of these for the loss of one Zero, which greatly increased their morale.

But 27 October was to be a day of discouragement for *Chujo* Onishi. His depression about Japan's position increased, and he told his senior staff officer Rikihei Inoguchi:

'The fact that we have to resort to kamikaze attacks shows how poor our strategy has been. This is certainly an unorthodox command.'

For Onishi and his senior staff kamikaze attacks were not to be contemplated as 'blind fanaticism', but as a decision based on the 'realities of war'.

A report that arrived in Onishi's in-tray 'for information' was to become a fundamental example in the history of the kamikaze for its illustration of the pilot's self-abnegation. It was written by *Tai-i* Naoji Fukabori, leader of the *Juncho* unit of 701st Air Group of 2nd Air Fleet, who had landed at Cebu. He had turned back from his sortie to Leyte Gulf with a jammed firing mechanism and it was too dark to operate:

'[27 October 1944]

'To: (1) *Chusa*, 701st Air Group, Nichols Field.

'To: (2) *Shosa* Ema, Mabalacat Eastern Field.

'Today I made an emergency landing at Legaspi [on Bohol, Philippines], because of trouble with my bomb fuse. After it was fixed I joined my unit and proceeded to Leyte, arriving there at 1850. We circled over the gulf at 1,000 metres but the sun had set and enemy ships were not distinguishable. Heavy ack-ack fire indicated their presence. The two planes with me appeared to have plunged into enemy ships, but there was insufficient light for me to identify a worthwhile target. I therefore abandoned the attack and headed for the airfield at Cebu.

'Landed safely at Cebu about 2030. It is my intention to fly from here early tomorrow morning and find a suitable target for attack. The following observations are made in the hope that they will prove of value to those who come after me.

'1. The bomb fuse lock should be checked carefully before departure.

'2. Loaded with one 250-kilogramme bomb and four 60-kilogramme bombs, a plane can cruise at 125 knots. Bearing this in mind it is essential to calculate the proper time of departure. Ship types cannot be recognised readily unless the target area is reached by 1820 at the latest. From the air it is difficult to find a target at sea, even in the brightest light.

'3. In a properly timed dusk attack I believe that even a Type-99 carrier dive-bomber can succeed in making a special attack.

'4. I recommend consideration of dawn attacks, using Cebu as a stopover base. In a dawn attack there is less chance of being caught by enemy fighters, and additional fuel in the plane will add to the destructiveness of the blow.

'5. Above all, do not lose patience. Wait until conditions for attack are satisfactory. If a pilot loses patience he is apt to plunge into an unworthy target.

'[Postscript]: The good faith of our pilots makes me confident that the Imperial Prestige will last forever. Our pilots are young but their behaviour is brilliant. There is no need to worry about selecting kamikaze pilots. I wish you the best of luck and good health. *Sayonara*.'

It is thought that Fukabori was successful with his suicide dive the day after he wrote this report; his target is presumed to have been the 10,000-ton light cruiser *Denver* (LC-58) which was hit on this date.

Targets became more and more plentiful as the American build-up in the Philippines continued. On 29 October Rear Admiral Gerald F. Bogan's Task Group Two (TG 38.2) struck at airfields around Manila, and claimed 71 Japanese aircraft shot down and thirteen potential kamikaze destroyed on the ground.

Now preserved as an integral feature of today's Manhattan scene at New York's West 46th Street and 12th Avenue, Captain J. F. Bolger's USS *Intrepid* (CV-11) – with Air Group 18 – was to win the dubious honour of being the first Allied capital ship to be struck by a kamikaze. Launched by Newport News Shipbuilding and Dry Dock Co of Newport News, Virginia, on 26 April 1943, the *Essex* Class *Intrepid* was commissioned in August 1943. With a complement of 360 officers and 3,200 men, she carried Grumman F6F Hellcats, SBD Dauntless scout bombers and Grumman TEF/M Avenger torpedo-bombers (and later SB2C Helldivers and F4U Corsairs). *Intrepid* had served during the preparation for the invasion of the Marshall Islands, the Truk Island attack and in the attack on Japanese airfields in the Palau Islands. During these last days of October 1944 she was attacked by kamikaze, one of which struck a gun battery, killing six men and injuring six others. Damage was superficial and the carrier continued to launch raids on Japanese airfields. There were to be at least two other kamikaze attacks on *Intrepid* but the vessel neither lost propulsion nor left station.

On 30 October, despite heavy AA fire, a kamikaze unit from Cebu managed to pin-point a squadron of Vice Admiral Marc A. Mitscher's Fast Carrier Force TF38, cruising some forty miles south-east of Suluan Island. In a flight of two groups of three, and attacking from different directions and at different altitudes, two aircraft of one group struck Captain J. M. Shoemaker's fleet carrier *Franklin* (CV-13) and blew a 40ft hole in the flight deck; the third kamikaze attacked Captain John Perry's escort carrier *Belleau Wood* (CVL-24), killing 56 men and destroying twelve aircraft. Both carriers withdrew to Ulithi.

From this point the kamikaze tacticians began to work on Appropriate Target Selection techniques which were to be honed to a high degree of success by a new kamikaze force.

CHAPTER NINE

THE SUICIDE CORPS EVOLVE

'We pray for the final victory of the Motherland. We will fight to the last man.' — *Taisa* Jiro Haneda, 931st Air Group.

Despite the failure of the *SHO-1* Operation, the Japanese High Command now considered the kamikaze corps too important to be disbanded. A new strategic objective was evolved and accepted at the highest level in the Navy: to assist and co-operate with the Imperial Japanese Army in destroying enemy forces. By November 1944 naval kamikaze units were effectively supporting the efforts of 16th Army Division at Leyte by attacking enemy transports.

By this time, too, the strains of war were telling on *Chujo* Onishi. His colleagues saw a personality change from confident efficiency to introspection, and as he was not eating well his weight loss became noticeable. All Onishi's time was now spent in formulating new methods of attack for his kamikaze. In early November the ailing Onishi flew to Imperial General HQ at Tokyo to give his assessment of the Philippine war and demand 300 aircraft to reinforce the Special Attack Force. Although Onishi's assessment of the situation was accepted, there were nowhere like that number of aircraft available; only some 150 were raised from the training bases at Omura in north-west Kyushu, the Japanese Korean colony of Genzan, Tsukuba, some forty miles north-west of Tokyo and Koh-no-Ike.

These aircraft were mostly Mitsubishi A6M *Zero-Sens* and Yokosuka D4Y *Suiseis,* manned mostly by reserve ensigns, most of whom had less than one hundred hours of flying training. They were augmented by instructors and student trainees. Consequently there were several en route losses as the aircraft were transferred to kamikaze commands. The pilots were incorporated into 1st Air Force and transferred to Formosa's (Japanese Taiwan) Taichu and Tainan airfields for extra training, flying there across the treacherous waters of the Satsunan archipelago at Amami-o-shima and via Okinawa. Their training was undertaken by *Tai-i* Inoguchi who had formulated a new instruction programme.

The syllabus began with a 7-day indoctrination and proficiency course. Days one and two were spent in take-off practice, from the receipt of the order to sortie to being airborne. Days three and four were devoted to formation flying, linked with more take-off practice, and days five, six and seven were for studying the approach to, and attacking of targets, with a number of practice 45–55 degree dives. Emphasis was also placed on navigational skill and Inoguchi insisted that no pilot should take off without an air chart and a personally drawn sketch of the Philippines. The final day's training also took in accurate bomb-release procedures. Too many pilots had failed to activate their bombs and, missing their target, the bomb went to the bottom with the aircraft and with no resultant damage to the target.

When flying the light, fast Zeros and *Suiseis*, Inoguchi recommended alternative approaches to the target: either from high or low altitude. To avoid enemy fighters the high-altitude approach from 6,000–7,000 metres was most effective; from here the pilot began to dive at an angle of 20 degrees as soon as the target was sighted. At 1,000–2,000 metres the dive was steepened to 45–55 degrees at 200 knots, directly on to the target.

In the low-altitude approach the aircraft would come in at a height of 10–15 metres where the US radar's range was limited to about ten miles, which made interception difficult. The pilot would then climb sharply to 400–500 metres above the target and come down in a steep dive. For both approaches the best point of aim (against aircraft carriers) was the central elevator, failing which, the forward or after elevators. Destruction of any of the elevators would reduce the vessel's operability. For small warships, transports and destroyers, a hit between the bridge and the centre of the vessel was thought most effective. As soon as each batch of trainees had fulfilled the training programme, Inoguchi sent them to the Philippines.

In the meantime *Tai-i* Iwamoto's *Manda Sakura* Army unit went into action officially on 5 November 1944, his unit usually consisting entirely of commissioned officers. As Onishi had given his units a pep-talk before flying, so did the Army Air Force senior officer *Chujo* Kyoji Tomonaga, as quoted by John Dean Potter in *A Soldier Must Die* (1963):

'When men decide to die like you they can move the heart of the Emperor. And I can assure you that the death of every one of you will move the Emperor. It will do more – it will even change the history of the world.

'I know what you feel now as you put the sorrows and joys of life behind you because the Emperor's fortunes are failing. Do not worry about what happens when you die and what you leave behind you – for you will become gods. Soon I hope to have the privilege of joining you in glorious death.'

Tai-i Iwamoto then led his pilots towards Leyte Gulf. Some eighty miles from Clark Field they encountered US carrier bombers on their way to attack Japanese bases. Iwamoto radioed back to say that he was engaging the enemy. He and his four pilots each targeted an aircraft and rammed it. Iwamoto entered the history of the kamikaze as a hero and even had a poem written in his honour.

The steady stream of reinforcements from Formosa helped to intensify the suicide attacks. On 25 November searching kamikaze units discovered Vice Admiral Mitscher's Task Force 38 off the coast of Leyte. By noon on that day Admiral Bogan's Group Two were at sea some sixty miles off Dijohan Point on the San Ildefonso Peninsula of Luzon. The kamikaze attack lasted some twenty-five minutes. Serious damage was done to the fleet carriers *Hancock* (CV-19), *Intrepid* (CV-11) and the light cruisers *Cabot* (CVL-28) and *Independence* (CVL-22). Admiral Frederick C. Sherman's Group Three, containing 15th Air Group, were also attacked with damage to *Essex* (CV-9).

Records show that one of the most destructive kamikaze raids in the Philippines campaign was flown on 27 November by both Army and Navy pilots. Some thirty kamikaze penetrated the fighter cover and made for Admiral T. D. Ruddock's Fire Support Unit North. At 1100 hrs – ninety minutes after leaving their base – they swooped. The light cruiser *St Louis* (CL-49) was the first casualty, her catapult and aircraft being damaged; this was followed by another light cruiser *Montpelier* (CL-57) which was hit by a quartet of kamikaze. In all eight aircraft attacked *Montpelier*, five scoring direct hits. The ship was able to retain formation, but the crew saw for the first time the carnage of a suicide hit; pilots' shattered body fragments were everywhere – a tongue, scalp, brains, knee-caps and other bones hanging among the wreckage were hosed into the sea.

By now some American naval personnel were becoming accustomed to the three-fold destructive effects of a kamikaze raid. First the explosion of the released bomb, followed by the impact of the crashing aircraft which could cut through armour plating, and finally the aircraft's exploding fuel tanks dousing everything with a burning stream of aviation fuel which flowed into every crevice of the ship's interior.

Two suicide attacks were made against US vessels of the amphibious force near the coast of Leyte on 28 November, but no real damage was done. As evening progressed on 29 November Captain H. J. Ray's battleship *Maryland* (BB-46) was performing the role of guide in the midst of the Task Force 77.2 formation, steaming on a northerly course in Leyte Gulf. *Colorado*

(BB-45) and *St Louis* (CL-49), with four destroyers, were stretched out to the east some five miles away. Sunset was overcast by intermittent rain squalls. Between the breaks in the clouds kamikaze appeared to give the tense, waiting seamen an incredible display of stunt flying.

Maryland was the first to be hit; the kamikaze crashed into one of her 16-inch gun turrets, killing 31 men and causing extensive damage. Meanwhile two kamikaze dived on the picket destroyers *Saufley* (DD-465) and *Aulick* (DD-569). The carnage in the latter was severe: the bridge was smashed and two 5-inch guns were destroyed, but more importantly 32 men were dead or missing and 64 were wounded – which meant that a third of the crew was incapacitated. NHK Radio in Tokyo hailed the attack on Task Force 77.2 as an *okii sensho* ('great victory').

By early December 1944 the frequency of Japanese attacks had noticeably decreased, and US strategists assumed that the Japanese were running out of aircraft. Strategically this was not the case; the High Command were holding back a reserve for an anticipated new major offensive by the Americans.

In early December the Americans were preoccupied with the imminent landings in the Japanese-held Ormoc area on the west coast of Leyte, and naval tactics were confined to sweep and counter-sweep. At 1100 hrs on 5 December an anti-submarine and radar picket patrol was being led by Captain K. F. Poehlmann in *Mugford* (DD-389) and Commander W. Thompson in *La Vallette* (DD-448), when a group of eight kamikaze appeared as the convoy was moving slowly through the Surigao Strait. Five were speedily shot down, but one successfully crashed amidships on LSM-20, sinking the vessel with eight crew deaths. Another ricocheted into LSM-23 to her great damage, while the eighth made for the destroyer *Drayton* (DD-366). Commander R. S. Craighill ordered open fire and rudder full left. The kamikaze passed down the vessel's starboard side at about 350 knots, its wing tip just missing the bridge. When the pilot realised that he was going to miss, he rolled his aircraft on to its starboard wing and struck the forward 5-inch gun. Although the greater part of the wrecked aircraft skidded clear, a portion of the wing and landing gear killed six and wounded a dozen crewmen. Aboard *Flusser* (DD-368), Captain W. M. Cole and his crew watched *Drayton's* plight. He later wrote this endorsement in *Drayton's* Action Report – the 'entire performance was observed with thrill and admiration'.

On 7 December a TG 78.3 Attack Group under Rear Admiral A. D. Struble was moving in to land troops of 77th Infantry Division south of the town of

Ormoc. A kamikaze unit was despatched to attack the convoy. At 0934 hrs twelve Japanese bombers and four fighters approached the picket destroyer *Mahan* (DD-364) and destroyer transport *Ward* (APD-16). Observers were to record of this, one of the most unusual and devastating of the kamikaze assaults of 1944, that the Japanese aircraft used torpedo-launching tactics, but when they had been hit (mostly by Lockheed P–38 Lightnings) they switched to kamikaze attacks, diving on *Mahan* and *Ward* simultaneously. Three Japanese bombers were shot down, but a fourth hit *Mahan* aft of the bridge, and a fifth hit her on the waterline. Another bomber, which had missed in a first pass over the destroyer, turned back to make a successful hit between waterline and forecastle deck. Captain Campbell ordered Abandon Ship; mercifully only ten men had been killed or were missing after the deadly attack. *Mahan* was scuttled. Lieutenant R. E. Farwell's *Ward* was attacked by three kamikaze and was struck by one, just above the waterline. A huge explosion ensued and the ship lay dead in the water. Abandon Ship was sounded and *Ward* too was scuttled. The two vessels had been dispatched inside fourteen minutes. As Admiral Struble ordered his ships to withdraw to Leyte Gulf, a flock of 'Zekes' pursued and one crashed into the bridge of *Liddle* (DE-206), killing her skipper Lieutenant Commander L. C. Brogger.

On 10 December the Japanese counter-attacked at Leyte Gulf with eight Mitsubishi G4M bombers; one suicide attacker dived on the destroyer *Hughes*; others scored on the Liberty Ship *William S. Ladd* and the *PT-323* and *LCT-1075*. The Japanese 'bag' was to be added to next day when Captain J. D. Murphy took the second US resupply echelon out of Leyte Gulf. They were attacked by a dozen or so Nakajima B6N2 *Tenzan* which scored successful hits on Commander Samuel A. McCornock's destroyer *Reid* (DD-369) and Commander D. R. Robinson's (flag) ship *Caldwell* (DD-605). Next day *Caldwell* was singled out by a group of three Mitsubishi A6M *Zero-Sen* in a perfectly planned and executed operation. Two of the aircraft attempted to bomb the ship, but were deflected by the destroyer's main armament. The third accelerated down the port side under a barrage of machine-gun fire and flew across the stern. The pilot then undertook a vertical bank but crashed. One wing hit the bridge and the fuselage crashed into the main radio antenna. While this was happening *Caldwell* was being bombed, one kamikaze scoring a hit near No 1 gun. Thirty-three men were killed or missing, and 40 were wounded. It took an hour to put out the fires, after which the ship rejoined the formation.

Operationally the Japanese Army Air Services committed more than 1,000 aircraft to the Leyte campaign. The Army disapproved of Onishi's tactics of using small groups of suicide pilots; they would have preferred massed kamikaze units operating under a combined Navy/Army strategy. Army leaders thought that Onishi spent too much time chasing Allied warships and not enough in targeting supply vessels and transports. The Army also decided to do away with bombing operations and concentrate on kamikaze efforts.

Throughout 1944 more and more of America's long-range heavy bombers, the Boeing B-29 Superfortresses, appeared over Japanese territory. They caused the Japanese great problems because they flew at such high altitudes (ceiling 33,600 feet) that current Japanese fighters could not cope with them. One officer who was increasingly frustrated by the success of the B–29s was *Shosho* Kiyaro Yoshita, acting commander of 10th Air Division based near Kyoto city. His brief was to defend Tokyo and the surrounding industrial areas of the Kanto Plain. Every time B–29s appeared over his area of command Yoshita sent up his entire force, but his aircraft could not reach the altitude of the bombers.

On 7 November 1944, when B–29s were crossing Yoshita's territory, one of them hit a wind current and lost height. One of Yoshita's pilots, who were impotently shadowing the tight formation of bombers, moved into position and rammed his fighter into the bomber at full throttle. The B–29 and the fighter plunged from 30,000 feet in a shower of wreckage. On reading the report of the encounter Yoshita reasoned that to have any future chance he would have to lighten his aircraft by stripping them of armour plating, bombing equipment, guns and ammunition so that they could reach higher altitudes and ram the enemy. At this date ramming was still a controversial affair, but Yoshita believed that it was the only way out. Consequently Yoshita established a number of such suicide units within 10th Air Division.

Yoshita reasoned that the tactical procedure would be simple. Each unit would be accompanied by a control aircraft whose pilot would chose a target for attack and order the unit in. If no quarry could be selected the unit would return to base. Located some fifty miles west of Tokyo, Squadron 47 of Yoshita's command was selected as a feeder for these special units. Army *Tai-i* Okuta of the 47th was chosen as commander of one of these units, and trained with seven young enlisted pilots. They called themselves the *Shinten* ('earth-shaking') unit.

On 27 November B–29 attacks began in earnest over Honshu. First blood for the *Shinten* was chalked up to *Gocho* (Corporal) Yoshinao Mita; he downed a B–29 with a direct ramming. As the raids on Tokyo itself escalated, more of the 47th's kamikaze scored direct ramming hits, like *Gunso* Shinobu Iketa and *Gocho* Kemoko Usui of the *Ran Hana* ('Orchid') Unit. By the end of the year *Shosho* Yoshita had recorded sixteen kills for his kamikaze units.

All the while Japanese strategists were worried that the Americans were planning an offensive to invade the western Philippines. This, if successful, would severely damage Japan's hold on the islands and ultimately threaten their control from Mindanao to Luzon. On 13 December the *Johohei* (Military Intelligence) reported a huge US Task Force steaming westwards through Surigao Strait (between Bohol/Leyte and Mindanao). So the Japanese decided to launch a powerful serial counter-offensive.

At dawn on 14 December eleven Japanese Navy aircraft set off to scour the seas south of Negros Island for US activity. None was reported, but two Kawanishi E15K1 *Shuin* ('Violet Cloud', code-named 'Norm') reconnaissance aircraft, 23 new Navy fighters – the Kawanishi NIK2-J *Shiden* ('Violet Lightning', code-named 'George') – 30 *Zero-Sen* and six new twin-engined Yokosuka PIYI *Ginga* ('Milky Way', code-named 'Francis') took off from Mabalacat. From a nearby airfield *Jun-i* Yonosuke Iguchi set off with three Yokosuka D4Y *Suisei* bombers. Together they made up the largest kamikaze group ever to take to the air. Their task was to fly to Negros Island and, if necessary, search the Mindanao Sea for American ships.

The kamikaze group was dispersed by Grumman F6F Hellcat fighters and poor weather, and most abandoned the mission. *Jun-i* Iguchi, however, did not return. He reported to base by radio that his bomb-release mechanism had jammed and that if he landed the bomb would explode. He said that he was now on the lookout for any likely target. None was apparently found, but over his radio the diving cry of *Tenno banzai!* (Long live the Emperor) was heard, then silence.

Elsewhere 'Divine Wind' elements had had greater success, kamikaze groups scoring in the Sulu Sea where the light cruiser *Nashville* (CL-43) was attacked and severely damaged; 133 men were killed and more than 190 wounded.

On 15 December a *taifu* (looked upon by the Japanese as a divinely inspired typhoon) hit the US Third Fleet east of the Philippines and caused great damage. Eight hundred men died, such vessels as the destroyers *Hull*,

Monaghan and *Spence* of the TG 30.8 At Sea Logistics Group sank, 186 aircraft were lost overboard and the fleet had to retire to Ulithi for repairs.

Meanwhile on Formosa the last group of 28 trainees were faced with a problem. There were only thirteen aircraft left. Although another twelve were cobbled together, Inoguchi decided that they could never be airworthy and he flew out with the last thirteen to Clark Field on 23 December. There he found that 1st Air Fleet HQ had been moved from Manila to Bamban Base at the northernmost end of Clark Field.

As 1944 drew to a close several kamikaze groups took off from Mabalacat and attacked supply convoys off Mindanao. One tanker, *Porcupine* (IX-126), was sunk, but none of these efforts delayed the US reconquest of Luzon.

CHAPTER TEN

THEY CAME TO LUZON

'There was a hypnotic fascination to a sight so alien to our Western philosophy. We watched each plunging kamikaze with the detached horror of one witnessing a terrible spectacle rather than as the intended victim ... And dominating it all was a strange admixture of respect and pity.'
— Vice Admiral Charles. R. Brown, US Navy

On 2 January 1945, the 164 ships of TG 77.2 Bombardment and Fire Support Group under the command of Vice Admiral Jesse B. Oldendorf aboard *California* set course for Luzon through the Surigao Strait. Their route was to take them through the Sulu Sea, past Bohol, Cebu, Negros and Panay, up into the Mindoro Strait and out into the South China Sea to head for the target area at Luzon, Lingayen Gulf. From a lookout point in northernmost Mindanao the Japanese caught sight of the fleet and a small kamikaze flight was dispatched from Sarangani on 3 January. Only one Aichi D3A2 (code-named 'Val') got through the intensive AA fire to inflict scanty damage on the oiler *Cowanesque* and the sortie was abandoned. For a while Japanese pilots kept a mainly watching brief.

During the afternoon of 4 January the kamikaze appeared again as the fleet rounded Panay Island east of Palawan. A few were shot down before they could make their dives. Again only one pilot was able to penetrate the barrage to crash-dive on to the deck of Captain H. L. Young's escort carrier *Ommaney Bay* (CVE-79); this time the damage was such that Young ordered Abandon Ship and *Ommaney Bay* was blown up by the destroyer *Burns*. One hundred and fifty-eight men had been killed and wounded.

By 5 January all available aircraft of 1st Air Fleet had been ordered to attack, and Army kamikaze were also scrambled. Following an intelligence report that 700 US vessels were west of Mindanao, *Tai-i* Shinichi Kanaya took off from Mabalacat with fifteen Zeros and two escorts. One aircraft was shot down by the protecting Grumman F6F Hellcats, but the others of the kamikaze flight eluded the fighters and made for the fleet.

In all some ten vessels were to suffer hits or be clipped. Rear Admiral Theodore E. Chandler's flagship, the heavy cruiser *Louisville* (CA-28) received a crash dive on No 2 turret; fires were quickly brought under control, but one seaman was killed and 59 were wounded. The heavy cruiser HMAS *Australia* received a kamikaze crash with bomb in place which killed 25 men and wounded 30. HMAS *Arunta* lost two men, and the radar antenna of the escort carrier *Savo Island* (CVE-78) was clipped. The escort carrier *Manila Bay* (CVE-61) was hit by two Zekes from 800-foot dives. One aircraft hit the flight deck and its bomb exploded in the upper hangar area; the other aircraft fell into the sea; 22 men were killed and 56 wounded. One kamikaze broke through the AA fire to strike *Stafford* (DE-411). The aftermast of *Helm* (DD-388) was clipped by a tumbling kamikaze. *Orca* (AVP-49), *Apache* (AFT-67) and *LCI(G)-70* also suffered damage.

Although Japan's aircraft factories were largely unhampered by bombing raids at this time, future shortages could not be far away. Zealous mechanics of 1st Air Fleet at Mabalacat cannibalised wrecked aircraft to get five Zeros into possible flying condition. It is interesting to note that ground staff from mechanics to radio operators heeded *Chujo* Onishi's remarks that they were kamikaze too; he had made it clear that it was not necessary to fly to be a 'suicide *samurai* for the Emperor'; to Onishi the kamikaze spirit was a state of mind despite specialised work. So these cobbled-up aircraft were inspected with dignity by *Shosa* Tadashi Nakajima; pronounced serviceable for one last raid, and permission to fly was given. Nakajima chose *tai-is* Yuso Nakano and Kunitane Nakao to command the units of three and two planes; the other flyers were *Jun-is* Goto, Taniuchi and Chihara.

At dawn on 6 January the US fleet anchored in Lingayen Gulf, and soon after first light the kamikaze began to attack. Of ten aircraft sighted, five were shot down, and no ships were damaged. The fighters withdrew, but just before noon they returned to attack in force. The battleship *New Mexico* (BB40), flag of the San Fabian Fire Support Group, was struck and sustained more than 100 dead and injured, including senior officer observers including Lieutenant-General Herbert Lumsden (Winston Churchill's personal liaison officer at General MacArthur's HQ). The destroyer *Walke* (DD-723) was struck by a kamikaze which set off serious petrol fires in which the ship's skipper, Commander George F. Davis, died. Fourteen were killed aboard the destroyer *Allen M. Sumner* (DD-692), and the fast minesweeper *Long* (DMS-12) and the transporter *Brooks* (APD-10) were sunk by Zekes.

In the late afternoon the Mabalacat kamikaze turned their attention to the Fire Support Column of Task Force 38 and crashed into the battleship *California* (BB-44). HMAS *Australia* received more hits as did *Louisville*. This time the kamikaze got themselves an admiral. Rear Admiral Theodore E. Chandler was on the flag-bridge of *Louisville* when the kamikaze hit the starboard side; the admiral was doused with burning petrol and died of burns next day.

These had been three black and demoralising days for the US Fleet; from 3 to 6 January the kamikaze had scored 25 ships sunk or damaged, and Admiral Oldendorf was pressed to comment on the increased amount of 'friendly fire' which had damaged the likes of Captain Smoot's flagship the destroyer *Newcombe*. He felt that it was operational carelessness during kamikaze raids, and issued this warning:

'A day which was characterised by brilliant performance on the part of many ships was seriously marred by indiscriminate, promiscuous and uncontrolled shooting. Ammunition was wasted, death and injury to shipmates inflicted, and material damage caused to our ships. All hands are enjoined to make certain that their guns are fired at the enemy and not at their shipmates.' (*History of United States Naval Operations in WWII*)

Japan's news reports of the events of these three days were backed with the voices of kamikaze singing the *samurai* song:

'In serving on the seas, be a corpse saturated with water.

In serving on land, be a corpse covered with weeds.

In serving the sky, be a corpse that challenges the clouds.

Let us all die close by the side of the Emperor.'

At this time too, *Chujo* Onishi summoned *Shosho* Tomozo Kikuchi, Chief-of-Staff of 2nd Air Fleet and *Tai-i* Inoguchi to a meeting with 1st Air Fleet Chief-of-Staff Toshihiko Odawara. He announced a four-point tactical plan. The 2nd Air Fleet were to be disbanded and its air units given over to 1st Air Fleet; the jurisdiction of 1st Air Fleet was to be extended to Formosa. The 1st Air Fleet headquarters staff, pilots and senior radio technicians were to withdraw to Formosa. Onishi dated the order to be effective from 8 January. Plans also included the defence of Clark Field from Bamba Hill by *Shosho* Ushie Sugitomo, commander of 26th Air Flotilla and *Chujo* Kazuma Kondo, chief of the Air Arsenal. In the meantime the kamikaze attacks were to continue where possible.

During the evening of 6 January, Onishi and Fukudome gathered their staff officers together at Bamban for a last meal together of dried *ika* (cuttlefish) and *sake* (rice wine). Later that evening two Mitsubishi G4M bombers landed for the senior staff's evacuation to Formosa. At dawn on 8 January *Chusa* Nakajima and *Tai-i* Takeshi Shimizu took off from Mabalacat on separate courses in two Yokosuka D4Y *Suisei* dive-bomber/reconnaissance aircraft to transfer the kamikaze records to Formosa. Shimizu's aircraft crashed near Takao in heavy fog, to his severe injury, but Nakajima reached Tainan in safety.

On 7 January Rear Admiral Daniel E. Barbey's Seventh Amphibious Fleet was attacked by a succession of single kamikaze. First a near-miss was recorded near the light cruiser *Boise* (CL-47) which had General MacArthur aboard. Another singleton Mitsubishi Ki–46 succeeded in sinking the minesweeper *Palmer* (DMS-5) with 28 killed or missing and 38 wounded. The kamikaze soon learned that US minesweepers were usually isolated and hadn't much in the way of AA protection, so they offered a much easier passage to the *Yasukuni-jinja.*

On 8 January Captain R. N. Hunter's escort carrier *Kadashan Bay* (CVE-47) was damaged by a lone kamikaze and had to return to Leyte. The cruiser *Australia* was again hit. The attack transport *Callaway* was struck in the starboard wing and 29 crewmen were killed and 22 wounded, to prove the devastation that could be caused by the fragments of an exploding aircraft. Before the day ended Admiral Theodore S. Wilkinson's Task Force 79 of troop transports was attacked and Rear Admiral Ofstie's flagship, the escort carrier *Kitun Bay* (CVE-71) was hit by a kamikaze below the waterline and had to withdraw in tow by the fleet tug *Chowanoc.*

On 9 January, the day of the US landings in Lingayen Gulf, Luzon, three kamikaze from Nichols Field attacked; one dived on the destroyer escort *Hodges* (DE-231), but the pilot miscalculated the angle of the dive, demolished the foremast and radio antennae and crashed into the sea with no shipboard casualties. The light cruiser *Columbia* (CL-56) was seriously damaged by a direct hit on the forward main battery director; 24 men were killed or missing and 63 were wounded. But the Japanese were becoming weakened in air strength, so the US troops landed without much opposition, except for two strikes. Just after 1300 hrs, two Aichi D3A2 kamikaze dive-bombers out of Tuguegarao made for the battleship *Mississippi* (BB-41) and HMAS *Australia*. In a very brief moment 23 men were killed or mortally wounded and 63 injured in *Mississippi* as one Aichi glided over the forecastle, hit the port side and carried on into an AA mounting before splashing into the sea. *Australia* sustained no casualties because the kamikaze pilot miscalculated his dive, just catching the foremast strut to be swung overboard in a square-dance swing of death.

US intelligence began to report that miscalculated dives were increasing. The Japanese were in fact scraping together pilot replacements from as far afield as Manchuria and Korea, and some of these men had less than forty hours of flying experience. Some could barely take off and land, and few had

had much gunnery practice. Navigation too was something of a mystery to tyro pilots. US intelligence noted that all Japanese units of whatever kind were likely now to become kamikaze. So it was during the hours of darkness on 10/11 January that the Japanese Imperial Army first used the 2–3-crew, 16–18.5ft, 2-ton 'suicide boat', the *Shinyo* (powered by car engines and carrying 260lb depth-charges), of which seventy were secreted at Port Sual, west of Lingayen. Ten US vessels were attacked but little damage was done.

Kamikaze attacks continued during 10–13 January, with such as the transport *Belknap* (APD-34) being damaged. The last of the successful attacks by the kamikaze in the Philippine marine war theatre took place on 13 January on the escort carrier *Salamaua* (CVE-96), although by the previous day the Japanese had lost every aircraft they had in the Philippines. The damage to *Salamaua* had been extensive because a kamikaze carrying two 250kg bombs hit the flight deck; fifteen men were killed and 88 wounded.

US intelligence formulated a table of successes in kamikaze attacks from October 1944 to 15 January 1945; here are their findings in simple summary: Sixteen vessels had been sunk (two carriers, three destroyers, five transports and six miscellaneous craft), and 87 vessels had been damaged (23 carriers, five battleships, nine cruisers, 23 destroyers, five destroyer escorts, twelve transports, and ten miscellaneous craft). US estimates, however, noted that with the last foray from Clark Field, the Japanese Army Air Service kamikaze lost 719 suicide pilots. The Navy Air Service had dispatched 480 kamikaze with escorts which never returned. Thus 1,198 lives had been spent to halt the US invasion by suicide attacks.

Consequently US Admirals King, Nimitz and Halsey continued to be concerned about kamikaze attacks. The truth was that more US warships had been sunk or damaged by kamikaze attacks in three months of operations in the Philippines than had been lost or damaged in the previous Pacific naval battles including Pearl Harbor.

The defence of the Philippines now fell to *Gensui Hakushaku* Hisaichi Terauchi and *Taisho* Tomoyuki Yamashita. Terauchi was based at Saigon in the old Union of Indo–China which the Japanese had taken from the French in 1940. Here was organised 3rd Air Army – with its headquarters in Singapore – which directed all Army air operations in SE Asia. By February 1945 the South West Fleet of the Imperial Japanese Navy had been disbanded and replaced by the 1st Southern Expeditionary Fleet of Shigeru Fukudome whose headquarters was at Singapore. On 1 January 1945 4th Air Army came under the direct control of the 14th Area Army.

CHAPTER ELEVEN

FORMOSA TRANSFER

'Kazunaranu sazare sho ishi no / Makogoro o tsumi kasanete zo / Koku wa yasukere' (Insignificant little pebbles that we are / The degree of our devotion does not falter / As for our country we move towards our final rest.) — Kamikaze 'Heroes Song'

Ilha Formosa (beautiful island) was the name given to modern Taiwan by the Portuguese navigators who came across it in 1590. At the end of the Sino–Japanese War China ceded Taiwan to Japan in 1895 by the Treaty of Shimonoseki. Both the Japanese and Chinese called it Taiwan, but in WWII Western war histories it retained the name Formosa. For the next fifty-one years after being ceded, the island prospered as a Japanese colony to include Penghu (Japanese *Hoko Shoto*, the Pescadores) some thirty miles west of Taiwan.

After 17 June 1895 Taiwan was ruled by a Japanese governor-general, and the economy was subject to Japan's needs, the colony being isolated from China and much of the outside world. The Japanese systematically fortified the island, turning it into an airbase, a military training-ground and a naval shipbuilding and repair yard. By the late 1930s much of the land that had been given over to pineapple cultivation had been planted with rubber trees in the interests of the war machine. By the early 1940s factories had been rapidly built to supplement Japan's military heavy industry.

Colonial Formosa served the Motherland well during the Pacific War as a source of labour, materials and military supplies. Formosa and Penghu were used as staging areas for the coastal occupation of China's Fujian (Fukien) Province and Guangdong (Kuongtung) from 1938, for the invasion of Luzon in December 1941 and Japan's subsequent thrusts into SE Asia. It was not until 1944 that the colony began to suffer from the direct effects of war after Allied submarines had interrupted shipping and heavy US air strikes began.

Chujo Onishi now established his headquarters in a fortified shelter east of Takao in south-east Formosa. When *Chujo* Soemu Toyoda's order to withdraw to Formosa had come, those of the 1st Air Fleet who had been left behind (because of shortage of aircraft) made their way to Aparri and Tugue-gorao in northern Luzon. There they had to wait for evacuation, and it had been Onishi's first main task to get these men to his Formosa base. Very soon after landing, however, he had formed a new kamikaze unit composed of veterans of previous suicide missions and young pilots from the Formosan training centres. Formosa was coming more frequently under attack from US carrier-based aircraft and B–29s (called *Bee-niju-kyu* by the Japanese) from free China bases, but evacuation from the Philippines was possible between enemy attacks.

At a ceremony on 18 January, Onishi inaugurated the new Formosan kamikaze unit at Tainan airfield. The theme of his address was simple:

'*Hongeki tai o Kamikaze* ... Even if we are defeated, the noble spirit of this kamikaze attack corps will keep our homeland from ruin. Without this spirit ruin would certainly follow defeat.'

The new unit was to be called *Kamikaze Tobetsu Kogekita Niitakatai* (Divine Wind Special Attack Bombing Squadron, Niitaka Unit), taking its name from the island's highest mountain, Mount Niitaka. Veterans like Onishi were aware of the historical significance of the unit's name. For the name of the mountain had been invoked in the coded message from *Gensui* Isoroku Yamamoto announcing the attack on Pearl Harbor on 7 December 1941: '*Niitakayama nobore*' (Climb Mount Niitaka). The inaugural ceremony was followed by a meal of corned beef and *ika*, vegetables and fruit. The habitu-ally stiff, haughty and distant Onishi was at his most affable and personally poured the traditional libation of *sake* for each volunteer.

When reports were received that the Task Force from Admiral Halsey's Third Fleet had been seen 200 miles east-south-east of the Bashi Channel, South Formosa, Onishi ordered the launch of *Niitaka* Unit for 21 January. For this the unit was divided into three sections to fly at minimum altitude: No 1, from Shinko, was made up of two Yokosuka D4Y *Suisei* and two Zero attackers and two escorts; No 2, from Taitung, sortied with two *Suisei*, two Zeros and two escorts; and No 3, from Taibu, with two *Suisei* and two escorts.

No 2 Section was reported as having encountered enemy Grumman Hellcats, the three escorts engaging while the *Suisei* continued to their target. No report was recorded on the other 2 Section aircraft. Nos 1 and 3 Sections' escorts returned to base with reports of direct hits by four kamikaze. US intelligence recorded two hits this day on the fleet carrier *Ticonderoga* (CV-14), one on the light carrier *Langley* (CVL-27) and one on the destroyer *Maddox* (DD-731). *Ticonderoga* and *Maddox* withdrew to the US base at Ulithi.

The kamikaze pilots regularly continued to receive messages of support from home with enclosures of mascots to take on last flights. One parent, however, made a more personal delivery to the 765th Air Group base at Kijin, Formosa. Madam Misao Kusanagi, the wife of *Saibankan* (Judge) Kusanagi of the High Court at Taihoku (Taipei to the Chinese) was met at the base as her rank demanded by *Taisa* Shogu Masuda. She gave him a parcel containing a scarf and a lock of hair from her student pilot son who had died from some illness before he could qualify as a kamikaze. She requested that the items be taken on a kamikaze mission. On the scarf she had written: 'I pray for a direct hit.'

On 2 February 1945 the High Command appointed the 54-year-old *Chujo* Matome Ugaki as the new commander of 5th Air Fleet. His new brief included the organising of the *TAN* (Sincere Loyalty) Operation – a major kamikaze attack on the Allied Fleet at Ulithi, north-west of the main groups of Caroline Islands.

When Ugaki took over his new command it consisted of 600 aircraft located west of the Osaka–Kyoto area, dispersed over thirty-six airfields (some disguised as farmland and country roads); but it was soon to move to the Kanoya Air Base in south Kyushu, with Ugaki's headquarters on the Osumi peninsula. Here Ugaki encountered for the first time the *Okha* suicide bombers which were soon to play such a devastating role.

On 5 February 1945, 1st Air Fleet was reorganised into four new air groups designated 132nd, 133rd, 205th and 765th. And on 13 February *Chujo* Teraoka of 3rd Air Fleet promised to train suicide pilots for the forthcoming Operation *TAN*.

CHAPTER TWELVE

KAMIKAZE AT IWO JIMA

'I leave for the attack with a smile on my face. The moon will be full
tonight. As I fly over the open sea ... I will choose the enemy ship that is to
be my target. I will show [my parents and sisters] that I know how to die
bravely.' — *Shojushi* Akio Otsuka (1922–45), crash-dived near Kateno.

As the war rapidly moved closer to Japan's main home islands, the High
Command regarded kamikaze sorties as being of the utmost strategic importance. By early February 1945, the 5th Air Fleet was mooted as a potential
attacker of the US forward base at Ulithi, north-west of the main groups of
the Caroline Islands. Before this could be set in motion, however, the
Americans achieved a rapid air attack in the Tokyo–Yokohama area of the
Kanto plain. Japan's strategists now concluded that the next US invasion
point would be Okinawa and Iwo Jima, for on 15 February reconnaissance
aircraft had sighted the US carrier fleet south of Iwo Jima, the largest of the
volcanic islands.

The Kanto attack prompted *Chujo* Kimpei Teraoka to form out of the
601st Air Group, under *Taisa* Riichi Sugiyama, a new Special Attack Force to
impede the possible Iwo Jima invasion. An announcement of the new
group's formation was made on 18 February, and flight officer *Shosa*
Shintaro Takeda selected pilots from eager volunteers. The new group's
commander was to be *Tai-i* Iroshi Murakawa, who had commanded carrier
bombers. The 32-strong group was named Unit No 2 *Mitate* ('Sacred Shield')
by *Chujo* Teraoka on 19 February, and consisted of twelve fighters, twelve
carrier bombers, four carrier torpedo-bombers, and four torpedo-bombers in
five groups numbered 1–5.

As an aside in the history of the kamikaze the following is interesting to
note with regard to Iwo Jima. In 1957 there appeared under the title *Samurai*
an autobiographical account by the former WWII air ace Saburo Sakai. Sakai
clearly speaks of an organised suicide attack before they became official. The
facts as he set them down are these.

Iwo Jima, the 'Sulphur Island', named for its volcanic origins, lies 760
miles from Tokyo; in 1944 it was to become strategically important to the

Americans because it was close to the midpoints of a route flown by B–29s from Mariana bases to bomb Japan. The defence of the island was the responsibility of Army *Chujo* Tadamichi Kuribayashi, Commander of 109th Division, and the Americans attacked the island for the second time on 24 June 1944, two days after Kuribayashi took up his command.

In the repeated US raids on Iwo Jima, the Japanese lost a great many of their defending aircraft and by 4 July there were only nine Zero fighters and eight Nakajima BN6 *Tenzan* torpedo-bombers left in *Chusa* Tadashi Nakajima's air command. It was decided that all these aircraft should be sent to attack the US fleet then lying 500 miles south of Iwo Jima; all the men who would take part in this knew that it would be a 'one-way mission'. The attack was to be led by Wing Commander *Tai-i* Kanzo Miura.

Flanked by a white banner fluttering from a pole and bearing the legend *'Namu Hachiman Daibosatsu'* (We believe in the Merciful Hachiman [God of War]) – a replica of a 16th-century Japanese warlord's banner – Miura addressed the pilots who were to attack the US Fleet:

'You will strike back at the enemy. From now on our defensive battles are over. You men are the fliers chosen from the Yokosuka Air Wing, the most famous in all Japan. I trust that your actions today will be worthy of the name of the glorious tradition of your Wing. In order for you to perpetuate the honour which is ours, you must accept the task which your officers have put before you. You cannot, I repeat, you cannot hope for survival. Your minds must be on the word *'kushu'* [air attack]. You are but seventeen men, and today you will face a task force which is defended perhaps by hundreds of American fighter aircraft. Therefore individual attacks must be forgotten. You cannot strike at your targets as one man alone. You must retain a tight group of aircraft. You must fight your way through the interceptors, and ...' Miura paused, then made it clear that it was to be a *jibaku* raid:

'... You must dive against the enemy carriers together! Dive – together with your torpedoes and your lives and your souls.'

Miura clarified the intention:

'A normal attack will be useless. Even if you succeed in penetrating the American fighters, you will only be shot down on your way back to this island. Your death will be ineffective for our country. Your lives will be wasted. We cannot permit this to be. Until you reach your target, the fighter pilots will refuse to accept battle with the enemy. No bomber pilot will release his torpedo in an air drop. No matter what happens you will keep your aircraft together. Wing to wing. No obstacle is to stop you from carrying out your mission. You must make your dives in a group in order to be effective. I know that what I tell you to do is difficult. It may even be impossible. But I trust that you can do it, that you will do it. That every man among you will plunge directly into an enemy carrier and sink the vessel. You have your orders.'

Never before had a Japanese air commander given such an order. Of the seventeen aircraft dispatched, four Zeros and one Nakajima returned. No shame or accusation of cowardice was attached to the pilots who returned; it was clear that they had not been able to line up targets to make their deaths meaningful went the reasoning. The *jibaku* raid was not reported to the High Command in Tokyo – such a thing unsanctioned would have been disapproved of – and in the US records it was logged as 'an ordinary enemy raid'.

Forward in time. On 21 February 1945 the five groups named by Teraoka as *Mitate* took off from Hitori air base, refuelled at Hachijo Jima in the Northern Bonins, and then launched attacks on Task Force 58 around Iwo Jima and the seas east of Chichi Jima.

The US Navy recorded these hits: Captain Lucian A. Moebus's carrier *Saratoga* (CV-3) of Task Group 58.5 confirmed Zekes in the area, and six of the ship's fighters 'splashed four' kamikaze. In poor weather (ceiling 3,500 feet) *Saratoga* catapulted several night fighters over a wide area. At 1659 hrs the ship was attacked by six kamikaze. Two were set on fire to crash blazing on the carrier's starboard side, their bombs bouncing into the vessel; these were compounded by a direct hit from the third. The fourth dived into the sea, the fifth hit the port catapult and the sixth crashed into the starboard crane. Observers noted that the attack was over in three minutes. Almost two hours later a group of five kamikaze attacked, but only one reached *Saratoga* to drop its bomb on the flight deck; the aircraft bounced overboard. The Action Report records 123 men killed or missing and 192 wounded, and 36 aircraft destroyed. *Saratoga* was out of action for three months.

In Rear Admiral C. T. Durgin's group, Captain J. L. Pratt's escort carrier *Bismarck Sea* (CVE-95) also came under attack. One kamikaze crashed abreast the elevator and the resultant fuel explosion wrecked the ship. Abandon Ship was ordered and after three hours she sank with the loss of 218 lives.

While this was happening the escort carrier *Lunga Point* (CVE-94) was attacked by four kamikaze torpedo-bombers. The third pilot launched his torpedo which missed the stern section, but his wing tip hit the island aft before he plunged into the sea. Fires were soon put out and there were no fatalities. The net cargo ship *Keokuk* (AKN-4) was hit on the starboard side by a Nakajima B6N2 *Tenzan* which wiped out a bank of guns; seventeen men were killed and 44 wounded. The LSTs 477 and 809 were also hit, but with little resultant damage.

Japanese records show that the leaders of the attacking groups Nos 2 and 3, *Tai-is* Iijima and Sakuraba, both developed engine trouble at Hachijo Jima, but transferred to other aircraft to complete their missions.

The Americans invaded the volcanic fortress island of Iwo Jima on 19 February 1945. It was defended by the merciless Army *Chujo* Tadamichi Kuribayashi with naval combatants under *Shosho* Toshinosuke Ichimaru. Kuribayashi's speech to his troops, a short while before the Americans landed has passed into the archives of the kamikaze because he was greatly inspired by the 'glorious example' of the suicide pilots:

'We are here to defend this island to the limit of our strength. We must devote ourselves to that task entirely. Each of your shots must kill many Americans. We cannot allow ourselves to be captured by the enemy. If positions are overrun, we will take bombs and grenades and throw ourselves under the tanks to destroy them. We will infiltrate the enemy's lines to exterminate him. No man must die until he has killed at least ten Americans. We will harass the enemy with guerrilla actions until the last of us has perished. *Tenno banzai!'*

The Battle of Iwo Jima (*Sakusen* to the Japanese) was to last for several bloody weeks. The Japanese were unable to put up much in the way of air support, and the Americans were occupying the airfields by 6 March, and had taken the island by the 16th. On the 27th the 60-year-old Kuribayashi committed ritual *seppuku*; on the same day *Shosho* Ichimaru was killed when emerging from his cave HQ.

Japanese intelligence – via a Nakajima C6N *Saiun* reconnaissance aircraft of 4th Fleet out of Truk – confirmed that the US task force was anchored at Ulithi. The pilot reported that he had seen five fleet carriers, three light carriers and seven escort carriers at the inner anchorage. He had also located eight other warships, 31 flying-boats and 54 transports. In the outer anchorage he had seen four carriers and a group of destroyers about to enter the lagoon. This intelligence stirred the High Command to launch their long-planned Operation *TAN-GO*. By 10 March the 4-step procedure had already been revealed to air commanders:

'Ichi. One flying-boat will leave Kogoshima Bay at 0300 hrs for weather reconnaissance along a course from Cape Sata, via Okinotori Shima, to Ulithi.

'*Ni*. Four land-based bombers will leave Kanoya at 0430 hrs and patrol in advance of the main force.

'*San*. Four flying-boats will leave Kagoshima by 0730 to guide the main force to Ulithi.

'*Yon*. The main force of 24 Yokosuka PIYI *Ginga* bombers will join the guide planes over Cape Sata and proceed to Ulithi to carry out *Tokkotai* attacks against enemy surface craft. Each plane will carry one 1,760lb bomb.'

The squadron that would make the *Tokkotai* attacks was named *Azusa* (the wood from which *samurai* bows were made) Special Attack Unit. The pilots were eager. On 10 March they assembled, *hachimaki* tied in place, to drink the Emperor's gift libation of *sake* and listen while *Shosho* Ugaki read the inspirational message from *Chujo* Toyoda:

'By order of the Commander of the Combined Fleet, based on authoritative reports, *Azusa Tokubetsu Kamikaze* will sortie today in accordance with previous instructions.

'The war situation grows daily more serious as the enemy *Bee-niju-kyu* raid the homeland.

'The enemy carrier force has twice struck the Kanto Plain without our being able to stop them.

'On Iwo Jima our comrades at arms are engaged in deadly battle, day and night, under conditions that indicate they will fight to the death.

'The Empire will survive or fall through the success or failure of this endeavour against the American Fifth Fleet.

'Let all hands of the *Tokubetsu Kamikaze* be diligent and do their very best to annihilate the enemy, the leaders to direct the unit to success, and the subordinates to do their utmost.

'You are first in our hearts as we bid farewell to you as you head over the sea in this most difficult expedition. As you reach your destination, you may be assured that your honour and greatness will be remembered. You have proved to be the greatest inspiration and we offer our appreciation as you go.

'After a month's operations, the enemy's carriers were seen yesterday and should be returning to port. The key to success in your enterprise is secrecy as you struggle to reach your destination in spite of the enormous difficulty with the weather.

'And to each unit commander: although success must be certain, if for some reason the plans go askew then we shall do our best to arrange for another attempt.

'Finally, remember there is no need for haste.

'Let the soul of the *Kami* be with you this day. We do not have to witness your unselfish loyalty and devotion. The many years of your training have provided a skill that makes it certain you will succeed with the aid of the Diving Spirit as you go to your eternal rest.'

A sortie was made on 10 March, after a delay caused by engine failure in the accompanying flying-boats. En route the aircraft were recalled after Ugaki received a message that the US fleet had disappeared from Ulithi. The message proved to be nonsense and a new sortie took off on 11 March.

The Americans had turned Ulithi into a huge repair, maintenance and supply base. So confident were they that they were beyond the range of kamikaze that there was no blackout in place and the Japanese pilots were able to identify their target from the bright lighting. The kamikaze of Operation *TAN-GO* had sortied from Kanoya, Kyushu, and flew east of Minami Daito Jima to Okinotori Shima, as planned, and through the Storm Zones to Yap, and thence east to Ulithi.

They reached their target after dark, but of the 24 *Ginga*s, thirteen developed engine trouble and dropped out, two of them ditching in the sea. The eleven remaining aircraft dived on their targets as the flying-boats returned home. Only one hit was made, on the fleet carrier *Randolph* (CV-15), but little damage was caused. Operation *TAN-GO* had been a failure and there were no more attacks on Ulithi. In Japan meanwhile, the B–29s were raining down hell on the citizens of Tokyo.

On 19 March *Shosho* Ugaki's reconnaissance aircraft sent back reports of more than a dozen enemy carriers launching aircraft against the Four Provinces of the *Seito Naikai*; Osaka, Kobe and Kure were in danger – the heartland of naval training bases and shipyards had become vulnerable. Ugaki sent an aerial fleet of Yokosuka PIYI *Ginga*, Nakajima B6N2 *Tenzan* and Yokosuka D4Y *Suisei* to make conventional attacks on the carriers. But several of his pilots were determined to be unofficial kamikaze.

Among Ugaki's forces were pilots nicknamed *kichikai* (madmen) who had taken up the 'suicide craze'; these *kichikai*, incidentally, called those not touched by the 'madness' *sukeibei* (letchers), deeming them to have renounced the honour of a place at the *Yasukuni* in favour of the comforts of the brothel and conventional living.

One such was the inexperienced and under-trained *Tokuso* Shoichi Yasui, who had been in the cadet corps for only a year. He was now assigned to the 536th Unit of the Matsushita Squadron. Kamikaze documents editor Naro Naemura quotes Yasui's last letter to his brother in

Bansei Tokkotai En no Issho (Writings of the Eternal Rest Suicide Squadron), Tokyo, 1978:

'Warmest greetings. I hope you are well. As for myself, more and more duty calls. What a fine reward determination is. It gives one piece of mind. After all, the body is only an attachment of the spirit.'

He included this poem:

> *'Sensei ni yoroshiku*
> *Mura no hito ni yoroshiku*
> *Ane san oya ni koko seyo*
> *Matsu otoko yo hayaku*
> *hikohei ni mare*
> *Goshin'*

(Remember me to Teacher/Remember me to all the villagers/Give filial piety to elder sister and our parents/Tell my friend Matsu to hurry up and be a flier/ May I achieve my instant sinking.) Shoichi Yasui was shot down at sea.

From the Japanese point of view the sorties to Ulithi were a failure mainly because of lack of pilot training. During 18–19 March some 308 personnel were lost to 1st Air Fleet in the air and on the ground. Ugaki summed-up in his diary: 'As a rule, improper actions and improper martial spirit as from time immemorial are the causes of fatal failure.'

During 19–21 March the Japanese lost 160 aircraft (including 69 kamikaze). As the operations which were leading up to the Battle of *Nansei Shoto* (Okinawa) developed, the advancing Allies left in their wake all the evidence of a rapidly diminishing Japanese air attack force.

CHAPTER THIRTEEN

OKINAWA DAYS AND NIGHTS

'Though my body decay in remote Okinawa, My spirit will persist in the defence of the homeland.' — *Shosho* Minoru Ota, Commander of Okinawa Naval Base Force, (*d.* by suicide, 1945).

Okinawa in the Ryukyu Archipelago was selected by the Allies as a suitable site for an advanced base from which the final push into Japanese home islands, some 350 miles distant, might be mounted. Operation 'Iceberg' was planned to capture this part of the inner ring of the Japanese defence perimeter.

Flanked to the east and west respectively by the Pacific Ocean and the East China Sea, the volcanic islands of the *Nansei Shoto* ('South-western Islands'), sub-titled the Ryukyus by the Japanese in their pronunciation of the Chinese characters for Loochoo, are made up of three *gunto* (groups) of which the central one is Okinawa. Inhabited by a native people of Chinese-Malay-Ainu origins, the latter being the original inhabitants of Japan, the islands had their own kings from early times until the annexation in 1879 by Japan. Okinawa was administered for Japan by a *chiji*. Political equality with the other forty-six Japanese prefectures was achieved in 1920 as Okinawa-*ken*. An important link in the military line of communication, leading south to Formosa, by 1941 Okinawa was within the totalitarian political control of the Imperial Japanese Naval Authority.

The Japanese built five airfields on the flat, infertile fields of Miyako and by the closing stages of WWII three full divisions of Japanese troops were quartered in the island. By 1943 Okinawa had become a part of 'Kyushu District', the last main defence line of Japan's *seishin*, whence it was believed the kamikaze would drive off and ultimately destroy the invading Allies.

The report to the British Joint Staff Mission, Washington, DC, of 18 April 1945, described Operation 'Iceberg' as 'the most audacious and complex enterprise yet undertaken by the American amphibious forces'. The four commanders, Admiral Spruance (Fleet Commander), Vice Admiral Mitscher, Vice Admiral Turner and Lieutenant General Buckner of US Tenth Army, planned to land on the west coast of southern Okinawa, between

Zampa-misaki and Kenzu-saki, next to the important air bases of Yontai and Kadena. Phase II would involve the seizure of the Motobu Peninsula and the large airfield at Ie Shima.

For the Operation to have any chance of success, mastery of sea and air would be vital. Little opposition was expected from the now 'decrepit' Imperial Japanese Navy, but Japanese air power had to be pared down as much as possible. The Allies were aware of the Japanese air bases in Okinawa and the nearby islands, and of the airfields some 150 miles away at Amami Gunto, those 230 miles away in the Sakishima Group, and the sixty-five airfields on Formosa and fifty-five on Kyushu. A well-organised kamikaze onslaught was expected.

In preparation for the anticipated Allied invasion, the Vice-Chief of the Naval General Staff in Tokyo, *Chujo* Seiichi Ito, had a meeting with *Shosho* Toshiyuki Yokoi, newly appointed Chief of Staff to 5th Air Fleet's Commander, *Chujo* Matome Ugaki, to brief him as to future intentions:

'The 5th Air Fleet will be composed of approximately 600 aircraft comprising the eight élite aviation units remaining in the Japanese Navy. Its area of operation will extend from Okinawa eastwards to a north–south line through the centre of the Japanese homelands. Your mission will be to break up enemy carrier striking forces by concentrating all power on suicide air attacks.'

Up to this time, a new important one in the history of the kamikaze, only *Chujo* Onishi's 1st Air Fleet had been officially involved in deliberate suicide missions, and this was a decided escalation of such. A reluctant Yokoi – who did not agree with kamikaze attacks at all – requested that the implementation of any such attacks be the entire responsibility of Matome Ugaki.

Records show that the Imperial Japanese Navy's airfields were re-organised on 11 February 1945. The 3rd Air Fleet's 25th Air Flotilla and other units were merged with the Combined Fleet's 12th Air Flotilla to form Yokoi's 5th Air Fleet. The residue of the 3rd was deployed around the Kanto Plain to guard the eastern approaches. On 13 February it was confirmed that the new headquarters of 5th Air Fleet should be located at Kanoya, Kyushu. On 1 March 10th Air Fleet was evolved, incorporating 11th, 12th and 13th Air Groups, to provide reserves for 5th Air Fleet.

So by early March the Naval Air Force was able to muster 2,100 aircraft: 300 in 1st Air Force at Formosa; 800 in the 3rd in Eastern Japan, focused on Tokyo; 600 of the 5th in Western Japan, focused on Kyushu; and the 400 of 10th Air Fleet in the home territories of Honshu. The fighting aircraft were a mix of different types; training and experience of pilots was poor to satisfactory. Imperial GHQ now decided that the ostensibly better trained 5th Air Fleet should be deployed against enemy task forces and the 10th against small vessels and transports.

In the preparations for the defence of Okinawa, the overall orders were clear: 'attrition' was the key, as laid down in the *Outline of Army and Navy Operations* (approved by the Emperor and promulgated on 22 January 1945):

'When the enemy penetrates the defence zone, a campaign of attrition will be initiated to reduce his preponderance in ships, aircraft and men, to obstruct the establishment of advanced bases, to undermine enemy morale, and thereby seriously to delay the final assault on Japan ... Preparations for the decisive battle will be completed in Japan proper in the early autumn of 1945. In general, Japanese air strength will be conserved until an enemy landing is actually under way or within the defence sphere.'

As usual the carriers were the prime targets, the escorts engaging the Grumman F6F Hellcats while the kamikaze selected their prey. During the Okinawa invasion period 19–20 March 1945, the TG.58 fleet carriers *Enterprise* (CV-6), *Franklin* (CV-13), the destroyer *Halsey Powell* (DD-686) and the submarine *Devilfish* (SS-2920) were early hits, but were not damaged enough to withdraw. The kamikaze of 10th Air Fleet were now called into action. One group of twenty *Suisei* bombers damaged the fleet carriers *Essex* (CV-9), *Wasp* (CV-18) and *Franklin* again; the latter, which suffered very heavy casualties, managed to limp back to the USA.

On 21 March a message was received from TG.58 that the US carriers had been spotted by a Japanese reconnaissance aircraft some 320 miles south-east of Kyushu. A total of 150 US fighters was launched including 24 from TG.58.1; this was to be the opening phase of the Allies' first encounter with a new Japanese suicide device. The new machine was the *Ohka* piloted bomb which had been designed to be launched from a twin-engined bomber flying at 20–26,000 feet, some twenty miles from the target. When released it would be guided to its target by a kamikaze volunteer. *Chujo* Ugaki issued the order for the *Ohka* unit's commander, the veteran naval aviator *Taisa* Motoharu Okamura, erstwhile commander of 341st Air Group (Shishi) at Tateyama, Tokyo, to use the new weapon.

The *Ohka* ('cherry blossom'), a gliding, piloted bomb was the brainchild of Special Service *Chu-i* Shoichi Ohta of 1081st Flying Corps (Aerial Transportation Corps), which he had perfected while stationed at the Atsugi Air Base. He reasoned that the winged bomb, steered into a fast gliding dive towards an enemy vessel, would be travelling so fast – aided by supplementary rockets – that it would be virtually impossible to shoot down. The huge, 2,340lb trinitro-anisol explosive charge would cause maximum damage on impact, and the launching medium bomber – usually a Mitsubishi G4M2e – stood a fair chance of survival for another mission.

Ohta had been working on his idea in 1943, and after a severe grilling from Technical *Shosa* Tadanao Miki of the Naval Aeronautical Research Laboratory's section on the Miura Peninsula in the spring of 1944, he was given leave to present the project. Although sceptical, the Ministry of Industrial Production accepted the concept and it was sent off through the tortuous bureaucratic system. Preliminary blueprints were drawn up by the Aeronautical Research Department of the Imperial University at Tokyo, and the bomb's tactical possibilities were formulated under Project *Marudai* 'Circle O', (i.e., from Shoichi Ohta's initial). By August 1944 the prototypes were being manufactured under the guidance of the *Kaigun Koku Gijutsu-cho* (Imperial Japanese Navy's Aeronautical Technical Arsenal at Yokosuka).

Summary of the *Ohka*'s particulars:

Length: 19ft 8½in

Span: 16ft 5in

Propulsion: three 588lb-thrust Type 4 Mk 1 Model 20 solid fuel
rocket motors

Weight: 970lb; 4,719lb (loaded)

Maximum speed: 570mph in final dive

Normal range: 55 miles approx.

Crew: one kamikaze

Armament: design weight of bomb 2,645lb approx.

The prototype MXY–8 *Ohka* appeared in the early autumn of 1944 from the factory of Nihon Hikoki KK; the first mass-produced training *Ohka* appearing as MXY–70 *Ohka*, Model 11, in October. On the 23rd a test of an unmanned *Ohka* took place and on the 31st the test of a manned *Ohka* proved favourable. The tests were carried out by the Yokosuka Naval Air Depot Flying Corps under *Shosa* Okamura. Further tests took place from 19 to 22 November, and on the 24th *Ohka* were shipped to the Philippines and Taiwan. (NB. Thus historically the suicide *Ohka* predated *Chujo* Onishi's kamikaze corps in concept and spirit.)

Fifty *Ohka*s were put aboard the aircraft carrier *Shinano* at Yokosuka in November 1944, but as the carrier was passing through Kumano-nada she was torpedoed by a US submarine and they were lost with the ship.

Above: *Chujo* Takijiro Onishi (suicide by *seppuku*, 16 August 1945), 'Father of the Kamikaze', photographed when Commander of 1st Air Fleet; he became Vice-Chief of Naval General Staff. (Japan Research Projects)

Below: *Shinto* priests and service personnel gather to honour the spirits of the war dead at the Yasukuni Shrine, Tokyo. A barrel of *sake* (rice wine) can be seen to the right of the altar; the wine was the last ritual libation of the kamikaze. *Gohei* (prayer papers to propitiate successful strikes) hang on a line around the altar. (Imperial War Museum)

Above: *Shosho* Masabumi Arima (killed while making kamikaze attack, 15 October 1944). Commander of 26th Air Flotilla. (JRP)

Above: Meiji Shrine, Tokyo, soon to be destroyed by enemy bombs, where troops have assembled to honour the spirits of the newly dead. The kamikaze received the regular prayers of the priests of Meiji at the end of WWII. (IWM)

Left: Japan's High Command mingle with young cadets and specially invited civilians to honour the war dead. Parents of kamikaze were given special invitations to join the military élite at prayer. (IWM)

Right: 'I will see you at the Yasukuni' was the kamikaze pilots' promise to their fellows. National Women's League representatives sponsored prayers for the kamikaze dead. (JRP)

Below: Air trainees enjoy rice and vegetables during their training as kamikaze. Rations were much better for those about to die. (IWM)

Top left: Mitsubishi A6M–5 *Zero-Sen* 52 fighter. This aircraft was the type regularly used in kamikaze attacks (JRP)

Centre left: Yokosuka D4Y–2 *Suisei* dive-bomber, used for kamikaze attacks. (JRP)

Bottom left: Yokosuka P1-Y-1 *Ginga*. Many were used in Operation *TAN-GO* against the US anchorage at Ulithi. (JRP)

Above: Air trainees at base camp performed various balancing exercises to prepare for kamikaze aerobatics. (IWM)

Below: A Yokosuka P1-Y-1 *Ginga* about to crash a US vessel. (JRP)

Above: The US Essex Class carrier *Bunker Hill* (CV-17) is hit by two kamikaze, 11 May 1945. (IWM)

Below: HMAS *Australia*, hit by kamikaze on port side of foremost funnel. (IWM)

Above: A kamikaze takes a last dive; a few seconds later it was struck by anti-aircraft fire. (IWM)

Below: A burning kamikaze skims the surface after attempting a dive on a US warship. (IWM)

Above: Propeller wreckage of a kamikaze aircraft aboard HMAS *Australia*. (IWM)

Below: Anti-aircraft fire knocks out a kamikaze; torpedoes fall harmlessly into the sea; an incident during the Marshall Islands campaign. (IWM)

Above: A US cruiser in the Santa Cruz Islands. One kamikaze can be seen splashing into the sea (right) followed by the second which moments later also plunged into the depths. (IWM)

Below: Anti-aircraft fire bursting above HMS *Formidable* before the successful kamikaze strike on 4 May 1945. (R. C. Sturtivant)

Top left: Seen from a sister ship, HMS *Formidable* ablaze after the kamikaze attack. (R. C. Sturtivant)

Left: Crew in HMS *Formidable* survey the damage caused by the kamikaze attack. (R. C. Sturtivant)

Above: Kamikaze attack on HMS *Indomitable*, 4 May 1945. (R. C. Sturtivant)

Below: Smoke clouds billowing after the strike on HMS *Indomitable*. (R. C. Sturtivant)

Above: Launching a Human Torpedo. (JRP)

Opposite page, top: Plans of a two-man submarine devised for kamikaze missions. (JRP)

Left: *Shosho* Sueyoshi Kusaba, commander of the 'divine wind' balloon Operation *FUGO*. (JRP)

Right: Ballast Gear and 5lb incendiary bomb for 'divine wind' balloons. (JRP)

Bottom right: An Imperial Japanese Navy 'Type B' 'divine wind' balloon being tested. (JRP)

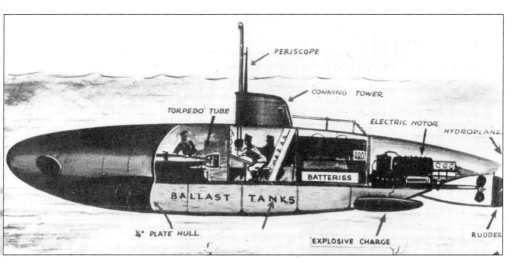

PERISCOPE

CONNING TOWER

TORPEDO TUBE

ELECTRIC MOTOR

HYDROPLANE

BATTERIES

BALLAST TANKS

¼" PLATE HULL

EXPLOSIVE CHARGE

RUDDER

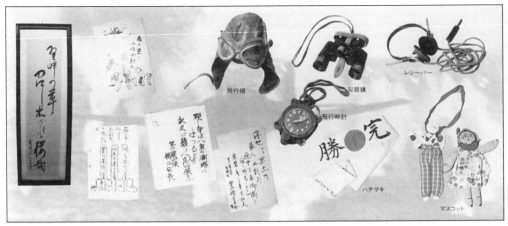

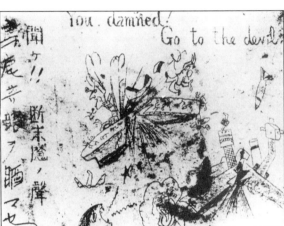

Above: An accumulation of kamikaze relics: cartoons, last testaments, goggles and helmet, lucky mascots and calligraphic *hachimaki* belonging to pilots of the Chiran Special Attack Force. (Peace Museum, Kagoshima)

Left: Japanese propaganda taunts Allies with the kamikaze threat. The calligraphy to the left reads: 'Listen to the Voice of Doom. Open your Eyes, Blind Fools.' (JRP)

Below: Mural showing the handmaidens of the *Kami* taking the soul of a kamikaze pilot to dwell forever in the pantheon of the Japanese Gods. (Chiran Collection, Peace Museum, Kagoshima)

Ohka Model 11 was to be the only operational version of the weapon; the Allies code-named it *Baka* (coining the Japanese word for 'fool'). Up to March 755 were completed, after which they were superseded by later models. These included the slightly smaller *Ohka* 22 of which fifty were built with a 110hp engine driving a Campini-style compressor to give 441 pounds of propulsive thrust. The *Ohka* 33, which was powered by a 1047lb s.t. gas turbine and was intended to be launched from the Nakajima G8N1 *Renzan* ('Mountain Range') bomber, was abandoned in favour of the similarly powered *Ohka* 43; the latter was designed to be launched from catapults and it is said that it was to have entered production in October 1945. The firm of Nihon Hikoki KK built two prototypes of a two-seater version of the *Ohka*, the MXY–8 *Kai*, but this model was never put into production.

From the blueprints of the day the *Ohka* is seen to have been a small, single-seat mid-wing monoplane of wood and mild steel, its fuselage having a bullet-shaped nose section. When examples of the *Ohka* were discovered by US aeronautical technicians after the war, they were astounded that these suicide bombs had such a large proportion of wood in their construction. The explosive charge was placed in the nose section within an artillery shell type casing to produce a perforating explosion. The cockpit housing the rudimentary controls and detonators was situated at the bomb's centre of gravity and was covered by a streamlined transparent bubble which featured a sighting ring to assist steering. The pilot would get into the cockpit from the mother aircraft's bomb bay when the area of attack was located. The tail section of the *Ohka* housed the rockets that increased the diving speed; this form of propulsion was based on data supplied by the Helmuth Walter Co in Germany. The *Ohka* rocket was a *Rogo*-type wherein condensed hydrogen peroxide reacted with hydrated hydrogen, a system developed by Mitsubishi Heavy Industries.

The *Ohka*s – also called *Jinrai* ('Divine Thunder') were to be accompanied to the target by what *Taisa* Okamura and group leader *Shosa* Goro Nonaka considered to be an insufficient number of escorts (only 55 fighters were available). But despite his reservations Nonaka insisted on leading the *Ohka* unit *Kaigun Jinrai Butai* ('Navy Thunder God's Corps') of 721st Naval Flying Corps himself, refusing to give way to Okamura who also wished to lead. *Tai-i* Kentaro Mihashi was selected as lead *Ohka* pilot. Incidentally it can be noted that the 721st had been born at Ronoike Base on 1 October 1944 to specialise in suicide attacks only; the unit was attached to the Yokosuka Naval Base.

To inspire his pilots *Shosa* Nonaka had a pennant flown at Kanoya Base depicting the five ideographs of *HI-RI-HO-KEN-TEN*. The pennant's calligraphy formed an *on*, a pronunciation in the Chinese literary style of a syllogistic philosophy much admired by the 14-century military patriot, Masashige Kusunoki, *shugo* of Kawachi to the Emperor Godaigo. It read:

HI was RI ni katazu (Injustice cannot conquer Principle,

RI was HO ni katazu Principle cannot conquer Law,

HO was REN ni katazu Law cannot conquer Power,

KEN was TEN ni katazu Power cannot conquer Heaven.)

On 21 March 1945 at 1165 hrs, *Chujo* Ugaki watched eighteen Mitsubishi Model 22 Type 1 bombers (sixteen laden with *Ohka* bombs and two to undertake radio and navigational duties) and the Zero escorts take off from Kanoya Base. The fifty-five fighters were soon reduced to thirty through stalling at take-off or engine trouble aloft. Some three hours later the Zeros broke flight to engage fifty Grumman F6F Hellcats. This first *Ohka* raid was to be a complete failure; fifteen of the carrying bombers were shot down and fifteen Zeros were destroyed; others crashed on the return flight to Kanoya. To jump forward in time. On 12 April 1945 the US Navy's 2,200-ton destroyer, Lieutenant Commander A. E. Parker's *Mannert L. Abele*, became the first ship to be sunk by an *Ohka*, and this was the first time that the device had been seen by US naval forces. *Abele* had been suicide dived by a Mitsubishi A6M *Zero-Sen* and was dead in the water when a minute later the *Ohka* hit the starboard side of the ship; six were killed, 73 were logged missing and 35 were wounded. In time the Allies developed effective defences against the ordinary kamikaze – the best way to deflect them was to fill the sky with flak – but they remained largely helpless against *Ohka* unless they could shoot them down. The Japanese hoped that the *Ohka* would frighten the Americans so much that they would call off their advance on the Japanese mainland. But fear itself was to have a callous and irreverent effect on many US seamen. Speaking in 1995 in a BBC interview about the kamikaze in the Okinawa campaign, Fred Murphy, who served as an Engineering Officer in the US Navy, recalled how one day he found among the wreckage on his ship the blackened right leg of a kamikaze pilot. As seamen were 'souvenir happy' at that time – anything Japanese was eagerly put aside – Murphy took the leg to the central store where such relics were stacked. Later the ship's craftsmen made rings, necklaces and ear-rings out of sliced bone from the leg. 'It sounds pretty bad,' said Murphy, who remembered how disturbed he felt after the war when musing on how the kamikaze's parents might have felt about the enemy making souvenirs of their son's body. Yet it seemed to be a natural act commensurate with the 'hardening' of the war.

On 25 March the Americans' first footing in the island chain of the *Nansei Shoto* was fifteen miles west of Naha port, southern Okinawa, in what is known as the Kerama Retto. The next day the Japanese launched Operation *TAN-GO* for the defence of Okinawa. The following day nine kamikaze unsuccessfully targeted vessels of the Western Islands Attack Group. The destroyers *Gilmer* and *Kimberly* were attacked by Aichi D3A2s with some damage and casualties. One kamikaze burst into flames over the battleship *Nevada* and its crashing fuselage hit the main deck killing eleven men and wounding 49.

On 29 March Commander P. J. Barnason's minelayer *Henry A. Wiley* was attacked by several kamikaze. On 1 April – the day on which the minelayer *Adams* was incapacitated by a kamikaze – the Okinawa campaign proper began with a US landing at Hagushi Beach near the airfields of Yontan and Kadena. British naval units patrolled the sea approaches from Formosa. The Japanese defence of two mixed brigades and two divisions was commanded by Army *Chujo* Mitsuru Ushijima, who watched the landings from the adjacent battlements of Shuri castle. The Army was supported by naval troops under the Commander of Okinawa Naval Base Force, *Shosho* Minoru Ota and *Taisa* Tanamachi's *Nansei Shoto* Air Groups, mustering 7,000 men.

When *Choju* Onishi began to use kamikaze in the Philippines he worked on a much smaller scale than *Choju* Ugaki at Okinawa. Aircraft production deficiencies meant that Ugaki had fewer aircraft at his disposal and his very young pilots were inadequately trained. And for the long term he would need a pool of experienced pilots for what he realised was to be the ultimate invasion of the main islands.

So his strategy was to fly non-formation sorties, using his oldest aircraft piloted by his least experienced men as kamikaze, retaining his experienced pilots as *hitsuji-kai* (shepherds) leading wave after wave of *mure* (herds). He ordered all old available aircraft to be salvaged and made serviceable, and by the beginning of the Okinawa campaign he had amassed a motley collection ranging from float-planes to outdated fighters.

Hitherto, traditional inter-service rivalry had kept the Army and Navy's air services apart, but now the Army's suicide units, the *Tokubetsu*, whose senior officer was Army *Chujo* Miyoshi of 6th Air Army, was brought under Ugaki's command. This co-ordination led to the *Kikusui* ('floating chrysanthemum') series of attacks, from 6 April to 22 June. The floating chrysanthemum (*kiku* = chrysanthemum) was the imperial symbol of spiritual purity, and its use in these circumstances represented the towering moral grandeur of the kamikaze in their air-sea operations. A half-*kiku* floating in water became the emblem of all Japanese suicide combatants in Okinawa. Although their main airfield was at Kanoya, *Kikusui* operations were flown from many airfields in Kyushu. All were carefully camouflaged and decoys such as dummy aircraft were widely used.

The US forces were dumbfounded to encounter little serious opposition to their landings. Ushijima had concentrated the bulk of his troops to the south, beyond the great escarpment which crosses Okinawa from shore to shore between Kadena and Shuri. His tactic was to draw the American troops into positions under the craggy heights of this line and subject them to sweeping fire, holding them there until reinforcements from Japan arrived. This was a bold decision, but within twenty-four hours about 50,000 American troops had dug in beyond the beachhead and were pressing across the eastern shore and Okinawa was divided.

Out at sea the US ships were being attacked at twilight, the kamikazes' favourite time to 'scatter the *kiku*'. On 1 April they crashed the transport *Alpine*, killing sixteen men and wounding 27, and the transport *Achernar* which lost five men being killed and 41 wounded. Next day a kamikaze crashed on the port quarter of *LST-884*, which was carrying 300 Marines; the vessel was engulfed in flames and 24 sailors and Marines were killed and 21 wounded. Another kamikaze holed the transport *Hinsdale* which lost power; sixteen killed and 39 wounded. On the same day the battleship *West Virginia* (BB-48) was crashed and four men were killed and two wounded; although the galley and laundry were wrecked the ship remained fully operational.

On 2 April a kamikaze (a Kawasaki Ki–45 *Toryu*) crashed the destroyer transport *Dickerson*, killing her skipper, Lieutenant Commander Ralph E. Lounsbury, his Executive Officer and 52 other officers and men, and wounding fifteen; the ship was scuttled on the 4th. Casualties and damage were also sustained by *Telfair* and *Goodhue*, and aboard Transdiv 50 flagship *Henrico*, Yokosuka P1Y1 *Ginga*s killed the skipper and the divisional commander, Captain W. C. France in a death dive. Next day *LST-599* was penetrated by a crashing kamikaze.

The first massed *Kikusui* attack took place on 6 and 7 April, 195 Navy and 160 *Tokubetsu* taking part. A dozen Nakajima Ki–43 *Hayabusa* and Nakajima B5N6s attacked the destroyers *Leutze* and *Newcombe* of Rear Admiral M. L. Deyo's fleet. Both vessels were harried for some considerable time and sustained great damage and casualties. The *Kikusui* kept up steady runs along the south-west coast of the *Nansei Shoto*, Commander G. R. Wilson's Destroyer *Colhoun* (DD-85) was hit by a *Zero-Sen* and left dead in the water by an Aichi D3A2. *Bush* (DD-529) too was vigorously attacked and sunk, while *Colhoun* was abandoned and sunk by friendly gunfire. The kamikaze continued to attack anti-submarine screening vessels and minecraft, crashes on *Witter, Morris, Rodman* and *Emmons* resulting in casualties.

Vice Admiral R. K. Turner's staff estimated that these *Kikusui* attacks had involved 182 Japanese aircraft in twenty-two groups (which was less than Japanese records suggest), and that 24 of them had been lost by direct kamikaze dives and the rest by gunfire. The Japanese claimed they had destroyed 60 ships and badly damaged 61. In fact the Americans lost three destroyers, one LST and two ammunition ships, and ten vessels had been badly damaged. Tacticians noted that comparative losses showed that the kamikazes were not as deadly as they had been over Lingayen Gulf just four months previously.

By 8 April Task Force 58 had taken up routine support of Operation 'Iceberg'. During the evening of the 9th, Commander G. B. Williams and the crew of *Sterett* were to witness a well-orchestrated attack by Aichi D3A2s. Five approached the destroyer in V-formation. The leader came under fire and with an impudent waggle of wings swerved out of range. His number two levelled out for a glide attack, but was hit by the destroyer's main battery fire and splashed on the starboard beam. The third was hit many times but collided with *Sterett* at the waterline. Out of the resultant smoke the fourth appeared off the starboard bow. Hit a number of times, a wing was sheared off and although the pilot righted the aircraft it crashed into the sea in a disintegrating mass, the pilot's body hurtling over No 2 gun. The fifth kamikaze was unaccounted for.

On 11 April the battleship *Missouri* (BB-63) was crashed by a kamikaze whose mutilated remains and those of the aircraft were scattered over the after section of the ship. All fires were brought under control in three minutes. The carrier *Enterprise* (CV-6) was attacked successively by two Yokosuka D4Y *Suiseis*; fires were quenched without difficulty, but fire damage to a catapult delayed flight operations for forty-eight hours.

In the second *Kikusui* attack of 12–13 April, 185 kamikaze sortied together with 150 fighters and 45 torpedo-bombers. The destroyer *Stanly* (DD-478) was attacked this day by an *Ohka* and, unusually for Japanese records, a strike was notched-up for *Tai-i* Dohi. The *Ohka* crashed into the starboard side of *Stanly*, and another hit the water 2,000 yards away, to be followed a little while later by a disintegrating Mitsubishi A6M *Zero-Sen*. During this action the battleship *Tennessee* (BB-43), the minesweeper *Gladiator* and destroyer-minelayer *Lindsey* were crashed and damaged by Aichi D3A2s, the destroyer *Zellars* (DD-777) sustained a port side kamikaze crash by a Nakajima B6N2 *Tenzan*, and a Nakajima Ki-27 crashed into the destroyer escort *Rall* (DE-304).

The third major *Kikusui* attack (165 aircraft) erupted on 16 April. The first target was Commander Frederick J. Becton's *Laffey* (DD-724) which was on AA picket duty. Beginning at dawn, the kamikaze came in from every angle and in a period of eighty minutes the ship sustained twenty-two separate attacks including five crashes; 31 men died, but nine kamikaze were downed by her guns. Most of the damage was inflicted abaft No 2 stack and the rudder was jammed; at the end she was towed to Hagushi anchorage by DMS *Macomb* and *Pakana*. A few miles away *LCS-116* was crashed by an Aichi D3A2 and lost twelve men. In *Bryant* (DD-665) 34 men were killed by a crashing kamikaze as she steamed to *Laffey*'s assistance. At another picket station the destroyer *Pringle* (DD-477), the minesweeper *Hobson* and *LSM-191* were attacked by Aichi D3A2s on the same day. One kamikaze crashed *Pringle* and the explosion sank the vessel. Thereafter the 'floating chrysanthemums' gave the radar pickets twelve days of respite.

During 27–8 April in a fourth *Kikusui* offensive 115 aircraft attacked the Okinawa invasion fleet and Task Force 58. The destroyers *Ralph Talbot* (DD-390) and *Rathburne* (DD-113) were hit but both made base at Kerama safely. The converted merchant vessel *Canada Victory* (loaded with ammunition) was not so lucky; hit in the stern by a kamikaze, she sank within ten minutes. The destroyer *Hutchins* (DD-476) was another early victim. On the 28th a kamikaze crashed into the (clearly marked and brilliantly lit) hospital ship *Comfort* (AH-6). The suicide attacks of April were completed with the sinking of the destroyer *Haggard* (DD-555).

In *Victory in the Pacific 1945* (1960), Samuel Eliot Morison writes:

'Few missiles or weapons have ever spread such flaming terror, such scorching burns, such searing death, as did the kamikaze in his self-destroying onslaughts on the radar picket ships. And naval history has few parallels to the sustained courage, resourcefulness and fighting spirit that the crews of these vessels displayed day after day after day in the battle for Okinawa.'

The fifth *Kikusui* onslaught of early May saw the targeting of these 'informers' (picket destroyers) which had alerted the invasion fleet of the suicide attackers' approach. The *Aaron Ward* (DM-34) was first damaged by shot-down kamikaze debris and was then crashed amidships, followed by a crash in the superstructure and another at the base of No 2 stack; 45 crew were killed or missing and 49 were wounded. On 4 May the offensive was intensified. The destroyer *Luce* (DD-522) and *LSM-190* were sunk and the destroyer *Morrison* (DD-560) was damaged; the minesweeper *Shea* (DM-30) was hit by an *Ohka*. During 3–4 May 1945, of the 305 aircraft (including 75 kamikaze) that took part in the assault, 280 crashed or were shot down. At Okinawa on 4 May Army *Chujo* Ushijima launched an offensive in the hope that US 10th Army would be defeated with the help of the fifth *Kikusui* mass attack.

As the Okinawa campaign developed the suicide attacks continued and on 11 May the sixth *Kikusui* attack was launched. The destroyer *Evans* (DD-552) was crashed by four kamikaze and had to be towed to Ie Shima. *Hugh W. Hadley* (DD-774) was crashed by a kamikaze and an *Ohka* and was also towed away. A lone kamikaze (independently of the massed *Kikusui* attack) managed to kill 41 of DD-470 *Bache*'s crew on 13 May. *Chujo* Ugaki stepped up operations; 160 *Kikusui* aircraft took off from Kyushu bases for their seventh offensive which lasted from 23 to 25 May in a series of attacks of more than usual ferocity. This was followed up with daytime kamikaze attacks.

The eighth *Kikusui* attack, numbering 100 aircraft, took place from 27 to 29 May. The destroyers *Anthony* (DD-515) and *Braine* (DD-630) were crashed as was *Drexler* (DD-741); the latter's casualties were heavy at 158 killed or missing and 51 wounded including the skipper, Commander R. L. Wilson. The kamikaze attacks continued on moonlit nights, *Shubrick* (DD-629) being one of their victims.

Among the ships of the Fast Carrier Force, Admiral Mitscher's flagship *Bunker Hill* (CV-17) was crashed by a *Zero-Sen* and a Yokosuka D4Y *Suisei*, leaving the vessel an inferno of flames, smoke and fuel fumes. By manoeuvring the ship much of the mixture was swept overboard. *Bunker Hill* suffered 353 dead, 43 missing and 264 wounded. Mitscher now transferred his flag and the rest of his personal staff to *Enterprise* (CV-6) which herself was to be crashed on 14 May. This was her third hit by a kamikaze and she had to be taken in for repairs.

A smaller *Kikusui* offensive (50 aircraft) was mounted from 3 to 7 June, but it was a comparative failure. On 19 June Army *Chujo* Ushijima sent farewell messages to Japan and ordered the remnant of 32nd Army to fight to the death. On the 21st US 10th Army entered Ara Saki, the southernmost point of Japan, and Major General R. S. Geiger announced that all Japanese organised resistance had come to an end. At 0300 hrs on 22 June *Chujo* Ushijima slit open his belly in traditional *seppuku* style and to complete the ritual the headquarters adjutant decapitated him. His spirit was deemed to have been joined that night at the Yasukuni by his Chief-of-Staff, *Taisa* Isamu Cho.

The tenth and final *Kikusui* operation was flown during 21–2 June and penetrated Kerama Retto to sink *LSM-59*. The kamikaze did not know that Okinawa had fallen. Until the end of the war US radar picket vessels remained a favourite target for single kamikaze.

In the vicinity of Okinawa kamikaze seriously harried US naval forces was on 29 July when Commander C. M. Bertholf's *Callaghan* (DD-792) was hit. The attack claimed 47 missing and 73 wounded and the vessel was abandoned and sank. Next night extensive damage was done to the destroyers *Cassin* (DD-793) and *Young* (DD-580). What the defenders found particularly galling about these raids was the fact that the kamikaze aircraft were elderly twin float biplanes made of wood and fabric.

Historians examining Japanese records of statistics for the suicide raids in the Okinawa theatre find a confusing number of listings, but the following, from Takushiro Hattori's *General History of the Battle of the Pacific*, gives a general outline. He lists these as the totals for kamikaze aircraft engaged from 3 March to 16 August: Navy, 1,637; Army, 934 (total 2,571). Hattori further mentions amongst Japanese 'kills' nine destroyers and four others sunk; nine battleships, ten aircraft carriers, four cruisers, 58 destroyers and 93 others badly damaged.

US Navy records set out the following vessels as having been sunk or badly damaged by kamikaze in the Iwo Jima and Okinawa theatres from 17 February to 30 July 1945:

FEBRUARY	*Wasp*	*LST-884* (scrapped)
18 *Blessman*	20 *Halsey Powell*	2 *Goodhue*
Gamble (scrapped)	26 *Kimberly*	*Henrico*
20 *LSM-216* (scrapped)	27 *Murray*	*Achernar*
21 *Saratoga*	*O'Brien*	*Dickerson* (sunk)
Napa	28 *LSM (R-188)*	3 *Wake Island*
Bismarck Sea (sunk)	31 *Indianapolis*	*Prichett*
28 *Whitley*		*Foreman*
	APRIL	*LST-599*
MARCH	1 *Adams*	*LCT-876* (scrapped)
18 *Franklin*	*Alpine*	6 *Howorth*
Essex	*Hinsdale*	*Hyman*

Mullany
Haynsworth
Fieberling
Rodman
Defense
Witter (scrapped)
Newcombe
    (scrapped)
Leutze (scrapped)
Morris (scrapped)
Bush (sunk)
Colhoun (sunk)
Emmons sunk)
LST-447 (sunk)
Hobbs Victory (sunk)
Logan Victory (sunk)
7 Hancock
    Maryland
    Bennett
    Wesson
8 Gregory
    YMS-92
9 Sterett
11 Kidd
12 Tennessee
    Purdy
    Cassin Young
    Zellars
    Rall
    Whitehurst
    Gladiator
    Lindsey   ·
    LSM-189
    LCS (L-57)
    Mannert L. Abele
        (sunk)
    LCS (L-33) (sunk)
16 Sigsbee

Intrepid
Bryant
Laffey
Bowers
Harding
Hobson
LCS (L-116)
Pringle (sunk)
18 LSM-28
22 Isherwood
    Swallow (sunk)
    LCS (L-15) (sunk)
27 Rathburne
    Ralph Talbot
    Canada Victory
        (sunk)
    Hutchins
28 Pinkney
    Comfort
    Haggard (sunk)
    Hazelwood
30 Terror

MAY
3 Macomb
    LSM (R-195)
    Aaron Ward
        (scrapped)
    Little (sunk)
4 Birmingham
    Ingraham
    Shea
    Carina
    Sangamon
        (scrapped)
    Luce (sunk)
    Morrison (sunk)
    LSM (R-190) (sunk)

LSM (R-194) (sunk)
9 Oberrender
    England (scrapped)
11 Bunker Hill
    LCS (L-88)
    Hugh W. Hadley
        (scrapped)
    Evans (scrapped)
13 Enterprise
    Bache
    Bright
17 Douglas A. Fox
18 LST-808 (sunk)
20 John C. Butler
    Chase (scrapped)
    Thatcher (scrapped)
25 William B. Allison
    Stormes
    O'Neill
    Butler (scrapped)
    Spectacle (scrapped)
    Roper (scrapped)
    Barry (sunk)
    Bates (sunk)
    LSM-135 (sunk)
27 Braine
    Anthony
    Rednour
    Loy
    LCS (L-119)
    Forrest (scrapped)
28 Sandoval
    Shubrick
    Drexler (sunk)

JUNE
3 Harry F. Bauer
    LCI (L-90)

(scrapped)	11 *LCS (L-122)*	*LST-534*
6 *Harry F. Bauer*	16 *Twiggs* (sunk)	
J. William Ditter	21 *Halloran*	JULY
(scrapped)	*Curtiss*	29 *Callaghan* (sunk)
10 *William D. Porter*	*LSM-59* (sunk)	30 *Cassin*
(sunk)	22 *LSM-213*	*Young*

The Tachiarai Joint Service Flight Training School was established in 1942 for volunteer student personnel to be trained as cadet officers. During 1945 Chiran became the southernmost kamikaze air base on the Japanese mainland. The number of 'juvenile personnel' killed in the Okinawa kamikaze operations has been logged at 1,035. They were particularly deployed from Chiran, Bansei and Miyakonojo, and were associated with the 8th Flight Division (Formosa) and the *Giretsu* Airborne Division in Kengun.

Okinawa kamikaze pilots are commemorated at the Peace Museum at Chiran, Kawabe-gun, Kagoshima Prefecture, Kyushu. The Peace Museum was built during 1973–5; its complex includes a bronze statue of a kamikaze pilot (1974), and incorporates the Heiwa-Kannon Temple wherein is a statue of the Goddess of Mercy Kwannon – depicted as the ideal of mourning for the dead kamikaze (1955). The museum displays one of the richest collection of kamikaze artefacts in Japan. Every year on 3 May groups gather at the Museum to participate in the memorial service for the kamikaze dead.

CHAPTER FOURTEEN

YAMATO MARU PLAYS THE KAMIKAZE CARD

'We live in the spirit of Jesus Christ, and we die in that spirit.
This thought stays with me. It is gratifying to live in this world, but
living has a spirit of futility about it now. It is time to die. I do not seek
reasons for dying. My only search is for an enemy target against
which to die.' — *Christian devotee Ichizu Hayashi, Genzan Air Group,
suicide crash, 12 April 1945.*

The largest battleship that the world had ever seen was earmarked by the
Imperial Japanese Navy – with the agreement of the *Gozen Kaigi* (Imperial
War Council) – to make one of the last kamikaze grand gestures. The
71,659-ton (full load) super battleship *Yamato* – named like the kamikaze
group for the province by which Japan was known in ancient times – was
the personification of the *unubore* (pride) of the Imperial Japanese Navy,
and was to be hopelessly sortied against the US Fleet off Okinawa to
become part of the kamikaze legend.

With a top speed of 27½ knots, and an overall length of 863 feet, *Yamato's*
main armament consisted of nine 18in guns which were designed and
constructed totally contrary to the terms of the Washington and London
Naval Treaties. *Yamato* was laid down as a part of the Third Reinforcement
Programme at a graving dock at Kure naval yard in 1937, three years after
design work had commenced at the chief naval test centre at Yokohama. She
was launched in August 1940 and commissioned in December 1941 to
become immediately the flagship of the most defiant and intrepid of Japan's
naval strategists C-in-C Combined Fleet, Isoroku Yamamoto.

Reputed the mightiest maritime machine of the war afloat, *Yamato* had
survived the battles of Midway, the Philippine Sea and Leyte Gulf. Now,
soon after Rear Admiral Richmond Kelly Turner launched the attack on
Chujo Mitsusu Ushijima's forces at Okinawa on the morning of Easter
Sunday, 1 April 1945, at 0406 hrs, *Yamato* took position in the Mitajiri
anchorage near Kyo Channel, *Seto Naikai*, to await developments.

On the morning of 5 April at Japanese Combined HQ at Hiyoshi, Kieo
University, C-in-C Soemu Toyoda gave the order to use *Yamato* as a

kamikaze. Toyoda's Chief of Operations, the excitable *Taisa* Shigenori Kami, gave the word to assembled staff officers:

'The 2nd Fleet [re-designated Special Attack Force *Tokko* duties] will participate [on 6 April] in *Kikusui Ichi*. The code-name will be Operation *"Ten-Ichi"* ['Heaven No 1']. Flagship *Yamato* will sail with cruiser *Yahagi* [*Taisa* Tameichi Hara] and eight destroyers ... to attack the American fleet and transports off Okinawa. After inflicting maximum punishment on the enemy, *Yamato* will be beached, using her main batteries as additional artillery to aid our defending forces. Surplus crew members will go ashore to reinforce the garrison.'

Despite deep misgivings among many of the senior staff of the Combined Fleet – such as *Chujo* Ryunosuke Kusagi, whose distaste for kamikaze tactics of any kind was undisguised – the sortie to Okinawa began at 1500 hrs on 6 April, with *Yamato* flying the flag of 2nd Fleet and with the force commander, *Choju* Seiichi Ito, and his Chief of Staff, Nobue Horishita, aboard. *Shosho* Kusaku Ariga (Commanding Officer) set a course through the Bungo Strait, round the south coast of Kyushu past the Osumi Group of islands and out to the open sea.

As the mighty vessel steamed out of the *Seto Naikai* the executive officer *Taisa* Jiro Nomura encouraged the crew with the shout: 'Let *Yamato* strike the enemy like a kamikaze'. The crew responded with three *banzai!* and a vigorous rendition of the *Kimigayo* and the Navy March.

Surrounded by her escort of willing 'kamikaze' followers, the light cruiser *Yahagi* and the destroyers *Fuyursuki* ('Winter Moon'), *Suyutsuki* ('Moon Bell'), *Yukikaze* ('Snow Wind'), *Kasumi* ('Spring'), *Isokaze* ('Shore Breeze'), *Hamakaze* ('Breeze off the Beach'), *Hatsushimo* ('First Frost of the Season') and *Asashimo* ('Morning Frost'), it had been decided that *Yamato* would act as bait to attract Allied aircraft away from the routes to Okinawa that the kamikaze would use. Most of *Yamato*'s crew knew that because of oil shortages at home there would only be enough fuel aboard for a one-way trip to Okinawa. In fact although the vessel's fuel capacity was 6,300 tons she was carrying less than 600 tons.

Hostile waters were entered a dozen or so miles south of Fukashima Island at the mouth of the Bungo Strait. US submarines were in the area. As the mid-point of the strait was reached *Yamato* was monitored out of gun range by patrolling Martin PBM Mariner flying-boat bombers whose observers were soon to be joined by Grumman F6F Hellcat fighters.

At about the time that the Grummans were preparing to attack *Yamato*, a group of kamikaze approached Task Force 58. These were Mitsubishi A6Ms from the Okinawa attack centre at Ranoya Base, Kyushu. They were too late to disrupt US plans to attack the Imperial Japanese Fleet and most of them were shot down without coming in sight of a target. Only a few of the *Zero-Sens* dodged the Grummans, and only one successfully targeted the 33,000-ton carrier *Hancock* (CV-19). Powering in from the starboard beam, surrounded by tracers, the kamikaze swung across the carrier's bows, aiming for the flight deck. A 520lb semi-armour-piercing bomb penetrated the port hangar as the kamikaze cartwheeled into parked aircraft and soon more than a dozen were ablaze from spilled fuel. Seventy-two men were killed and 82 injured. During the *Yamato* chase, only desultory kamikaze attacks were undertaken by small groups of Yokosuka *Suisei* D4Y1s with only the pilots aboard. In all these later sorties only one came close to a hit (on *Essex*).

During the morning of 7 April the US Task Force 58 began to move on the Japanese fleet in the East China Sea. At 1230 hrs the destroyer *Asashino* was sunk, and one hour later medium bombs and twelve torpedoes had found their mark on *Yamato*. At about 1400 hrs three medium bombs hit *Yamato* port amidships and the vessel's doom was but twenty minutes away. The end came with three armour-piercing bomb hits, then two torpedoes to port aft and amidships and one to starboard. At 1417 hrs two torpedoes hit starboard amidships.

On No 1 bridge *Choju* Ito saluted his senior officers for the last time. 'Save yourselves', he said. 'I shall stay with the ship.' He locked himself in his sea cabin. *Shosho* Arima ordered Abandon Ship as *Yamato* listed, circling help-lessly with damaged steering. The attacking Grummans kept up a hail of cannon and machine-gun fire as they repeatedly swooped over the stricken ship. At 1423 hrs the mighty battleship sank in the East China Sea some 130m west-south-west of Kagoshima.

Yamato's mission was unaccomplished; her dead numbered 3,063 including Ito and Arima, and in the escort force 1,187 officers and men lost their lives. Each is remembered every year on 7 April at the *Yasukuni-jinja*, as is the ship herself whose passing signalled the end of the Imperial Japanese Navy.

CHAPTER FIFTEEN

KAMIKAZE VERSUS THE WHITE ENSIGN

'The English never yield, and though driven back and thrown into confusion, they always return to the fight, thirsting for vengeance as long as they have a breath of life'. — *Giovanni Mocenigo, Venetian Ambassador to France, 1588.*

The role of the White Ensign in the WWII Far East campaigns began on 8 December 1941 when Rear-Admiral (Acting Admiral) Sir Thomas Spencer Vaughan Phillips, C-in-C Eastern Fleet, set sail from Singapore in the new battleship HMS *Prince of Wales*, accompanied by HMS *Repulse* and four destroyers, to attack the Imperial Japanese Navy's amphibious forces which had made landings at Signora on the north-east coast of Malaya. Next day the British ships were attacked by 34 high-altitude bombers and 51 Japanese torpedo-bombers from Saigon, French Indo–China. On 10 December *Repulse* and *Prince of Wales* were sunk within 45 minutes of each other; Admiral Phillips lost his life. This blow crippled Allied power in the western Pacific and gave the Japanese near undisputed dominance of the sea.

Admiral Sir Geoffrey Layton took over from Phillips and, with hardly any fleet to command, set up his new command, called ABDA, in Java, to liaise with US Admiral Thomas C. Hart's motley fleet of submarines, cruisers and destroyers. ABDA's prime task was to help with the reinforcement of Malaya and the Dutch East Indies.

Into the campaign now sailed one of the players who would dance the naval jig of death with the kamikaze. The 23,000-ton fleet aircraft carrier HMS *Indomitable* – completed in October 1941 by Vickers-Armstrong, Barrow – flew fifty Hawker Hurricane F.36/34s to airfields in Java. But by 17 February 1942 Singapore had been surrendered by Lieutenant-General A. E. Percival, GOC Malaya, to his rank equivalent, the Class A War Criminal and Military Commander of Malaya and Sumatra, Tomoyuki Yamashita.

The Allied naval forces in this theatre consisted of five British, US, Australian and Dutch cruisers and ten destroyers of mixed nationalities. All were under-trained tactically and, lacking air support, were no match for the

Japanese. During 27–8 February *Shosho* Shoji Nishimura and *Shosho* Raizo Tanaka triumphed at the Battle of the Java Sea.

A new Eastern Fleet, under Admiral Sir James Somerville, scraped together by the Admiralty, was deployed to thwart *Chujo* Chuichi Nagumo's anticipated attacks in the Indian Ocean, and *Chujo* Isaburo Ozawa's presumed targets in the Bay of Bengal. By 12 April the Japanese *chujo* were withdrawing to Singapore and were entering the period that would mark the decline of the Imperial Japanese Navy's ascendancy.

The Eastern Fleet continued diversionary movements in the Bay of Bengal. Following the Casablanca Conference of January 1943, the twin offensives from the Solomons and New Guinea to break through the Bismarck Barrier into the open seas towards the Philippine Islands saw the Americans re-organising their 3rd and 7th Fleets and being joined by the surviving Australian and New Zealand warships. And another British vessel, which was to brave kamikaze action, the *Illustrious* Class HMS *Victorious* – completed by Vickers-Armstrong on the Tyne in May 1941 – joined US 3rd Fleet.

Somerville's Eastern Fleet was run down for European duties, and in July 1943 the New Zealand cruiser *Leander* – the last major White Ensign vessel to serve in US 3rd Fleet – was severely damaged by a torpedo. By 21 June 1944 the Eastern Fleet had been reconstituted; a carrier air attack was launched on the Andaman Islands, and *Victorious* and *Illustrious* launched aircraft at Sabang on the northern tip of Sumatra. On 23 August Somerville was replaced by Admiral Sir Bruce Fraser, erstwhile Commander-in-Chief Home Fleet, and the Eastern Fleet carrier crews continued their assault on Japanese installations. By now Admiral Fraser was C-in-C of the newly formed British Pacific Fleet with HQ at Sydney, and the countdown to the return of the White Ensign to the Pacific was under way. The CCS Report for President Roosevelt and Prime Minister Winston Churchill on the status of the British Fleet read:

'We have agreed that the British Fleet should participate in the main operations against Japan in the Pacific, with the understanding that this Fleet will be balanced and self-supporting. The method of employment of the British Fleet in these main operations in the Pacific will be decided from time to time in accordance with the prevailing circumstances.' (16 September 1944. CCS 680/2)

On 4 January 1945 *Victorious* and *Indomitable* were attacking oil refineries in Sumatra during Operation 'Iceberg', and with them was another participant in forthcoming kamikaze attacks on British vessels, the 23,450-ton *Implacable* Class HMS *Indefatigable*, which had been completed at John Brown's in April 1944. It should be noted here that on 6 January, while sailing from Sydney to Langayen in USS *New Mexico*, Admiral Fraser narrowly avoided death in a kamikaze attack.

During mid-March the British Fleet was being readied to support the invasion of Okinawa, and British Task Force 113 (designated TF.57 when it came under US 5th Fleet), under Vice-Admiral Sir Bernard Rawlings, were to give support in operations against the islands of Mijako and Ishigaki in the Sakishima group. The British Fleet comprised:

TF 113: 1st Battle Squadron, Vice-Admiral Rawlings: HMSs *King George V* and *Howe*.

1st Carrier Squadron, Rear-Admiral Sir Philip Vian: HMSs *Indomitable*, *Victorious*, *Illustrious* and *Indefatigable*.

4th Cruiser Squadron, Rear-Admiral E. J. P. Brind: HMSs *Swiftsure*, *Black Prince*, *Argonaut*, *Euryalus*, New Zealand's *Gambia*; fifteen destroyers under Rear-Admiral J. H. Edelston.

TF112: Service Squadron, Rear-Admiral Douglas B. Fisher, with tankers, salvage and repair ships.

This well-balanced British Fleet was served by air groups mustering more than 200 aircraft including US Grumman F6F Hellcats, Grumman TBF Avengers, Chance Vought F4U Corsairs, and British Supermarine Seafires (the Navy version of the Spitfire) and Fireflys.

On 15 March Admiral Rawlings sent this signal to US Admiral Nimitz:

'I hereby report TF 113 and TF 112 for duty in accordance with orders received from C-in-C British Pacific Fleet ... Anticipate TF 113 with units of TF 112 be ready 1200 17 March to sail from Manus as you may direct ... It is with a feeling of great pride and pleasure that the British Pacific Force joins the US Naval Forces under your command.'

The experienced carrier skipper Captain E. C. Ewen, USN, was to act as liaison officer between Admiral Rawlings and US 5th Fleet, and the British Fleet very smoothly assumed its role within the Allied fleet.

During the period 6 April to 9 May 1945 four British ships were to be involved in kamikaze attacks: *Victorious*, *Indefatigable*, *Indomitable* and the 23,000-ton *Illustrious* Class *Formidable*, which had been completed by Harland & Wolff in November 1940. The sequence of action went like this.

On 26 March Admiral Rawlings took position off the Sakishima group of islands, his strategic objective being to deny to the Japanese the six airfields that were being used as staging-posts for kamikaze and other aircraft from Okinawa. Rawlings's strike force comprised 218 bombers and fighters (embarked in carriers), and on 26–7 March the first attacks on Japanese positions took place. Meanwhile the US attack groups approached Okinawa to touch down on 1 April.

The first successful kamikaze strike in retaliation took place on 6 April. Kamikaze were first detected at a distance of 75 miles east of the fleet, closing at 210 knots and at a height of 8,000 feet. Low cloud and poor visibility gave the Japanese pilots the advantage. The kamikaze split formation around 40 miles from target. The wing tip of a kamikaze struck the flight deck of *Indefatigable* at the base of the island and the 550lb bomb exploded on impact, damaging arrester gear and radar installations; 21 men were killed and 27 wounded. Three other kamikaze were shot down and, alas, a Seafire was shot down by friendly fire. In this action the destroyer HMS *Ulster* was damaged and had to be towed to Ulithi for repair. Admiral Sir Philip Vian commented:

'The armoured flight deck, which was a feature of British Fleet carriers, paid a dividend on this occasion. In spite of the direct hit *Indefatigable* was able to operate aircraft again within a few hours. American carriers similarly struck were invariably forced to return to a fully equipped Navy Yard for repair.'

During the evening of 6 April a Japanese squadron comprising *Yamato*, eight destroyers and one cruiser sailed from the *Seto Naikai* to attack the Allied fleet. Next morning US Admiral Mitscher launched his carrier air crews and the Japanese were vanquished. History records this 'Battle of the East China Sea', of 7 April 1945, as Japan's last chance to challenge Allied control of the sea approaches to the Motherland.

On 12-13 April the British ships attacked the airfields in northern Formosa from where the Japanese were flying bombers to attack invasion shipping off Okinawa, after which they retired to Leyte for replenishment.

Kamikaze were doing a great deal of damage to offshore shipping at Okinawa, and on 1 May the British Fleet re-entered the fray out of Leyte. By 4 May Admiral Rawlings was again assaulting targets on the Sakishima Gunto and now the British vessels came under more sustained kamikaze attack.

Kamikaze successes of 4 and 9 May were to be credited to the 205th Air Group which had been organised on 5 February 1945 at Taichu (Taichung), Formosa, and then sent to 1st Air Fleet. The unit was made up of three elements: Fighter *Hikotai* 302, 315 and 317, each mustering 48 carrier fighters. Their commanding officer was *Chusa* Asaichi Tamai. The kamikaze of the 205th were dubbed *Taigi-tai* ('Noble Cause Unit').

On 4 May a lone kamikaze bounced off *Indomitable*, causing superficial damage, but missing the bridge by ten yards. A single-engined aircraft machine-gunned the ship, killing one rating and wounding two officers and four ratings. *King George V* was also strafed by the same aircraft but no serious damage was caused. Twenty kamikaze attacked in four groups, diving steeply from a great height. On that day two kamikaze hit *Formidable*. The worst damage was to the flight deck, where an armour splinter cut several steam pipes in the centre boiler room. Eight men were killed and 27 wounded.

On 9 May the *Fiji* Class cruiser *Gambia*, which had been transferred to New Zealand in 1943, opened fire with both 4in batteries against a targeting kamikaze. *Formidable* was hit again, by the fifth of a group of eleven kamikaze; it struck the flight deck and set fire to the after aircraft park, destroying 23 US Chance Vought F4V Corsairs and seven Grumman TBF Avengers. Two pom-poms were put out of action but the vessel was back to full speed in fifteen minutes.

Victorious was also attacked on 9 May, by four kamikaze, one of which was brought down by fighters. A second dived steeply wing-tipped the flight deck forward. A third shallow-dived and glanced off the deck to fall into the sea. *Victorious* sustained a hole in the flight deck by the forward accelerator and 10 per cent of the armament was put out of action. She was able to operate a few aircraft within the hour, but was obliged to return to Sydney for a month-long repair programme, after which she went back to sea. The fourth kamikaze shallow-dived the battleship *Howe* but was hit by gunfire from the ship and crashed into the sea.

After 9 May the striking position of TF.57 was moved eastward and the British fleet was not again seriously attacked. On 27 May US 5th Fleet again became 3rd Fleet; TF.58 became TF.38 and the British TF.57 became TF.37.

In the South East Asia Theatre, during that phase when British naval units were active in the Bay of Bengal (leading to the occupation and build-up of the Cocos Islands as an advanced air base), SE Asia Command ships were attacked by kamikaze for the first time. On 26 July 1945 three of the suicide pilots were shot down by the cruiser HMS *Sussex* and the assault carrier HMS *Ameer*. Another kamikaze hit the minesweeper HMS *Vestal* causing a fire which led to the sinking of the vessel.

CHAPTER SIXTEEN

JINRAI BUTAI – THE DIVINE THUNDERBOLT CORPS

'Even my own flesh falls from me like a cherry blossom from the bough /
But my spirit will still defend the skies of Imperial Japan.' — *Tanka* poem
by the *Ohka* pilot Itto Hiko Heiso Noriyoshi Sugimoto.

During early June 1944, *Chujo* Shigeru Fukudome, Commander of 2nd Air
Fleet, with 6th Base Air Force, in Formosa, was inspecting 341st Air Group
Shishi (Lion) of 1st Air Fleet, when he was handed a report by the group's
commanding officer, *Taisa* Motoharu Okamura. An erstwhile fighter pilot,
Okamura suggested in the report that there be formed a special unit that
would do nothing more than train for and take part in suicide missions.
Fukudome took the report to Imperial Japanese Navy HQ and the suggestion was given detailed discussion; the outcome was a positive acceptance of
the proposal.

Thus was developed the Air Group Fighter Squadron 721, known in
kamikaze history as the *Jinrai Butai*. In Japanese the character for *shin* is often
read as *jin* and means 'divine/heavenly'; the character *rai*, often read as
kaminari, means 'thunder'; in this grammatical combination the 721st became
known as the Divine Thunderbolt Corps. Recruitment for the corps was from
units of the Imperial Japanese Navy; and in all the corps was to comprise 600
personnel.

The 721st was to utilise the suicide weapon known as the *Ohka*, and
their main escorts were to be the Mitsubishi A6M *Zero-Sen* Model 52
aircraft, dubbed *Kembu* ('building up *samurai* spirit'). The unit insignia of
Jin was used on their fighters from October 1944 to August 1945, and the
Thunderbolt Corps' fighters had a black nose, yellow wing edges, dark
green and light grey two-tone body and white insignia. The *Ohka* (slung
under Mitsubishi G4M2s) was painted a brilliant blue, with a *sakura* motif
on the nose.

On 1 October 1944 the 721st was stationed at Hyakurigahara Naval Air
Base in Ibaraki Prefecture, East Central Honshu. Their Commander-in-Chief
was Motoharu Okamura, with *Shosa* Goro Nonaka as Chief Flight Officer,
and *Shosa* Kunihiro Iwaki as Chief Aviation Officer. The corps was made up

of four *Ohka* squadrons: 1. *Tai-i* Akira Hirano (replaced *Tai-i* Tsutomu Kariya); 2. *Tai-i* Akira Shinzo (replaced *Tai-i* Kentaro Mitsuhashi); 3. *Tai-i* Morimasa Yunokawa; 4. *Tai-i* Fujio Hayashi

To be really effective, said *Chujo* Misao Wada, commander of the *Kaigun Koku Gijutsu-cho* (co-builders of the prototype *Ohka*), the 721st would have to have adequate fighter support. So the 48 aircraft of *Shosa* Hachiro Yanagi-sawa's Fighter *Hikotai* 306 were attached to the 721st. (It should be noted that during the Battle of Okinawa, Fighter *Hikotai*s 305 and 307 were also attached). Thus the corp's four squadrons initially had at their disposal fifty *Ohka* and *Kembu* fighters (equipped to carry 1,100lb bombs). A bomber wing was organised for comprising 708th and 711th squadrons of eighteen Mitsubishi G4M2s each.

On 7 November the 721st was moved to Konoike Naval Air Base in Kashima, Ibaragi Prefecture, and intensive training began. Senior officers were charged with giving the pilots a pep-talk on the rightness of the *Ohka* missions. Such a talk might begin:

'The *Jinrai Butai* is the true *Yamato Damashii*. It is the ultimate weapon that Japan's divine soldiers can arm themselves with to destroy the enemy. Regardless of flight training you are undergoing, you must prove your loyalty to the Emperor.'

Work was inspected on 13 November by Commander of the Yokosuka Naval Base, *Chujo* Mitsutaro Totsuka. Plans were afoot to send the *Jinrai Butai* to an advanced base in the Philippines, and the vanguard of the corps was intended to go under *Tai-i* Tsuji. At Yokosuka fifty *Ohka* bombs were stowed aboard the carrier *Shinano*, but when she was passing through Kumanonada, she was torpedoed by a US submarine and the *Ohka*s went down with the ship. Plans for the vanguard flight were scrapped. It is recorded, too, that by mid-November the 1st Squadron's commander, *Tai-i* Tsutome Kariya, was the first *Ohka* casualty when he lost control of his craft during a test flight.

The *Jinrai Butai* was visited on 1 December 1944 by the Imperial Japanese Navy Commander-in-Chief, *Chujo* Soemu Toyoda, who presented each member of the corps with a *hachimaki*, emblazoned with the calligraphy of the *Jinrai*. He also presented each pilot with a short ceremonial sword indi-vidually engraved with the recipient's name. A paraphrased transcription of his speech survives:

'I'm very glad to see that you are all in good health. Everyone of you here has volunteered for duty in this corps and has been selected from among many applicants. Indeed, you have every right to be proud of yourselves. I must say that I was also greatly moved by your firm determination and learn that you have never been the least bit hesitant in your willingness to sacrifice yourselves for the sake of His Imperial Majesty and the nation.

'As all of you are well aware, we have recently been engaged in a series of crucial encounters. Eventually victory in this war rests squarely on your shoulders. The enemy is trying hard to defeat us by relying on the strength of his superiority in material resources. For our part, however, we are confronting him with such irresistible power as the *Kamikaze Tokubetsu Kogekitai* that will unleash such might that even the gods will tremble at it. At the present time, it is impossible for we Japanese to compete with the enemy in terms of sheer quantity of material. We have no alternative but to fight him on the basis of what he neither possesses nor can perform. This, then, is the situation that brought the *Jinrai Butai* into being.

'I am convinced that the *Jinrai Butai* will unleash a power several times stronger than that of the kamikaze units – crash-diving with old planes with 550-pound bombs attached. We Japanese as a nation are solidly united in our patriotic fervour. But only deeds achieved by our great fighting spirit and firm martial discipline will be able to determine the final outcome of the war. I hope that all of you will try to reach the heights of your best possible performance. I'm reminded of an old saying that goes something like this: "It's easy to die unwillingly; the difficult thing is to die submissively."

'Don't die until you have dealt the enemy a deadly blow. The physical and spiritual damage that the *Kamikaze Tokubetsu Kogekitai* has inflicted on the enemy has been enormous. Its actions have also inspired the entire nation to make even more strenuous efforts than before. Regardless of how you die, your death will make a deep impression on the public mind, but unless it's productive, it won't cause any damage to the enemy. This means, therefore, it behoves you not to give up your life unless you are sure of achieving a positive result. I sincerely trust you will all do your utmost.'

When speeches such as this were studied after the war, some historians suggested that for example Toyoda's underlining of 'volunteers' was pure propaganda. The documentation gathered by the *Hagoromo-kai* in the years following the Japanese surrender gives the lie to the suggestion that kamikaze were drugged, forcibly strapped-in to their cockpits by *Kempeitai*, or pressured by blackmail that their families would be punished for any default to carry out *shutsujei meirei* missions. This documentation includes holographs by pilots who write of 'being destined to die', 'sacrificing my life with joy', 'peacefully reposing' in a 'different world' reserved for kamikaze, 'long hoped-for sortie to attack the enemy', and 'our fleshly body is nothing when protecting the Emperor'. And as *Chu-i* Hirokazu Ushikubo was to write: 'If I can be of any service to our Emperor there is absolutely no reason to spare my life in the sky war. One enemy ship sunk by my single soul.'

Two days after the Corps had been visited by *Chujo* Toyoda, the importance of the pilots was underlined by a personal visit from the *Kaigun Daijin* Mitsumasa Yonai. During the three days of 4–7 January 1945 representatives from each squadron of the *Jinrai Butai* said prayers in front of the *Kyujo*, the *Yasukuni* and the *Meiji-jinja*, for individual success. Ten days later the Corps had a visitation from a personal representative of the Emperor and were treated to displays by *sumo* wrestlers and *samurai* epics by the Toho Motion Picture Co.

On 28 January the *Jinrai Butai* began the move to Kyushu, but 1st squadron (*Tai-i* Akira Hirano) stayed behind at Konoike to form the nucleus of a new 300-pilot *Ohka* unit, the 722nd Naval Air Corps which was to be called *Tatsumaki Butai* (Tornado Corps); it was embodied on 25 February under *Taisa* Isao Watanabe.

Some of the pilots of the *Jinrai* were sent to Izumi Naval Base and others to Miyakonojo. From these bases they redeployed to Tomitaka, Usa, Oita and Kanoya. Training continued. Leisure activities ranged from swimming to *kendo*, *judo* and tennis, all calculated to promote peace of mind before the final *shutsujei meirei*. A precedent was the fact that, where possible, parents were allowed to visit the pilots before their last mission (in true Japanese fashion, all behaving as if no such missions were to take place; though some parents were known to present their sons with funeral clothes to wear when making their final mission). From time to time reporters from NHK visited the pilots and recorded their last messages to parents (all edited to highlight self-sacrifice for Emperor and nation).

From Naval HQ in Tokyo senior officers were advised to hone-up their skills in 'final words of encouragement' for departing *Ohka* pilots. Commanding Officer Motoharu Okamura was skilled in the style; here is an extract from one of his talks:

'For the past eight months since you joined our Corps with the ultimate aim of sacrificing your lives, being unable to bear the sight of our country's growing poverty and its suffering from a critical shortage of materials, your valuable training has continued unabated until this day of all days. Although we were preceded by the kamikaze in the Philippines, our heroic resolution was already made before they departed. Truly, we have long been waiting this day, continuously contemplating death for eight months.

'I don't intend to let you go alone. Although there is a difference of precedence and delay, I will be going without fail. [It is likely that Okamura intended to fly an *Ohka* himself; in the event he committed suicide when Japan surrendered.] I now temporarily part with you after joining you in a final cup of *sake* in the firm hope that you will successfully carry out this *Kikusui* Operation and help decide the destiny of our nation. Do not worry about the results of your part in the battle. I will report to you at *Yasukuni-jinja*. Be stout-hearted and cheerful. *Sayonara*.'

By 21 March the first *Ohka* of the *Jinrai Butai* was at Kanoya as a part of 5th Air Fleet. Henceforth in kamikaze history they were to be known as the 'Cherry Blossom Squadrons' (with a prefixed number). US carrier aircraft had been sighted on 19 March, and the Fighter *Hikotai* 305 was deployed to Tomitaka Naval Air Base to intercept enemy aircraft; they claimed 22 kills, but lost 23 fighters themselves.

A US presence being confirmed south of Shikoku, *Choju* Ugaki sent Attack *Hikotai* 711 to accompany a large *Ohka* group; a total of 137 pilots and crew in sixteen bombers with fifteen *Ohka* attached, led by Chief Flight Officer, *Shosa* Goro Nonaka, and about thirty escorting Zeros led by *Tai-i* Mutsuo Urushiyama a divisional officer of the 307th. Poor maintenance and other reasons cut down the number of serviceable aircraft, but in the event all were shot down en route by sixty Grumman F6F Hellcats some fifty miles from the US Task Force. The first *Jinrai Butai* attack was a total failure.

By the end of March Japanese defensive measures were well in place on Okinawa and it was decided that the 721st be used as a fighter-bomber unit to breach enemy patrol zones. *Chusa* Nakamura was assigned to command and train the new unit, and a change in tactics was made. Instead of flying in large formations, the *Ohka* would now be deployed in what the strategists called *tenteki kogeki* (constant dribble), mingling with other kamikaze. By 1 April the 2nd Cherry Blossom Unit had moved up to Kanoya, and night *Ohka* attacks were undertaken during which fourteen pilots died crash-diving enemy vessels.

The first success achieved by the *Ohka* was to take place on 12 April, the day on which the 3rd Cherry Blossom Unit advanced to Konoya to take part in the *Kikusui* Operation 2. Thirty-five pilots and crew crashed to their deaths. From the records of the *Hagoromo-kai*, the following sequence of events of the Cherry Blossom Squadrons and *Kembu* bomber units can be plotted to the end of hostilities:

1-12 April. 1st *Kembu* Bomber Unit advances to Kanoya to prepare for assaults on any enemy vessels found in the Okinawa area. 2nd *Kembu* Bomber Unit deploys to Kanoya to follow through attacks on US shipping.

12 April. 3rd *Kembu* Bomber Unit moves to Kanoya.

*c.*13 April. 4th *Kembu* Bomber Unit in place at Kanoya as is the 5th.

14 April. 4th Cherry Blossom Unit at Kanoya. Preparations for *Ohka* attack. Forty-eight pilots and crew reported killed either by direct hits or by being shot down en route to targets. The 6th *Kembu* Unit in place.

16 April. 5th Cherry Blossom Unit advances to Kanoya for *Ohka* attacks. Twenty-eight pilots and crew killed in crashes, fighter attacks or by naval gunfire. 7th *Kembu* Bomber Unit moves up to Kanoya. 8th *Kembu* Bomber Unit in position at Kanoya.

28 April. 6th Cherry Blossom Unit forms up for *Ohka* attacks.

29 April. 9th *Kembu* Bomber Unit in position.

4 May. 7th Cherry Blossom Unit advances to Kanoya. Thirty-five pilots and crew killed en route or at target.

11 May. 8th Cherry Blossom Unit advances to Kanoya. Twenty-one killed in action.

14 May. 11th *Kembu* Bomber Unit moves up.

25 May. 9th Cherry Blossom Unit in place. Twenty-four pilots and crew killed.

5 June. Anticipating enemy onslaught on Japanese home islands, all Cherry Blossom Squadrons (except No 1) sent to Komatsu Air Base at Ishikawa Prefecture, Western Honshu. 1st Cherry Blossom Squadron posted to Konoike Naval Air Base and others to Matsuyama Air Base, Shikoku.

22 June. Last *Ohka* mission. 10th Cherry Blossom Unit takes part. Thirty-two pilots and crew killed.

11 August. 12th *Kembu* Bomber Unit advances to Kanoya.

Statistics compiled and assessed from the records of the *Hagoromo-kai* suggest that 467 *Jinrai Butai* personnel were killed in this form of *Ohka* and *Kembu* kamikaze attacks.

Like other *Tokko-tai,* the *Jinrai-Butai* were disbanded when the Japanese surrendered on 15 August 1945.

CHAPTER SEVENTEEN

PORTRAITS OF THE KAMIKAZE

'Umi narazu / Tataeru mizu no / Soko made mo / Kiyoki kokoro wa / Tsuki zo terasamu' (Not the sea / yet to the very bottom of these brimming waters / the moon will illumine a blameless heart.) — Poem 'from *Shinkokinshu'* attributed to *Sugawara no Michizane* (845–903) found on the body of a kamikaze pilot.

Because there was no tradition of statistically recording each kamikaze 'kill', or the singling out of individuals, it has always been difficult for historians in the West to build up biographical data concerning Japan's suicide pilots of WWII. Some basic research was possible through the *Zengun Fukoku* (All Units Bulletin) because individual kamikaze pilots were identified with a double rank promotion at death. Seminal work in tracing biographical data was done by Professor Ikuhiko Hata of Takushoku University, Tokyo, and Dr Yasuho Izawa, associate professor at Yamanashi Medical College.

In their book *Nihon Kaigun Sentoki-tai* (1970), Hata and Izawa state that between 7 December 1941 and 21 October 1944, eighteen 'key fighter pilots' deliberately used their aircraft as (by this date still unofficial) kamikaze weapons. Their records list the following as 'key' Special Attack Force suicide pilots from 21 October 1944:

Chu-i Yoshiyasu Kuno. Fighter *Hikotai* 301; 21 October 1944; off Leyte.

Sho-i Naohisa Uemura. 201st Air Group; 21 October 1944; off Leyte.

Tai-i Yukio Seki. Fighter *Hikotai* 301; 25 October 1944; off Leyte (with his two crewmen *Itto Hiko Heiso* Nobuo Tani and Iwao Nakano).

Itto Hiko Heiso Tamisaku Katsumata. Fighter *Hikotai* 301; 26 October 1944; off Leyte.

Chu-i Korekujo Otsuji. Fighter *Hikotai* 163rd Division; 12 November 1944; off Leyte (with crewman *Joto Hiko Heiso* Yaozo Wada).

Sho-i Munesaburo Takahashi. 341st Air Group; 18 November 1944; Tacloban.

Chu-i Yoshita Toda. 221st Air Group; 19 November 1944; Leyte.

Chu-i Mikihito Sakamoto. 352nd Air Group; 21 November 1944; by ramming, Omura.

Sho-i Yoshimi Minami. Fighter *Hikotai* 305; 25 November 1944; Philippines.

Chu-i Tatsu Nagato. Fighter *Hikotai* 305; 26 November 1944; Philippines.

Hiko Heisocho Yasunori Ono. 252nd Air Group; 27 November 1944; Saipan (with *Tai-i* Kenji Omura)

Tai-i Tetsuro Yano. Fighter *Hikotai* 316; 7 December 1944; Philippines.

Joto Hiko Heiso Ushi-o Nishimura. Fighter *Hikotai* 302; 8 December 1944; Iwo Jima.

Tai-i Shin-ichi Kanaya. 201st Air Group; 5 January 1945; Philippines.

Joto Hiko Heiso Shigenobu Manabe. 252nd Air Group; 7 January 1945; Philippines.

Hiko Heisocho Yoshio Yamazaki. Fighter *Hikotai* 902; night-fighters; Balik-papan.

Tai-i Minoru Kawazoe. Fighter *Hikota* (Group Leader); 21 January 1945; off Taiwan (with *Tai-i* Sei-ichi Saito).

Chu-i Hidenobu Sumino. 201st Air Group; 25 January 1945; Lingayen Gulf.

Tai-i Mutsuo Urushiyama. Fighter *Hikotai* 307; 21 March 1945; off Tosa. On the same day and at the same location the following kamikaze of Fighter *Hikotai* 306 died: *Tai-i* Yu-ichi Izawa; *Joto Hiko Heiso* Kojiri Murakami; Goro Tsuda; Ichizen Kobayashi; Toshikazu Nakano. They were all in the *Jinrai* Special Attack Escort.

Tai-i Nao Sugisaki. 352nd Air Group (Group Leader; *Jinrai* Escort); 31 March 1945.

Itto Hiko Heiso Iwao Fumoto. 721st Air Group; 1 April 1945; Okinawa (*Ohka* Special Attack Force).

Tai-i Yozo Tsuboi. 302nd Air Group (Divisional Officer) Kanto Plains (*Ohka* Special Attack Force).

Joto Hiko Heiso Hiroyuki Fujishima. 601st Air Group; Okinawa (*Ohka* Special Attack Force; with *Joto Hiko Heiso* Tatsu Nakatani).

Joto Hiko Heiso Yu-ichi Kobayashi. 205th Air Group; 5 April 1945; Okinawa (*Ohka* Special Attack Force).

Tai-i Kunio Kanzaki. Fighter *Hikotai* 312 (Group Leader); 6 April 1945; Okinawa (318th Air Group). On this day and at the same location *Tai-i* Hiroshi Matano, Fighter *Hikotai* 312, and pilots of the Omura Group dived to their deaths. Names recorded: *Tai-i* Noboru Yamakawa; *Joto Hiko Heiso* Shinzo Tabata; Kazuo Tanio. The latter flew in 13th Air Group, *Kaga*, 15th Air Group, Tainan Air Group.

Chu-i Tenshin Suzuki. Yatabe Air Group; 14 April 1945; Okinawa. *Chu-i*
Tadashi Omoto. Yatabe Air Group; 14 April 1945; Okinawa (also *Sho-i*
Hachiro Sasaki and *Nito Hiko Heiso* Hideo Sumihiro).

Koku Heisocho Nobuo Saito. 205th Air Group; 17 April 1945; Okinawa.

Koku Heisocho Yoshio Oishi. 205th Air Group; 4 May 1945; Special Attack
Force *Zuikaku*.

Koku Heisocho Tei-ichiro Hayashida. Omura Air Group; 4 May 1945; Special
Attack Force *Shoho*.

Joto Hiko Heiso Hideaki Maeda. 205th Air Group; 9 May 1945; off Taiwan.

Sho-i Hiroshi Nemoto. Yatabe Air Group; 13 May 1945; Okinawa (Special
Attack Force, with *Nito Hito Heiso* Gi-ichi Hoshino).

Chu-i Shiro Okajima. 721st Air Group; 11 August 1945; Okinawa (Special
Attack Force, with *Itto Koku Heiso* Minoru Hoshino).

Tai-i Sadao Oshio. 343rd Air Group; 12 August 1945; Kyushu.

Joto Hiko Heiso Kazumasa Sagara. 302nd Air Group; 13 August 1945; off
Honshu.

From the files of Professor Hata and Dr Izawa the following kamikaze and
their colleagues can be mentioned as typifying the 'suicide spirit'; but first a
portrait of two *kyoshi* (instructors).

Hiko Heisocho Kazuo Sugino. (Born in Yamaguchi Prefecture, SW Honshu,
1921. He survived the war to serve in the Maritime Self- Defence Force,
which replaced Japan's navy after the war.)

A cement factory operative, Sugino volunteered for the Navy in 1939. He
began aviation training with the *Hei* (Aviation Student Class) 3rd Flight
Reserve Enlisted Training Class, completed his training in the 17th training
course in March 1942, and was posted to 6th Air Group at Kisarazu Base,
which was to form part of 26th Air Flotilla. At the Battle of Midway he was
serving in the carrier *Akagi*, and was among those rescued when it sank.
After service in *Kasuga Maru* he became a *kyoshi* in the Omura Air Group;
and in 1943 he was serving in the carrier *Zuikaku*.

Sugino underwent intensive training in air combat and dive-bombing
tactics. Until his return to Japan he took part in daily interception operations
with 253rd Air Group (the former Kanaya Air Group Fighter Squadron). He
served as a *kyoshi* with the Tsukuba Air Group, and after combat duty in
Taiwan and the Philippines returned to Taiwan in 1945 to train kamikaze of the
Hakata Air Group until the end of the war. He was credited with 32 'kills'.

Chu-i **Keishu Kamihara.** (Born Yokohama, 1920. He died in 1970 while piloting a Maritime Safety Agency helicopter near Hakodate City, Hokkaido.)

A Yokohama Second High School graduate, Kamihara was recruited into the *Ko* (Aviation Student Class) 1st Flight Reserve Training Class, of which he was one of the first students after its foundation in 1937. After serving in the Oita, Omura and Yokosuka Air Groups he was posted to 12th Air Group Fighter Squadron and served in the China theatre, after which he was posted to the Tainan Air Group.

Kamihara saw action in the Philippines and Dutch East Indies and in 1942 joined 6th Air Group for the Aleutian operation in which he served in the 24,140-ton carrier *Junyo* ('Falcon Hawk') ex-*Kashiwara Maru*. He served again in the Oita Air Group as *Hiko Heisocho* and after 1943 transferred to 381st Air Group and took part in the air defence of the Celebes and Borneo. Using the Type 3 aerial bomb, Kamihara intercepted B–24s and P–38s with great success. Wounded, he returned to Japan to train kamikaze.

Given below are some details of Japanese pilots who are known to have conducted ramming operations:

Itto Hiko Heiso **Masajiro Kawato.** (Born into an agricultural family in Kyoto Municipality in 1925. Returned home after POW internment.)

Graduating in 1943 from the *Hei* 12th Flight Reserve Enlisted Training Class and the 28th Flight Training Course, Kawato had become a Zero pilot in 253rd Air Group by the end of the same year. Only eighteen when he made his first ramming attack, he earned a reputation for recklessness while engaging North American B–25 Mitchells over Rabaul. On one occasion, after a hectic shoot-out he attempted to close beneath a burning enemy aircraft, and then rammed it. He baled out and was rescued from the sea unscathed.

His second ramming took place during an intercept battle on 11 November 1943, in which he again baled out but was wounded and grounded for a month. On 17 December Kawato made a head-on attack on a Bell P–39 Airacobra, collided and parachuted into the sea. It was his ambition to ram the tail of a B–24 which he succeeded in doing on 6 February 1944 over Rabaul, after which he again parachuted to safety.

When most of the fighter units were withdrawn from Rabaul, Kawato and a few others remained. In cannibalised Zeros they conducted guerrilla interception raids, reconnaissance sorties and attacks around the Admiralty and Green Islands. When 253rd Air Group was dissolved Kawato's unit became the 105th Air Base Support Squadron. On 9 March 1945, while piloting a Zero on a B–25 interception raid, he was reported missing presumed dead in action. He was later reported to have attacked an enemy destroyer and ditched in the sea. Despite severe injuries he was able to reach the shore where he was taken prisoner by the Australians.

Itto Koku Heiso **Masu-Aki Endo.** (Place of birth and date unknown. Suicide, 7 June 1943.)

An October 1941 graduate of the Otsu 9th Flight Reserve Enlisted Training Class, Endo was to take up duties with the Tainan Air Group in February 1942. He was to play a role in the air battles over the Solomons and New Guinea from bases at Rabaul and Lae. Re-organisation of his group led Endo to return to Japan in May 1943 where he joined 251st Air Group and its programme into the south-eastern area. A member of *Tai-i* Ichiro Mukai's air group, Endo shot down a Lockheed P–38 Lightning fighter-bomber. Surrounded by Bell P–39 Airacobras, he rammed one of them and died in the collision.

Sho-i **Shigetaka Omori.** (Born Yamanashi Prefecture, Kofu, Honshu, 1916. Suicide, 26 October 1942.)

Omori enlisted in the Imperial Japanese Navy in May 1933, and graduated from the 33rd Pilot Training Class in September 1936 to become a fighter pilot. Two years later he joined 13th Air Group Fighter Squadron and was sent via Cheju Island to Kunda airfield, Shanghai, which was then being bombarded. He scored his first hit on 25 February 1938 during the attacks on Nanchang, and then saw service in the Central China theatre.

After service in the converted carrier *Akagi* and with the Tsukuba and Ominato Air Groups, the outbreak of war in the Pacific found him in the 7,470-ton carrier *Hosho* ('Flying Phoenix') and then again in *Akagi*. During the Battle of Midway Omori was *shotai* (leader) of *Akagi*'s fighter *chutai* under *Sho-i* Shirane. On escort duty his flight was intercepted by US fighters and he shot down two Grumman F4F Wildcats. He led several battle sorties and when *Akagi* caught fire (and was lost on 5 June 1942) he landed on the 17,300-ton *Hiryu* ('Flying Dragon'). Flying in defence of *Hiryu* (which was also lost at Midway), he was forced to ditch but was picked up by the light cruiser *Nagara*.

Returning to Japan, he was assigned to the 25,075-ton *Shokaku* ('Flying Crane'). He was assigned to combat air patrol on 26 October 1942 during the

125

Battle of Santa Cruz where a force of four Japanese carriers took on an American carrier flotilla half the size; it was a tactical victory for the Japanese, but they lost more than 100 naval aircraft which would be difficult to replace. Omori rammed a dive-bomber that was about to bomb *Shokaku* and died instantly. *Shokaku* was sunk by a US submarine on 19 June 1944 at the battle of the Philippine Sea.

KAMIKAZE ESCORT PILOTS

Joto Hiko Heiso **Kunimichi Kato.** (Born 1923, Aichi Prefecture, Honshu, he served until the end of the war.)

A January 1943 graduate of the *Hei* 10th Flight Training Course, Kato was posted to the Omura Air Group in 254th Air Group, Hainan Island. He took part in the attacks on mixed P–38, Consolidated B–24 Liberator, Curtiss P–40 Warhawk and North American B–25 Mitchell raids from south-west China bases, over Kwangtung, Hong Kong and Hainan, his first 'kill' being a Lockheed P–38 Lightning fighter-bomber. Kato was hailed as 'top ace' of the 254th, and transferred to 210th Air Group in 1944 to play a vigorous part in home defence from Meiji Base. He was then sent to Kokubu base and became an escort pilot for the Okinawa Special Attack Force operations.

Hiko Heisocho **Minpo Tanaka.** (Born Nagasaki Prefecture, 1923. After WWII he became a civilian pilot for Zen Nippon Kuyu (ANA – All Nippon Airways) and was still in their employ in 1970.)

Tanaka joined the Otsu 11th Flight Reserve Enlisted Training Class in June 1939, and graduated from the 23rd Flight Training Course in September 1942. In June 1943 he was posted to 261st Air Group *Tora* ('Tiger'), 1st Air Fleet.

In 1944, with the situation worsening for the Japanese in the Marianas, he was posted to *Sho-i* Ichiro Higashiyama's *buntai* and took part in various air battles (also in Peleliu under *Tai-i* Ibusuki).

Tanaka is particularly remembered for his expertise in intercepting the US maritime patrol and reconnaissance Consolidated Vultee PBY Catalinas in the Marianas campaign. He made himself the master of what the Japanese aviators called the *shikaku no zen-kaho kogeki* (frontal, downward dead-angle attack). He also took part in the pilot preparation programme for the Battle of the Marianas.

During the interception of US convoys off Saipan, Tanaka flew escort to the *Ginga-tai* ('Milky Way' Unit), and was credited with downing two

Grumman F6F Hellcats. He was one of the few pilots left on Guam to harry the invading Americans, and eventually escaped to the Marianas and thence to Cebu.

On transfer to 201st Air Group he played a prominent role in escorting kamikaze Special Attack Units from the Philippines, and saw service in home defence of the Kanto Plain and Kyushu Island in 252nd and 203rd Air Groups.

UNOFFICIAL KAMIKAZE ATTACKS

Tai-i **Isamu Mochizuki.** (Born Saga Prefecture, W. Kyushu,1906. Suicide, 6 February 1944.)

Mochizuki enlisted in the Imperial Japanese Navy in 1925 and graduated from the 9th Pilot Training Class in November 1926. He saw service in the carrier *Honsho* and the 29,600-ton carrier *Kaga* before her final conversion (1935), and was then posted to the Omura Air Group. From 1932 to 1936 he served with the prestigious Yokosuka Air Group. When the 'China Incident' occurred on 7 July 1937 (whereby war between Japan and China began again), Mochizuki was posted to 13th Air Group at Kanda Base in Shanghai.

His age now tempering his role as an active combat pilot, he returned to Japan to become an instructor in various air groups. In 1943 he became Divisional Officer of the newly formed 281st Air Group at Maizuru Air Base under *Chusa* Shigehachiro Tokoro, to be stationed in the Kurile Islands.

With the deteriorating situation in the Marshall Islands, Mochizuki transferred to Roi Base. US forces landed during February 1944 and official entries show that Mochizuki made a *gyokusai* (personal *banzai* attack) from Roi.

Sho-i Jiro Chono. (Born Ehime Prefecture, W. Shikoku, 1907. Suicide, 21 February 1941.)

An early WWII suicide role model, Chono entered the Imperial Japanese Navy in 1927 and graduated as a fighter pilot in the 15th Pilot Training Class in 1930. When the 'China Incident' erupted, Chono was a *shotai* leader of the fighter squadron in the carrier *Kaga*. He first appears in combat documents on 11 November 1937 as assailing Northrop A-17 light attack bombers off the Maanshan Islands. Chono participated in the 1938 attack on Canton leading Nakajima carrier fighters, and in other China theatres. It was during the attack on Kunming that he made his kamikaze attack.

Cho-i **Osamu Kudo.** (Born Oita Prefecture, N. Honshu, 1915. Suicide, 3 March 1942.)

In 1931 Kudo joined the Otsu Flight Reserve Enlisted Training Class, and in April 1935 he finished the 2nd Flight Training Class Course and was posted to the Omura Air Group. He too saw service with 13th Air Group at Shanghai.

During the attack on Nanking, he had to ditch in the Yangtze River but was rescued. On returning to Japan he was posted to *Kaga* to fly in attacks over southern China. In the attack on Nan-yung on 30 August 1937, he shot down two British Gloster Gladiators.

Kudo followed this with service in *Akagi* and was posted to the Hyakuri-gahara Air Group; he was transferred to 3rd Air Group just before WWII broke out. He took part in the attack on Luzon, and in March 1942, during the air attack on the port of Broome in Western Australia, he died in a suicidal low-altitude strafing pass.

Kamikaze historical records throw up, from time to time, 'air aces' who were well known in Far Eastern aviation circles, and who contemplated and enacted *ad hoc* kamikaze dives before they became official policy.

Chu-i **Hiroyoshi Nishizawa.** (Born Nagano Prefecture, W. Central Honshu, 1920. Died 1944 aboard a transport aircraft. Kamikaze role model.)

A textile worker, having had a formal education, Nishizawa volunteered for the *Yokaren* (Flight Reserve Enlistee Training Programme) and qualified in 1936 as a student of the Otsu 7th Class. He completed his training in 1939 and served with the Oita, Omura and Susuka Air Groups. Immediately prior to the outbreak of WWII he was posted to the Chitose Air Group Fighter Squadron, just in time to be deployed to Micronesia (Inner South Sea Area) under overall commander *Taisa* Fujiro Ohashi.

Nishizawa was then transferred to 4th Air Group and scored his first kill over Rabaul; he was soon posted to the Tainan Air Group for service in New Guinea. Following the US attack on Guadalcanal, he saw service during the Battle of the Solomon Islands.

It was during an air battle on 7 August 1942 that Nishizawa chose to set up a suicide attack. After having shot down six Grumman F6Fs, he realised that his aircraft had been hit. Ironically, he unsuccessfully sought an enemy target, but made it back to base with a rapidly disintegrating aircraft. He was to see service in the 251st and 253rd Air Groups before returning to Japan.

By the time he was assigned to 203rd Air Group, Nishizawa was probably the most skilful of all Japanese fighter pilots. In the 203rd he was sent from

Atsugi base to take part in the defence of the Kuriles, and on 24 October 1944 went to Mabalacat, Luzon, to take part in Operation *SHO-GO*. There he flew as escort during the first kamikaze attack. While returning to base in a transport aircraft on 26 October, he died when Grumman F6Fs made an attack over Calapan, Mindoro Island.

Nishizawa was a much-lauded exponent of aerial skill and was honoured far more than a Japanese NCO could expect. He received a ceremonial sword from *Chujo* Jinichi Kusaka, Commander of SE Asia Fleet: the weapon bore the legend *Buko Batsugun* ('For Conspicuous Military Valour'). He was honoured with a ceremonial funeral on 2 December 1947 (the course of the war having delayed his gazetting in the *Zengen Fukoku*); he was dubbed *Bukai-in Kohon Giko Kyoshi*, a Zen Buddhist title hinting that within the military spirit Nishizawa was 'an honoured Buddhist person'.

Tai-i **Yoshimi Minami.** (Born Kagawa Prefecture, Honshu. Died as kamikaze, October 1944.)

Minami enlisted in the Imperial Japanese Navy in 1933 and immediately volunteered for flying duty. Graduating from the 30th Pilot Training Class in 1935, he was posted to 13th Air Group, thence to the 12th, via the Omura Air Group, within a period of two years. He won valuable experience in the air attacks on Nanchang and Hankow and was declared 'top ace' of 12th Air Group. Having survived a ramming raid over Hankow, he returned to Japan in 1938, to be assigned to the Saeki and Oita Air Groups and served aboard the carrier *Hiryu* and the 11,262-ton *Zuiho* ('Auspicious Phoenix') ex-*Takasaki*. In 1941 Minami was transferred to *Shokaku* and served in sea battles from the Indian Ocean to the Coral Sea.

In 1942 he was transferred to 601st Air Group and served in the newly completed 29,300-ton *Taiho* ('Great Phoenix'). Having survived a number of dogfights, he was seriously wounded when *Taiho* was sunk by a US submarine on 19 May 1944 during the Battle of the Philippine Sea, and returned to Japan. There he was attached to 653rd Air Group Fighter Squadron and became a kamikaze with the Kasagi Unit. He died diving on a vessel of the US Task Force off the Philippines.

Sho-i **Ichiro Yamamoto.** (Born Ehime Prefecture, W. Shikoku, 1918. Suicide, 19 June 1944.)

An Imperial Japanese Navy enlistee, Yamamoto was selected for the 50th Pilot Training Class in December 1939 and graduated in June 1940. His first postings were to the Oita and Sasebo Air Groups in *Zuiho* and *Shokaku*.

Yamamoto took part in the attack on Pearl Harbor (screening his carrier) and saw service in the Indian Ocean and Coral Sea. On 8 May 1942 he was assigned to the fighter escort command of *Tai-i* Takumi Hoashi. His service was to continue with the Battle of Santa Cruz where he clocked up hours in combat patrols and interception raids. He notched up 'kills' against US torpedo- and dive-bombers.

In November 1942 he became a *kyoshi* with the Oita Air Group. In *Zuikaku* (601st Air Group) his skill was put to use in Operation *A-GO*, and he became *shotai* leader of the carrier's fighter squadron. En route to a target he was intercepted by Grumman F6Fs and made a kamikaze dive.

Sho-i Saburo Kitahata. (Born of agricultural stock, Hyogo Prefecture, S. Central Honshu, 1915. Suicide, 23 January 1943.)

An Imperial Japanese Navy enlistee in 1932, Kitahata joined the 21st Pilot Training Class in 1933 and graduated the same year to enter the Omura Air Group. He was serving in the 10,600-ton carrier *Ryujo* ('Fighting Dragon') at about the time of her first conversion in 1934, and thence in the Kasumigaura Air Group. Kitahata served two tours of duty in *Ryujo* and then joined the Saeki Air Group, with service in various China theatres. By 1938 he was in *Soryu* and took part in the Kwangtung battles.

In 1939 Kitahata transferred to the Yokosuka Air Group and, via 12th Air Group, saw more action in China. April 1942 saw him in *Junyo* and he played a part in the raid on Dutch Harbor, to win accolades for spirited defence sorties against Curtiss P–40 Warhawks which attacked the carrier.

Kitahata remained in *Junyo* and took part in the attack on Guadalcanal and the Battle of Santa Cruz. From the air base on Truk Island, he sortied against Consolidated B–24 Liberators and dived suicidally into a flight of three aircraft.

Chusa Aya-o Shirane. (Born Tokyo, 1916. Suicide, 24 November 1944.)

A graduate of the *Kaigun Heigakko*, Shirane had influence at the highest level, being the son of (a later appointed) Secretary to the Cabinet, Takesuke Shirane. In 1939 he became a fighter pilot after completing his training with the 31st Aviation Student Course. Later in the same year he joined 12th Air Group and saw action in China until 1941.

After war in the Pacific began, Shirane took part in attacks on Darwin and in the Indian Ocean, and at the Battle of Midway transferred to *Zuikaku* and won huge praise for efforts during the Second Battle of the Solomon Sea and at Santa Cruz. He was posted to Yokosuka Air Group, and promoted Group Leader of 341st Air Group. Here he began to fly the fighter-bomber Kawanishi Kokuki KK N1K2–J *Shiden* ('Violet Lightning') known as George 11 to the Allies, a development of the N1K1 *Kyofu* float-plane.

During the course of 1944 Shirane became leader of the *Shiden* unit which he trained – Fighter *Hikotai* 701 – operating from Mabalacat. On 24 November he was attacking the USAAF 433rd Squadron's Lockheed P–38 Lightnings when he turned kamikaze to die over Leyte.

Hiko Heisocho **Wataru Nakamichi.** (Born Osaka City, 1922. Survived the war as an *Ohka* support pilot.)

Formerly a worker in a tin can factory, Nakamichi enlisted at Kure Naval Base Barracks in 1940. He volunteered to be a pilot and joined the Tsuchiura Air Group, graduating with the *Hei* 4th Flight Reserve Enlisted Training Class, to get practical training with the Kasumigaura and Oita Air Groups. He served in *Junyo* and by 1943 was in 204th Air Group operating out of Buin.

Nakamichi enters kamikaze history as an 'ace' who did sterling work as a pilot of the *Jinrai* ('Heavenly Lightning') 721st Fighter Squadron directly supporting the *Ohka* Special Attack Force units.

CHAPTER EIGHTEEN

KAITEN, KORYU, KAIRYU, SHINYO:
A QUARTET OF OCEAN KAMIKAZE

'May my death be as sudden and clean as the shattering of crystal ...
like cherry blossoms in the spring, let us fall clean and radiant ... Most
important, do not weep for me ...' — Thoughts of an anonymous
suicide *Kaiten* operative (1945)

The Allies were to discover that the spirit of *jiketsu* was not to be confined
to Japan's airmen, for *jibaku* was to be just as ruthlessly undertaken on and
under the sea as well as in the air. When *Choju* Onishi's kamikaze operations in the Philippines became known, there was pressure from ordinary
naval ratings to train as marine kamikaze. The technology for this to
become feasible was to be found in Japan's arms manufacture of decades
earlier.

For twenty years before the outbreak of WWII, Japan had rankled at what
the nation perceived as the injustice of an international agreement on the size
of her navy. This discontent led to a devious plan. The Washington Conference of 1921 had forced Japan to agree to limit her navy to the 10:3.5:6
Formula. For every ten tons of US or British warship, and for every 3.5
French or Italian tons, Japan could maintain no more than six tons. Experts
from Japan's Navy General Staff scoured the agreement for loopholes, and
found that the tonnage did not apply to torpedoes and submarines. So these
were to be the areas in which Japan intended to excel, and these were also to
be the founts of *jibaku* activity.

By the 1920s torpedoes had been taken to their maximum of performance
in the navies of the world's maritime powers. New propulsion systems were
needed. Britain and France had spent time on such research but nothing
much had been invented. Oxygen as a propellant had been looked at, for
instance, but had been discarded as being too dangerous. Yet Japanese
engineers were keen to exploit the fact that oxygen in a torpedo offered a
wider range of distance propelled and speed achieved, and set to work on
the exploitation of a workable system.

In 1933 *Chujo* Toshihide Asaguma – soon to be Chief Naval Designer at
Kure Naval Arsenal – and *Shosho* Kaneji Kishimoto – Chief of the Torpedo

Department at Kure – were honoured by Emperor Hirohito for their five years spent in developing of the wakeless torpedo, 24 inches in diameter, 30 feet long and 6,000 pounds in weight. It was called the Type 93 because it was calculated that 2,593 years had elapsed since the foundation of the Japanese Empire. Later to be dubbed 'Long Lance', the torpedo's warhead could contain 1,000 pounds of high explosives, which was twice that carried by US and British torpedoes.

Eventually all Imperial Japanese Navy destroyers and cruisers were equipped with Long Lance and the requisite bulky oxygen-producing technology. Their installation was carried out in great secrecy, the oxygen generators being described as 'air-conditioning' to those without security clearance. The torpedoes were used for the first time on 27 February 1942 (with little real success but with naval enthusiasm) against an Allied force at the Battle of the Java Sea, but the loss of so many ships that could have taken the weapon into war areas meant that the stocks remained unused at Imperial Navy Ordnance Depots.

By December 1941 Japan had built sixty-four large I-Class submarines, and twenty midgets. The history of the latter had begun during the Russo–Japanese War of 1904–5, when the two-man craft had been used in, for example, the attack on Port Arthur. Called by the Japanese *hai* ('flies'), they could remain submerged for five hours, and although not initially a *jibaku* weapon in the kamikaze sense, they were risky to operate.

The first IJN experimental models of mini submarines, the Types A–1 and A–2, were built at Kure in 1938. After successful trials two other prototypes, Ha–1 and Ha–2, were built. These shore-based or ship rechargeable mini submarines were 78.7 feet long and displaced 46 tons; with a two-man crew they had a range of 80 miles at 2 knots, or 20 miles at 19 knots. Two 18in torpedoes were carried in the bows. By January 1942 a fleet of 42 of the Ha–3 to Ha–44 Series had been built at Urazaki, near Kure.

During the spring of 1942 the Japanese High Command decided to use mini submarines for 'to the death' coastal defence and the original models were modified to become the Series Ha–46 to Ha–61. During the Philippines campaign of late 1944 – early 1945, they were used around Surigao Strait and Mindanao, but to little effect.

In October 1942 the Type B Ha–45 mini submarine was produced; this was 80.4 feet long, displaced 50 tons and was able to recharge its own batteries. It carried a crew of three and had a range of 350 miles at 6 knots surfaced, or 120 miles at 4 knots submerged. The prototype was developed and produced in a series of fifteen, called Type C Ha–62 to Ha–76. Production ceased in 1944. These too were intended for coastal defence.

These midgets were transported to their station by I-Class submarines, which could release and recover them while surfaced. They were used at Pearl Harbor on 7 December 1941 in what was virtually a kamikaze mission, long before the word had evolved in all its horror, for although the seamen involved were not told specifically that they were suicide volunteers, the inference that they were was more than apparent in mess and ratings' quarters. Experienced operators knew that any provision for their ultimate rescue was only a paper gesture.

When Japanese analyses of mini submarine activity at Pearl Harbor had been completed, it was evident that their operations had added nothing tactically to the destructive capacity of air sorties. But log-books recorded that the midget submarine was a valuable weapon because of its capability to penetrate even a competently defended enemy harbour, and the kamikaze potential was noted – and would be re-assessed in 1944. Japanese naval strategists held that the ever present possibility of these mini craft striking at distant targets regardless of consequences to themselves would engender feelings of insecurity and fear in the enemy. The kamikaze principle if achieving little else would certainly lower enemy morale. So from 1941 work went on in IJN research departments to facilitate the accommodation and release of the mini-submarine from a mother vessel while submerged.

By 1942 Japanese senior naval staff officers were individually looking at the potential of the mini submarine for reconnaissance and strikes in areas of active enemy deployment from Sydney, Australia to Diego Suarez, Madagascar. Under the command of *Shosho* Noburo Ishizaka of 8th Submarine Flotilla (to be known as Submarine Special Attack Group, Kure) mini submarine training had begun by the last days of April 1942, with an envisaged operational date of 31 May 1942.

Submarines *I–16, I–18* and *I–20* made their way via Penang and the east coast of Burma to the first target strike area of Madagascar, with the intention of launching two-torpedo *hai* (from the series Ha–3 to Ha–4) as near as possible to the entrance to Diego Suarez harbour. There they would negotiate the anti-submarine nets and attack enemy vessels. If they failed to make a strike the vessels were to be scuttled, and the men were to return to their mother submarine. The written order included the latter sentence to mask the kamikaze element of the operation. As the mother submarines were to remain some ten miles away from the targets, it would have been a nonsense to expect tired men to swim so far. In the event the submarines reached their position, and *I–18* prepared to launch her mini; the engine refused to start. *I–16*'s and *I–20*'s minis were launched, but one sank at the harbour entrance – cause unknown. The remaining mini submarine moved on to target. At this time the British were occupying Madagascar and were not expecting enemy activity, so no real defence was offered. The *hai*'s pilot followed the route that had been planned for him from reconnaissance reports and entered the harbour. Finding no ships at this point he moved farther into the harbour. The silhouette of a tanker appeared, and although the short range made it risky a torpedo was launched. Ten seconds later the torpedo hit *Loyalty* amidships, the backlash of the explosion nearly capsized the mini submarine and the two crewmen were thrown against its sides. Toxic gas from damaged batteries began to pollute the interior, the craft began to lose speed, but made its way painfully towards the Eastern Fleet battleship HMS *Ramillies* now illuminated by the blazing tanker. The second torpedo was fired and hit HMS *Ramillies* but she was able to steam to Durban in East Africa for repairs. The mini submarine drifted to shore where the crew were found dead, asphyxiated by battery gas. Their story was pieced together by surmise and known events.

While this first strike was being made, the second target area was being approached by submarines *I–21*, *I–22*, *I–24*, *I–27* and *I–29* under command of *Taisa* Sasaki. Aboard *I–21* was a collapsible Aichi E16AI *Zuin* ('Auspicious Cloud' – Allied code-name 'Paul') reconnaissance float-plane.

At about 1630 hrs the submarines hove-to some seven miles away from Sydney, Australia, and four mini submarines were launched. As they slowly approached North Head, the *hai* pilots saw that the anti-submarine net was open. One of the minis became irretrievably entangled in the net but the other three proceeded to the target area. Soon two heavy cruisers were encountered, the USS *Chicago* (CA-29) and HMAS *Canberra*, with a supply vessel nearby.

Chicago was the first to be sized up; one suicide pilot pressed his firing button, but the torpedo (it was later surmised) stuck in its tube and exploded, destroying the *hai*. Allied ships were alerted and erratic gunfire began as the two remaining minis unleashed their torpedoes. The *hais* were forced to the surface by 8in shellfire and destroyed; one torpedo ran to shore and another hit and sank a ferry. The Sydney operation was a disaster.

Naval historians note that the last unit of the suicide *hai* – four craft based at Dumaquete in the Philippines – were scuttled on 20 March 1945, as the Americans moved on Davao.

During the winter months of 1942–3 Naval *Tai-i* Kuroki and Sekio Nishina, with the naval architect Hiroshi Suzukawa put together a design based on the Long Lance torpedo, which incorporated a cockpit fitted with steering gear and periscope. By the spring of 1943 their design was complete for a new manned torpedo with a warhead consisting of 3,410 pounds of TNT and a range of 40 nautical miles.

Japan's *Sensui Butai* (submarine force) was more perceptive about the country's deteriorating fortunes than any other branch of the armed forces, and several senior officers such as *Shosho* Chumi Takema were advocating 'certain death' attacks long before *Chujo* Jisaburo Ozawa's carrier fleet was destroyed at the Battle of Cape Engano on 25 October 1944. Indeed in the early months of 1943 Takema drew up a plan to revive the 'human torpedoes' of the Russo–Japanese War. His report to IJN General Headquarters fell on deaf ears.

Yet the torpedo option was what the IJN's General Staff really needed, and ideas regarding the construction and deployment of 'human torpedoes' continued. For instance, *Tai-i* Makoto Chika, navigational officer of the submarine *I–165*, made suggestions on the subject to his commanding officer *Tai-i* Kimi Izawa, who passed them to Fleet HQ in the form of a petition (written in blood!). Designers Kuroki and Nishina continued their work and called their 54-foot, 40-knot manned torpedo *Kaiten*. The literal translation is 'Heaven Shaker', but the inference of its calligraphic symbols suggests a ground-moving shift of ideas.

At first the General Staff rejected the *Kaiten* as a fantastic and expensive weapon, but following the US successes at Saipan from 15 to 30 June 1944, the *Kaiten* plans were revived. Although Kuroki and Nishina were to underline the importance of their design with a petition (again written in their own blood!), events alone stirred the Navy's General Staff to order manufacture of a prototype under the project *Maru Roku Heiki* (Circle Six Mountain). At this stage, though, the 'suicide' element was not popular and it was insisted that an escape hatch be incorporated in the design. During February 1944 the prototype was approved and a yard was set up for its manufacture at Otsujima Island, near Kure, and close to the Headquarters of the IJN's 6th Fleet submarine force.

There were to be four *Kaiten* types. Type 1 (based on the standard Type 93 torpedo, with matching explosive charge, air chambers and motor) displaced 8.3 tons and was 48.2 feet long with a beam of 3.3 feet. Its range varied according to speed, from 14 miles at 30 knots to 48 miles at 12 knots. Propulsion (at 550bhp) was fuelled by a mix of petroleum and oxygen. The usual automatic directional equipment of a torpedo was replaced by a cockpit and small conning tower surmounted by a short periscope. (Initial US intelligence on *Kaiten* reported erroneously that the operators straddled the torpedo rather than sitting within). Beneath the cockpit was an escape hatch.

At first the *Kaiten* were intended for coastal defence, and submarines were adapted to carry four to six of them (the *Kaidai* -Class *I–54* carried five on deck). Eventually the escape hatch was connected to the interior of the mother submarine by a tubular passage set within the flooding chamber so that the operator could enter the *Kaiten* while the submarine was submerged. This made launching easier and reduced the chance of detection. Records show that in practice few operatives tried to escape.

The Type 1, the most commonly deployed of the *Kaiten*, was mass produced in yards at Yokosuka, Hikari, Maizuru, Kure and Sasebo; purists might add that it was the only one built because the small number of later versions did not come into production until the war was ending. Types 2, 3 and 4 were 55 feet long and had a beam of 4.5 feet; they displaced 18.3 tons and had a top speed of 40 knots. They were propelled by hydrogen peroxide motors (1,500–1,800bhp) and carried an explosive charge of 3,300–3,690 pounds of TNT. The later models had a larger conning tower and horizontal fins, and were crewed by two men.

During the month of June 1944 a few *Kaiten* were produced in a programme that was given the utmost secrecy, but as Japan's fortunes deteriorated in the Marianas the IJN General Staff ordered production to be stepped up. A second order followed rapidly calling for volunteers to operate a new *Kyukoko heiki* (national salvation weapon). The inference of the order was that the weapon's missions would be one-way, but it seems likely that there was no lack of volunteers, and the Navy set out four criteria for recruitment. The volunteer must be unmarried; be physically and psychologically well; evince a strong spirit of patriotism; and have a minimum of dependent family responsibilities (i.e., not be an only son, or a family's sole source of income).

'Base P', the *Kaiten* depot at Otsushima, an island off the coast of Yamaguchi Prefecture, south-west Honshu, was to be the place where the volunteers were to be indoctrinated with *Yamato damashii*, and they were not allowed leave before training was completed. *Tai-i* Kuroki and Nishina supervised the training of the first volunteers.

Familiarisation with the construction and function of Type 93 torpedoes was followed by dry-run sorties in simulated programmes. Then came submerged dives aboard vessels at anchor in Tokuyame Bay. Finally an operational dummy run was carried out aboard a submarine. At this point training was considered to be complete. Number One Special Base Squadron was duly recruited from 6th Fleet (the Japanese submarine service) and training began in September 1944; volunteers were selected from the flight schools of Tsuchiura and Nara.

Records show that on 6 September 1944 the *Kaiten* programme claimed its first casualty. Kuroki's training *Kaiten* stuck in the mud in the calm water of the *Seto Naikai,* and more deaths were to be logged in training and in accidents while on operations. One such was that of Minoru Wada. Copies of his diary entries survive in kamikaze collections, and in this transcription one can read the very rare testimony of a *Kaiten* operative:

[Diary leaves of Tokyo University graduate Miroru Wada (1920–45)]

'18 November 1944. Yesterday I heard the air-raid warning. Enemy aircraft were over the banks of the Kawadana River. Today a lorry of the naval construction sector crushed a mother and her two children to death. Kudo and I happened to see to it. Why should a creature a-quiver with life be transformed into an inert mass within a moment?

'1 February 1945. For the first time in my life I got into a *Kaiten,* a human torpedo. I have just re-read *Kokoro* [*The Heart,* 1914: a study in loneliness] by Soseki [Natsume Soseki, 1867–1916, Japan's most popular modern novelist] and *Jindo no Kigeki* [*Human Comedy*] by Shiro Ozaki [1898–1964]. These two novels were of great interest to me, for my entire life is permeated by a scent of death. I enjoy perusing a literary work. Even if the style is not perfect it always moves me.

'The consolation, the encouragement, the noisy manners of the Army and all its rhythmical songs make me feel sick. I wish I could find again the kind of emotion that used to move me to tears in bygone days, when we lived in peace. Have I lost the faculty to judge myself dispassionately? The idea of dying for my country in the spring does not move me in the least. I must remain calm and try to find the best way of living in the meantime.

'Father, Mother – that is where I have got to now. Can you remember the red velvet that Wakana wore on the day of her concert recital? It glittered, illuminated by the spotlights, and now the sea is like it, sparkling in the sunlight. It is a muggy afternoon.

'I am in charge of a 400-ton tug. I have my binoculars round my neck and, on my left sleeve, a green chrysanthemum blossom, the emblem of the 'Special Attack' crews. In an hour we will arrive at Sahuku. The old tug-boat captain is continually dozing and nodding his head. A lieutenant called Miyoshi was killed. He tried to dive his torpedo under a boat and bumped against it. The water seeped through the upper hatch. When they fished him up his body was already inert and his face covered with blood. When the torpedo was inverted, the water that flowed out was rust-coloured. It must have been tinted with his blood.

'It has been raining, and last night we were all drunk, including our commander. The storm took us by surprise at about 11 p.m. Two torpedoes were cast up on to the shore by the gale and the violence of the waves. We at once became sober and rushed down to save them, but it was too late.

'18 April 1945. I have only a month left. I feel as though I am about to sit for an end of term exam. In a month I will have crashed myself against the enemy. I do not feel that I am about to die. After all, we are fortunate: we are neither responsible for our life nor for our death. I do not talk like [the group leader] who indulges in long speeches of which every word is bursting with passionate and ardent patriotism. I detest these kind of manifestations; I prefer peaceful meditation.

'I attempt to transform all that is passion into reflection. You may say that this kind of meditation has no value whatever and is unnecessary. But we are students and have been taught to think. It is a burden which we will never succeed in laying aside, but it will help me to draw up the balance-sheet of my life.

'"My heart is becoming cold. Around it stretches dismal solitude", said the heroine of Ishikawa in his collection of morbid verses. [Takuboku Ishikawa, 1885–1912, a consumptive, impoverished poet. Minoru Wada is referring to Ishikawa's *Ichiaku no Suna* (*A Handful of Sand*), 1910] Is this coldness of my heart caused by my cowardice? My comrades are worried by my apathy. I only attempted to discover a meaning for my death. When I had found it, my heart turned to ice.

'In a month's time, the order will come. Perhaps it will put an end to this meaningless existence? The hours move relentlessly on.

'When the decisive moment for my last attack comes I shall undoubtedly be afraid. The calm, cool manner I have adopted until now is only affectation. Now, for the first time in my life, my past seems really confused to me.

I have made desperate efforts to discover myself during these last months. And I already have the impression that I no longer exist.

'I have already been inside the torpedo that crawls at the bottom of the sea at a depth of 105 feet and never surfaces. I piloted another and plunged into the sand at a depth of ninety feet at an angle of forty degrees. I could see my comrade's head under my shoes. When I opened the hatch of a third, a white-vapour suddenly escaped from it and I felt as though I am "a hell of a fellow". And yet at every moment I should like to burst into tears.

'12 June 1945. Those who can no longer put their trust in humanity deserve to be pitied. Since we left for the attack, we have spent ten days in idleness. To see us joking together, anyone would think we were quite indifferent to death. As a matter of fact, it is merely the natural reaction which makes us avoid looking each other in the face.

'Now I am waiting for the enemy at Urushi, on the great supply route of Okinawa. Sometimes I feel happy during the night. I can see, above the bridge, the Great Bear on the right, the Southern Cross on the left, both of them twinkling brilliantly, and the Milky Way looks to me like white cloud. 26 July 1945. I have returned alive. It is no use assuming an air of bravado when faced with the frailty of our daily life. In order to become detached one's mind must be clear and one must work at this detachment continually.

'My life has been nothing but vanity and cowardice. This month of meditation which was given to me, and my return alive, will mark a turning-point in my life and I hope it will lead to a change in my actions and my state of mind. I have had the opportunity of seeing myself as I really was.

'My past consists only of superficial actions (as, for instance, my infatuation with Shiro Osaki's *Human Comedy*). My opinions on life and death may possibly have also been the expression of such a state of mind. I need more time to think, I must make greater efforts ...'

From initial training at 'Base P', *Kaiten* operators were given honorific nlcknames ranging from '*Samurai no kami*' (Warriors of the Gods) to the cumbersome 'Group for the Promotion of *Bushido*'.

All the I-Class submarines extant were fitted-out to carry 4–6 *Kaiten*. As the target was approached the pilots would climb into their craft and be sealed in; telephones linked them with the submarine's captain. As the optimum minute was reached the *Kaitens*' engines would be fired and they would be launched at five-second intervals. The pilots would then steer them to the target. When 500 yards away the pilots would switch the craft to automatic and prepare for final acceleration to full speed, to impact at a depth of about twelve feet.

When talking to the author in 1961, Toshio Inari remembered his son's account of his *Kaiten*:

'It was just as well that I was small for inside the *Kaiten* even a small man was cramped. Even though the controls were simple, it took all my training skills to operate the craft efficiently.

'Just below my feet was a minute box of emergency rations and a small *uisuki ippon* (bottle of whisky). As I sat in the cockpit directly in front of my vision was the viewing glass of the short, chunky periscope which I could raise and lower with a crank lever to my right. Also to the right, and above my head, was a valve to regulate the oxygen flow to the motor which was located immediately behind my seat. Overhead, and to the left, was another lever connected to the *Kaiten*'s diving planes which controlled the rate of descent or elevation underwater. Below this lever was a valve for letting in sea water. This valve was necessary to maintain the vessel's stability when the oxygen fuel was used up. The rudder control lever, to steer right or left, made up the controls. The latter would be the last that we pilots would adjust as we went for target; thus it was known as the "dead man's handle". As I sat in my first *Kaiten* I thought that to operate this efficiently I would need half a dozen hands, and the same number of eyes to monitor the control panel. As well as the periscope there was a gyro-compass, a clock, and depth and fuel gauges. And I found that any rapid change in the controls or contact with an underwater object led to a sharp rap on the head from one of these instruments. So around Otsushima there was always a goodly number of bandaged heads.'

After training was complete each man was given leave to return to his home; ostensibly to bid a kamikaze's farewell to his family. Then the pilots would return to the submarine bases at Otsushima or Hikari on the Sea of Suo, *Seto Naikai*. Here they passed their days before missions in some indulgence with extra rations and the delights of 'comfort women'. Each operational mission was preceded by an evening party in the presence of the highest ranking Imperial Submarine Fleet officer available. Next day the pilots would parade in 'number ones', and their belongings were sent back to their families. Each pilot sported a *hachimaki* with the name of the *Kaiten* group and a suitable slogan. The climax of departure was the ritual drinking of *sake* and a stand-to-attention for the *Kimigayo*. Thus did the *Kaiten* warriors depart for kamikaze missions.

The first *Kaiten* attack was prompted by the US seizure of Ulithi Atoll in the Carolinas on 22 September 1944 under the command of Admiral Chester

W. Nimitz. A dozen newly trained suicide mariners were chosen for the sortie including the inventor of the *Kaiten*, *Tai-i* Nishina, who placed at his feet the ashes of *Tai-i* Kuroki, his co-inventor.

Before the mariners departed, a dedication ceremony took place at Otsushima on 7 November, supervised by Commander of 6th Fleet, *Chujo* Shigeyoshi Mura, who briefed the *Kaiten* pilots. Three Fleet submarines were to be used to transport four *Kaiten* apiece to the neighbourhood of Ulithi where intelligence had located a concentration of US vessels. The orders were to sink the largest ships possible. Each *Kaiten* pilot was toasted by Mura and given a short ceremonial sword; they were to be called the *Kikumizu* ('Chrysanthemum Water') Unit.

The submarines appointed for the mission were: *I–36* (*Shosa* Teramoto); *I–37* and *I–47* (*Shosa* Zenji Orita). The *Kaiten* were towed to the submarines by four cables. At 0900 hrs on 8 November 1944, the submarines were led out of Otsushima by *I–36* to a chorus of *banzai!* from ships' crews in the bay. The *Kaiten* pilots took part in the hourly routines of the submarine crew. Survivors were to note how assured, resolute and scathing of death they were. Once out of port the submarines split up: *I–37* made for Kossol Passage in the Palaus; *I–36* and *I–47* set course directly for Ulithi, 900 miles south of Leyte.

I–37 did not reach her target; monitored by the US destroyer *Nicholas* (DD-449) on 12 November, she was picked up by sonar while preparing to launch her *Kaiten* on the 19th and destroyed by depth-charges from USS *McCoy Reynolds* (DE-440) and *Conklin* (DE-439). *I–47* made a slow and steady 20-knots surface passage to the area where US patrols were anticipated. She then lay submerged, surfacing by night to charge batteries and monitor radio messages from 6th Fleet HQ at Kure. *I–47* and *I–36* were in constant communication with Mitsubishi Ki–46 reconnaissance aircraft from Truk.

On 17 November *I–47*'s radio operator reported receiving a message from control – relayed by Tokyo – that the Ki–46s had seen a large concentration of US vessels at Ulithi, twenty-four hours before, one reported battleships and carriers in three groups of miscellaneous ships. Fifty miles west of Ulithi *Shosa* Orita surfaced to verify bearings, the substance of the message received and to check the *Kaiten* which were all logged as being in a satisfactory state. *I–47* moved close to the entrance of Ulithi lagoon on 19 November. At midnight Orita inspected the *Kaiten* operators, formally accepted their wills and last letters home and the four suicide pilots donned their *hachimaki*. *Sho-i* Akira Sato and Kozo Watanabe climbed into their

Kaiten, while *Tai-i* Nishina and Fukuda waited, because they could gain entry to their craft from within the submarine. As soon as Sato and Watanabe were in place, *I-47* submerged and slowly made her way to the entrance of the lagoon. The two *Sho-i* had an uncomfortable three hours in their *Kaiten*, linked only by telephone. At 0300 hrs Nishina and Fukuda squeezed through the access tubes to their *Kaiten* Nos 1 and 2. The attack quartet of suicide killers was ready.

At Ulithi US repair engineers were working on damaged vessels. *Shosa* Orita steered *I-47* towards their welding lights' glare. At 0415 hrs on 20 November 1944, *Tai-i* Nishina was given the order to go and his *Kaiten* No 1 moved off. His orders were to penetrate the anchorage as far as possible, raise his periscope and select a target. At 0430 hrs *Sho-i* Sato and Watanabe and *Tai-i* Fukuda set off at five-minute intervals to enter the lagoon and fan out right and left of Nishina's position; but Fukuda was to attack as soon as he entered the lagoon. The intention was to instil panic by blowing up vessels over a wide range.

Shouts of *Tenno heika banzai!* crackled over the telephone links between the *Kaiten* and *I-47* as the four pilots ploughed their way towards their targets. Orita repositioned *I-47* to the south-east of Ulithi Atoll. At 0507 hrs the first explosions were heard and clouds of smoke rose over Ulithi. While *I-47* dodged a US destroyer by submerging, three explosions were monitored – had three *Kaiten* struck? At 0600 hrs Orita presumed that all four pilots were dead; he offered prayers for their souls bound for the *Yasukuni* and set course for Japan.

Aboard *I-36*, *Sho-i* Taichi Imanishi and Yoshihiko Kudo had entered their *Kaiten* at about midnight; by 0300 hrs *Tai-i* Kentaro Yashimoto and Kazuihisa and Touozuni were in place. But on the very point of launching, *Kaiten* Nos 1 and 2 stuck fast in their racks with engines started, and No 4 was reported to be leaking seriously. At 0454 hrs *Sho-i* Imanishi in No 3 was launched. *I-36* now made ready to return home as soon as the *Kaiten* pilots got back. The crew listened to hear if *Sho-i* Imanishi had been successful, and explosions were heard between 0545 and 0605 hrs; but when depth-charges began to rock *I-36*, *Shosa* Teramoto gave the order to move off submerged. They were to remain submerged for nineteen hours breathing foul air before it was safe to surface and return to base.

On 30 November *I-47* and *I-36* arrived back at Kure; three days later a debriefing conference was held aboard 6th Fleet's Flagship *Tsukushi Maru*. Some 200 naval staff had assembled to hear the reports prepared by *Shosa*

Orita and Teramoto. A staff officer summarised the reports: Crew of *I–47* had observed two fires; crew of the *I–37* had heard explosions. Photographs taken by a Mitsubishi Ki–46 from Truk, three days after the *Kaiten* attack were set alongside the written reports. A final analysis was placed in the IJN records: '*Tai-i* Nishina sunk an aircraft carrier, as did *Tai-i* Fukuda and *Sho-i* Imanishi. *Sho-i* Sato and Watanabe each sank a battleship. The report was received with the usual *banzai!* As news of the operation spread the morale of tyro *Kaiten* pilots soared. The success, though, was a propaganda lie; the only US vessel sunk at Ulithi was the tanker *Mississinewa* (AO-59), lost with her crew of 150.

A new and more ambitious *Kaiten* offensive was now planned which would involve six submarines: *I–36* (*Shosa* Teramoto); *I–47* (*Shosa* Zenji Orita); *I–48* (*Shosa* Zenshin Toyama); *I–53* (*Shosa* Seihachi Toyamasu); *I–56* (*Shosa* Masahiko Morinaga); *I–58* (*Shosa* Mochitsura Hashimoto). Each would carry four *Kaiten* that would attack US shipping fleets simultaneously but in locations that were quite widely separated. A target of twenty-four US capital ships was pencilled-in. The immediate goal was to arrest the US impetus and give Japan time to re-group her forces, increase the production of kamikaze weapons and train pilots.

The two dozen *Kaiten* pilots recruited for the offensive were dubbed the *Kongo* Group, after the mountain where the military leader of the Northern and Southern Courts, Magashige Kusunoke (*d.*1336) had trained his *samurai*. There was no air of secrecy about the *Kongo* mission, the hours before their departure taking on the atmosphere of *kyoen* (festive merrymaking). An armada of small craft swarmed around Otsushima Bay whose occupants chanted the names of the *Kaiten* pilots almost as a Buddhist mantra.

On 3 January 1945 the submarines sailed out of Otsushima through the Bungo Strait and into the Pacific. *I–36* would return to Ulithi Atoll for another go; *I–47* would head for New Guinea where the Japanese forces were struggling; *I–48* was sailing as a back-up for *I–36* but she is recorded as missing (presumed sunk at Ulithi) on 22 January. *I–53* had been ordered to attack the shipping lanes off the Palaus; *I–56* to harry US and Australian ships in the Admiralty Islands; *I–58* (famous in IJN messes for her role against the British Force Z of the Malay campaign) was destined for Guam. By now it was clear from intercepted radio messages that the Allies knew of the *Kaiten*, so the submarines spent a great deal of time submerged.

All these vessels were to make 'simultaneous attacks', and the day chosen for launching was 11 January. To add to the pressure on the Japanese in all theatres at this time, the *Kaiten* had a spate of back luck. *I–36* ran into an underwater shelf while submerged and was only dislodged with much effort. Her four *Kaiten* were launched and made the usual claim of four kills. *I–47* ran into an anti-submarine patrol, but launched her *Kaiten* in Humboldt Bay, New Guinea; again four kills were claimed, as was the supposed tally of *I–48* at Ulithi, but the submarine vanished on about 21 January. On the 23rd, however, *I–48* re-appeared north-east of Yap Island and was attacked and sunk by the destroyer escorts *Corbesier* (DE-438), *Raby* (DE-698) and *Conklin* (DE-439).

The comings and goings of Allied vessels in the Kossol Passage in the Palaus gave *I–53* a selection of prime targets. One of the four *Kaiten*, however, would not start so three were launched. Just as it ejected one *Kaiten* exploded so that only *Sho-i* Ito and *Itto Koku Heiso* Arimari rode to their target (and made the usual reports of 'kills').

I–56 got to the Admiralty Islands undetected, but became stuck in a submarine net. After a difficult extraction she returned to base with her *Kaiten* still aboard. *I–58* also arrived safely at Guam and *Tai-i* Ishikawa, *Sho-i* Kudo and *Itto Koku Heiso* Mori and Mitsueda were given credit for sinking two transports and an escort vessel.

Overall, 6th Fleet Command declared the operation a success and increased the weapons and training programme, with a new centre at Hikari for 200 new suicide squad recruits. The only flaws in the future plans were the shortage of technicians to service the *Kaiten* and a directive to conserve high octane fuel (used in 'mother' fast patrol boats employed in training exercises).

The impending US attack on Iwo Jima led to 6th Fleet HQ complying with Combined Fleet HQ orders to step-up *Kaiten* activity in the area. On 22–3 February 1945, *I–368* and *I–370* departed with ten *Kaiten* from the *Chibaya* Unit (named after the castle near the ancient capital of Nara) from Otsushima and Hikari to take up positions off Iwo Jima. Both submarines were sunk: *I–370* by Lieutenant Commander H. Huffman's destroyer escort *Finnegan* (DE-307) on 26 February; *I–368* by aircraft from Captain G. C. Montgomery's carrier *Anzio* (DVE-57) on 27 February.

On 23 February *I–44* (*Shosa* Genbein Kawaguchi) sailed with five *Chibaya Kaiten* aboard, bound for Iwo Jima. Records show that she returned on 9 March with the *Kaiten* unused, having been unable to break through the tight anti-submarine patrols. Kawaguchi was relieved of his command by *Chujo* Shigeyoshi Miura, Commander 6th Fleet submarines, for not having sacrificed his ship and crew as kamikaze. These events were to be the IJN's sole contribution to the defence of Iwo Jima.

During the early days of March, I–58 and I–36 left base for Iwo Jima again with ten *Kaiten* of the *Shimbu* ('God's Warriors') Group to form the *Kamitake* ('Peak of the Gods') Unit. They returned having achieved nothing. Sixth Fleet HQ decided that a concerted *Kaiten* offensive was necessary in a large *banzai* operation, but only four submarines were available. Nevertheless *Kaiten* of the *Tatara* Group (named after the beach in north Kyushu where the Mongol Fleet was wrecked by the *kamikaze* of antiquity) embarked aboard I–44, I–47, I–56 and I–58, with I–47 as flagship. I–56 was to carry six *Kaiten* (against the others' four) for an attack on warships off Okinawa.

On 26 March *Shosho* Mitsuru Nagai toasted the *Kaiten* pilots of the *Tatara* Group as *Samurai no Umi* ('*Samurai* of the Sea') with the usual *sake* libation. In his speech he said:

'I hope each of you will strike the enemy.

'At that moment your souls will fly to *Yasukuni*, there to watch forever over the Kami country of Japan. Please be assured that all remaining in the Sixth Fleet will do everything possible to comfort those you leave behind.'

Like the *Shimbu* operation, that of the *Tatara* was a complete failure. While the *Kaiten* submarines were approaching the US forces were storming the beaches of Okinawa, and some 150 destroyers were shielding the invasion fleet and it was impossible for the four submarines to get through. The sequence of action was: I–47 sailed from Kure on 29 March and as she emerged from the Bungo Strait was attacked by US aircraft. On the 30th she was detected by destroyers and subjected to a depth-charge attack which resulting in a fuel leakage. She surfaced and repairs were effected near Tanega Island. The fuel leak was exacerbated when she was bombed by a US night patrol; unable to submerge, she returned to Kure.

On 3 April I–44 and I–56 left Kure and made for Okinawa. Aboard were supplies for a month and orders were to cruise Okinawan waters and wait for an opportunity to strike. Two weeks passed unsuccessfully trying to evade the attentions of the Americans, and they were constantly attacked by US planes. Disturbed by the presence of Japanese submarines, the Americans increased air and sea cover. On 18 April, just east of Okinawa, I–56 was cornered by five destroyers: *Collett* (DD-730), *Mertz* (DD-691), *McCord* (DD-534), *Heermann* (DD-532) and *Uhlmann* (DD-687). The submarine was heavily buffeted by depth-charges but remained submerged as night fell; eventually she was sunk by an aircraft from the carrier *Bataan* (CVL-29).

Although *I–44* was subjected to several attacks, she sustained no serious damage, but her commander had been thwarted in selecting a target. On 29 April she surfaced to recharge batteries, but was attacked by US aircraft, one of which, from the carrier *Tulagi* (CVE-72), scored a direct hit near the conning tower and *I–44* disappeared for ever.

By 2 April, *I–58* had departed for the Okinawa arena, but she was attacked so frequently while running on the surface that by 6 April she had only got as far as Amami-oshima. In an endeavour to shake off US patrols, she went north and approached Okinawan waters on a different tack. By 14 April her compressed air was alarmingly low. With no target in sight, the *Kaiten* pilots' morale was falling and because they were forced to submerge for such long periods the vital maintenance of the *Kaiten* was not being carried out which rendered them unstable. At last, on 25 April orders were received to return to Kure; no *Kaiten* attack had been achieved.

Records show that other Japanese submarines carrying *Kaiten* were continually harassed by US patrols. On 25 April, for instance, *RO–109* was approaching Okinawa when she was detected and sunk by the armed transport *Horace A. Bass* (APD- 124).

As April drew to a close there were not enough submarines left to accommodate all the *Kaiten* pilots who had been trained. Most of them were re-deployed in what was dubbed 'Base *Kaiten* Attack', the idea being to place the *Kaiten* all along the coast of Japan where the US forces would be likely to attack. There the *Kaiten* pilots would wait, camouflaged and on constant alert. Then, on orders from IJN HQ, they would launch suicide attacks on any US vessel that appeared. This tactic was much disagreed with by torpedo expert *Chusa* Tennosuke Toresu. He believed that all *Kaiten* should be at sea as much as possible, to perpetrate as much disruption as could be achieved on the US lines of communication. At last IJN HQ agreed for two submarines to take up such duties to evaluate the potential of a future battle plan. So *I–47* and *I–36* were sent on 20–23 April to test the waters as the *Amatake* ('Heaven Peak') Unit. Each submarine sported six *Kaiten*. *I–47* made for the routes US vessels had to take from Ulithi to Okinawa, and *I–36* sailed for the Saipan–Okinawa routes.

A little after dawn on 27 April, *I–36* encountered a convoy of thirty US vessels bound for Okinawa. At a distance of 8,000 yards all six *Kaiten* were launched. Two jammed in the racks, but *Tai-i* Yaki and *Itto Koku Heiso* Abe, Matsuka and Ebihara made for their targets. Within ten minutes four explosions were heard, and that evening Tokyo received a radio report that four

US 'transports or cargo ships' had been sent to the bottom. *Tenno heika banzai!* – it was a fine birthday present for Emperor Hirohito, aged 44 on 29 April. In reality only a single vessel was sunk, the SS *Canada Victory*, and historians believe that all four *Kaiten* had somehow aimed at the same vessel.

On 1 May, *I–47* came up with a convoy; and as *Kaiten* had difficulty operating in the dark, skipper Orita ordered an attack by conventional torpedoes. But twelve hours later *Kaiten* pilots *Tai-i* Kakizake and *Itto Koku Heiso* Yamaguchi were launched. Two explosions were heard at a distance of three miles. *Itto Koku Heiso* Furukawa's *Kaiten* was then launched, after which an explosion was heard. All souls were deemed bound for the *Yasukuni*.

On 5 May two of *I–47*'s remaining three *Kaiten* were launched carrying *Tai-i* Maeda and *Itto Koku Heiso* Shinkai. Orita had not given the order for *Itto Koku Heiso* Yokota's *Kaiten* to be launched because the telephone link had failed. Orita consoled the abject and angry Yokota by saying: 'To live, at times, is much more difficult than to die ... A lot of patience is required to wait until the best possible moment for dying comes.'

Both submarines returned to Japan and IJN HQ now came round to the opinion that *Chusa* Toresu had been right. All submarine operations would now be left entirely to the discretion of 6th Fleet HQ; nevertheless, *Shosho* Nagai ordered the remaining I-Class submarines on *Kaiten* missions.

By mid-July 1945 six of the submarines had been sunk. But on 29 July a deadly scenario was to be played out. The heavy cruiser *Indianapolis* (CA-35) had been crashed by a kamikaze and undergone extensive repairs at Mare Island. Now under Captain Charles Butter McVay III she was proceeding without escort from Guam on a course for Leyte. In a choppy sea, she came into the track of *Shosa* Hashimoto's *Kaiten* submarine *I–58*. Neither radar nor lookout officers aboard *Indianapolis* picked up *I–58*'s presence. Among maritime historians a controversy remains as to exactly what Hashimoto did. Certainly at 2332 hrs, by his own admission in his own narrative, he ordered six torpedoes to be fired; submariners aver that in reality he had launched the *Kaiten*.

The torpedoes travelling at 48 knots covered the distance between *I–58* and *Indianapolis* in 85 seconds. Two hit on the starboard side forward (one under No 1 turret, the other under the wardroom), causing severe damage to communication links. *Indianapolis* began to list and SOS was keyed – but with communications largely destroyed, no message was received. *Indianapolis* sank a few minutes before midnight. Of the 1,199 crew, 350–400 were lost.

Incidentally Hashimoto was to enter naval history under a further heading. After the war it was rumoured that *Indianapolis* had an atomic bomb aboard, it having been intended to drop a third atomic bomb (on Niigata, an important port on the Sea of Japan at the mouth of the Shinano River). Although US Secretary of State for War, Henry Stimson, hotly denied the rumour, President Truman says in his memoirs that the story was true. Nevertheless, Captain McVay was court-martialled for 'hazarding his ship's safety', but was acquitted. Hashimoto was a witness at the trial.

Tokyo boasted that *Kaiten* had sunk fifteen tankers and transports, two cruisers, five destroyers, one seaplane tender and six miscellaneous vessels in the closing days of the war. The Allies declared all these 'kills' a fantasy because no firm submarine/*Kaiten* contacts had been recorded, though on 14 May the fleet tug *Sioux* did destroy a *Kaiten* by 40mm gunfire. The fact remains that eighty *Kaiten* pilots were recorded killed.

Out of the research for the *Kaiten* was to develop the *Koryu* submarine, which was an upgrading of the Type C/*Kaiten* built as a prototype Type D Ha–77. Basic design work was begun in June 1944 and was completed in January 1945. Nicknamed *Koryu* ('[The Nation] rising up') the 86-foot-long submarine with a displacement of 60 tons had space for a crew of five and had a range of 1,000 miles at 8 knots surfaced, 320 miles at 6 knots submerged; the *Koryu* could dive to 330 feet. The IJN High Command were impressed with the vessel's performance and ordered 540 of them for the defence of Okinawa, but the shortage of materials inhibited production and only 115 had been completed when the war ended.

The design of the *Koryu* was such that it could be put into the water by a crane or launched along rails fitted in various ships. As the end of the war approached there was a dearth of torpedoes so the *Koryu* was modified and in place of torpedoes the bows were packed with an explosive charge, which means that it was intended as a kamikaze weapon from the very beginning, as was well known to the operators. A number of *Koryu* had a second periscope fitted and an instructor's seat in the conning tower for training purposes. The weapon was not used in large numbers and no significant destructive missions can be credited to it.

The paternity of the nautical kamikaze known as the *Kairyu* can be traced to an experimental version of the Type A *Kaiten* which was being worked on at the end of 1943. Differences from the Type A included a horizontal fin on each side of the hull to give additional stability and ease of handling. By 1944 a modified version of this had been built and given a thorough testing.

The *Kairyu* emerged as a 55.8-foot-long craft of 19 tons displacement, with a range of 450 miles at 5 knots surfaced, 36 miles at 3 knots submerged. Two 18in torpedoes were carried, one on each side of the lower hull. The two-man vessel's diving depth was 480 feet (330 feet with torpedoes in place). Surface propulsion was by an 85hp Izusu automobile petrol engine, and an 80hp electric motor when submerged.

In February 1945 production began, the craft being constructed in three sections, each by a different manufacturer, for final assembly at Yokosuka Naval Base. Twenty of the initial production line were earmarked for training, two periscopes and an enlarged conning tower being fitted to these. Again, shortage of torpedoes meant that the bows were packed with 1,320 pounds of TNT, torpedo spaces being used for ballast and extra fuel. The design of a *Kairyu* 2 of 40-tons displacement was begun, but was not completed before the end of the war. No details of *Kairyu* deployment or effectiveness are known.

In October 1944 a new torpedo school was opened at Kawatana, Kyushu, and later that month it was visited by *Taisa* Toshio Miyazaki, senior instructor of the torpedo school at Oppama; he was to talk to the 400 students about a new concept in suicide torpedo-boats.

The Japanese had failed to realise the usefulness of the torpedo-boat until they saw what the US versions could do. And by 1944 their technology gap was such as to make it impossible to build a fleet of boats that would match the US equivalents in quality and numbers. Nevertheless crews were being trained in torpedo-boat operations. As the High Command studied all aspects of suicide vessels, the torpedo-boat began to interest them. The current Japanese torpedo-boats were too slow to be effective in the kamikaze role, but smaller ones could be built and crammed with explosives for ramming. It was this concept that Miyazaki was propounding at Kawatana.

He described how the torpedo-boats would be used, and he rounded off what he had to say by revealing a new idea. It was planned that groups of frogmen, in light diving gear, would place delayed-action explosive charges under the hulls of enemy ships at anchor. They would be dropped off from small boats as close as possible to the target, move along the sea bed, place their charges, and return to the boats. If they were unable to return to the boats ...

When Miyazaki had finished his briefing, the rostrum was taken by the commander of the school, *Taisa* Tameichi Hara, part of whose speech is reproduced in his book *Japanese Destroyer Captain* (1961):

'I have no orders for you.

'You came here to prepare yourselves for conventional torpedo-boats. You have just learned of two other weapons that have been authorised for study in this school. Starting tomorrow one of the three courses of study will be open to you. You have a free choice of which class you wish to attend, according to your own aptitude and inclination.

'I want your choice to be made, without compulsion or influence from any one, according to the dictates of your own conscience. This is my ruling. I will be in my office this afternoon and evening, as long as is necessary. Each of you will report to me personally of your choice. There will be no questions asked, or explanation required as to why you make the choice you do. That is all.'

Hara retired to his office to await the reaction. One by one the students paid him a visit to lodge their willingness to serve. When the final tally was taken, 50 per cent of them had chosen to continue their training for conventional torpedo-boats; 38 per cent had volunteered for the new suicide boats – which Miyazaki said were to be called *Shinyo* ('Ocean Shakers') – and 12 per cent had decided to become the suicide frogmen dubbed *Fukuryu* ('Crawling Dragons').

When the concept of the *Shinyo* had been agreed by the High Command, it was suggested that to overcome manufacturing slowness civilian pleasure boats be utilised. They would be ready, it was argued, as soon as the explosive charges had been put in place, but the idea was abandoned almost immediately when it was realised that it would mean using boats of different styles, sizes and capacities which would have led to a great variation in performance. A programme of custom-built *Shinyo* was begun.

Three types were to be built. Type 1 had a flimsy wooden frame covered with plywood. Its length was 16–17 feet, and its unloaded weight was 2,470–3,740 pounds. An automobile engine produced a speed of 26 knots. The explosive charge in the bows consisted of 3,300 pounds of TNT. Type 2 was a variation of Type 1.

Type 3 had a steel frame, covered with light metal, length was 18 feet and unloaded weight was 4,730 pounds. It was powered by two automobile engines which gave a top speed of 30 knots when loaded with 4,400 pounds of TNT. Some of the Type 3 carried two depth-charges of equivalent explosive power. Each Type had a pilot's cockpit (close to the stern}, steering wheel, throttle and arming-lever to engage the explosive charge before impact. The craft were equipped with two 5in incendiary rockets in the stern to thwart the aim of enemy gunners bent on destroying the *Shinyo* before a ramming could take place.

Operational use of the *Shinyo* can be plotted in greater detail than can that of the other suicide vessels. During the early days of January 1945, the *Shinyo* pilots and their craft assembled along the north-west coast of Luzon, Philippines, to await the US landing in Lingayen Gulf. Forty *Shinyo* attacked the US invasion fleet on the night of 9 January. A large number were destroyed by gunfire, and some were repelled or lost in the darkness. Six of them broke through to hit two LCIs and four LCTs; one LCT sank. On 31 January another group attacked US auxiliary vessels; one *Shinyo* survived the defensive fire and sank the submarine-chaser *PC-1129*.

On 15 February US amphibious forces landed on the Bataan Peninsula. That evening three *Shinyo* penetrated the supply fleet. Two were sunk by gunfire, but one hit a US ship and caused great damage. When the US forces landed and occupied Kerama Retto the Japanese were taken by surprise and were unable to sortie the 400 *Shinyo* which the Americans found secreted in caves.

The IJN set up two *Shinyo* bases on Okinawa: one in the centre at Hagushi Beaches and one in the north on the Motobu Peninsula, which consisted of botched piers in the estuary of the River Bisha Giwa. These became the operational locations for seven sea raiding battalions of *Shinyo* under the overall command of Army *Chujo* Mitsuru Ushijima of 32nd Army. Certain that the US forces would land at Hagushi, the Japanese planned a counter-offensive directly offshore. The Americans approached Hagushi on 31 March and were assailed by 50 *Shinyo*. The bulk of them were destroyed by very accurate fire or were swamped by shells exploding in the sea. Only one survived to hit *LSM-12* which, although repaired, sank on 4 April.

It may be noted that at the re-occupation of Hong Kong by Rear-Admiral C. H. J. Harcourt (Flag Officer, 11th Aircraft Carrier Squadron, British Pacific Fleet), when the minesweepers and destroyers preceding his flagship, the cruiser *Swiftsure*, entered harbour on 30 August 1945, three *Shinyo* moved out of the suicide boat base at Lamma Island to attack. They were sunk or strafed by aircraft; the remainder of the fleet were bombed and sunk, or else beached themselves.

Once the existence of *Kaiten, Koryu, Kairyu* and *Shinyo* attack units was known, the Allied response was to form units of fast ships and minor craft, all equipped with surface radar, searchlights and starshells. Some of these defensive units were positioned near the exits of suspected Japanese bases, and others patrolled the most likely sea lanes.

The results obtained by the suicide craft in the Luzon, Iwo Jima, Okinawa and Kyushu campaigns were more than disappointing for the Japanese. The rivalry and consequent lack of co-operation between Army and Navy was detrimental to any kamikaze endeavour. Unlike kamikaze pilots, though, the large majority of suicide boat volunteers died before they could reach their target. All in all the use of the suicide craft was brought about through under-estimation of Allied strength, technological supremacy and mastery of sea and air, and the Japanese belief that they held the moral high ground in 'liberating' the Far East.

CHAPTER NINETEEN

EXPLOITING THE PACIFIC 'DIVINE WIND'

'The "government" was contacted and we were told ... to take no pictures ... It was to be kept extremely hush-hush ... no publicity ... so the Japanese would not know their balloons had arrived.' — Jerrine Brooks May, reporter from the *Sentinel*, Goldendale, Washington.

In Japanese thinking, the concept of *Kami Kaze*, the essence of the 'Divine Wind', occupies a broad canvas in which the suicide pilots form but a small element. The *Shinto* faith has in its pantheon about three thousand *Kami*, and the wartime Kamikaze had as their spirit leader one of that celestial number, *Fujin*, God of the Winds. On kamikaze talismen he appears running with an elongated bag around his shoulders carrying his four winds; *Fujin* and one of those winds, *nishi kaze*, the West Wind, was to be summoned up to play a part in one of the most curious naval offensives of the war.

The project was called *FUGO*, the vehicles were made of paper and silk, and the pilots were the *Kami* themselves. The extent of Operation *FUGO* was not made known to the Western public until long after the war was over, but for the USA it began on Saturday, 5 May 1945.

At about 1030 hrs that day a large explosion was heard, 5,000 feet up on the southern slopes of Gearhart Mountain, a few miles east of the timber community of Bly, Oregon. The land on which the explosion was heard belonged to the Weyerhauser Timber Co. The local sheriff was informed and gossip soon spread that the wife of the Revd Archie Mitchell and five children aged between 11 and 13 had been killed in a violent explosion while picnicking. These six people were to enter WWII history as the sole known fatalities of enemy action on mainland USA. Later on that Saturday, military sources confirmed that the explosion had emanated from an IJN 15-kg anti-personnel high-explosive bomb.

What the American public were not told was that the Japanese had been bombing the western seaboard of North America since 6 December 1944, and the Gearhart Mountain bomb was the 240th recorded by the military authorities. Reports revealed that the first explosion had occurred some dozen or so miles south-west of Owl Creek Mountain near Thermopolis, Wyoming.

There followed reports of mysterious balloon descents at Holy Cross, Alaska, and Kalispell in western Montana, and fragments of wreckage sent to the US Naval Research Laboratory were found to be of Japanese origin. The military were puzzled as to how Japanese-made bombs could be exploding in America, and the US Office of Censorship requested a news blackout.

Military intelligence knew that the Japanese had used balloon warfare from the time of the Russo–Japanese War and they had been experimenting with 'upper air current bombing' since the 1930s. A plan had been mooted to bomb the Russian naval base at Vladivostok from bases in occupied China, but although balloons had been made and tested for this purpose, the raids never took place.

Prompted by the Doolittle Raid of 1942, the Japanese decided to try to bomb the US mainland. During early September 1942 the IJN High Command ordered the bombing of Oregon, they selected targets from maps of the state and coastal navigation charts which they had captured at Wake Island. Submarine I–25 was dispatched to the southern coast of Oregon, and on 9 and 29 September catapulted a two-seater Yokosuka E14Y1 reconnaissance aircraft to drop incendiary bombs over the Siskiyou National Forest; result, a small conflagration on Mount Emily.

By late September, the Japanese balloon warfare ideas had been resuscitated and by 1943 a series of unmanned paper balloons, with 20-foot envelopes, were ready for launching from two modified submarines, I–34 and I–35. An arsenal of 200 balloons (with a range of more than 600 miles) was ready by August 1943, but as the situation deteriorated for the Japanese, no submarines were available for such a hit-and-miss enterprise and the IJN dropped the idea.

Several months before the Gearhart tragedy of 5 May 1945, a US aircraft had shot down a balloon which landed intact some thirty miles west of Alturas, California. At Moffitt Field, Sunnyvale, California, it was examined by aeronautical boffins who analysed its characteristics:

Dimensions: A true sphere of about 100 foot circumference.

Structure: Below the balloon the payload capacity was suspended from nineteen 49ft shroud lines; three aneroids triggered a battery-powered circuit which controlled altitude.

Capacity: Inflated to 19,000 cubic feet of hydrogen.

Lifting power: 1,000 pounds at sea-level; 200 pounds at about 36,000 feet.

Construction: Paper construction; 64 gores (sectors of the curved surface) to form the gas envelope. Four laminates of paper glued with *Konnvaku*, a Japanese equivalent of a hydro-cellulose adhesive made from potato paste. Waterproofed with a nitrocellular lacquer to limit gas loss.

Payload: Two 11lb thermalite incendiary bombs; one 33lb anti-personnel fragmentation bomb, suspended from a large dural ring.

Where had these bombs come from? Initial conclusions were pencilled in as the Japanese mainland, 7,000 miles away.

Although the Navy had aborted their balloon incentives, the Imperial Japanese Army continued research, and the balloon strategy became the responsibility of *Shosho* Sueyoshi Kusaba. He had supervised the design of hand-made paper balloons, and it was one of his devices that had caused the Gearhart Mountain tragedy.

Research was continued by 9th Military Technical Research Institute, and notes were compared with scientist H. Arakawa of the Central Meteorological Observatory at Tokyo, an expert on high-altitude winds, and with the naval ordnance engineer *Shosa* Kiyoshi Tanaka who had also studied wind currents over the Pacific. An entirely new research team was put together involving academics, industrial scientists, experts from the Fujikura Rubber Co, Seiko (Horological), and Toshiba Electronics, all to harness the power of the sacred *nishi kaze*. Their project was to be called Operation *FUGO* ('Windship Weapon').

Kusaba's designers produced three types of balloon: A 30ft diameter paper balloon for winter winds; a 45ft one for summer winds; and a 30ft balloon known as Type A. At this time Kusaba combined Army and Navy balloon experimentation and the IJN produced a 27ft rubberised silk balloon, called Type B, to be used for upper air testing.

Because the balloons had no mechanical propulsion and no steering technology (they were deemed to fly at the behest of the *Kami*), once they were launched into the atmosphere the maintenance of altitude and course, and effecting an explosion at the right time was a very hit-and-miss affair. Flying at 30,000 feet they were difficult to detect from ground/sea level observation or radar, and most US fighter aircraft could not reach them. Once the bomb payload was released the balloon was designed to self-destruct.

Once the US authorities had identified the origins of the balloons, they had to decide what to do about future attacks. Should they alert the public (because of the bomb payloads)? Japanese intelligence would soon pick this up and realise that their balloons had reached America and were effective. Or, should they keep a tight security blackout and hope that the Japanese would think that their balloons had been lost in the Pacific. They compromised with Operation 'Firefly'.

The US 4th Air Force was ordered to make aircraft available for balloon spotting. The agricultural community was told in a low-key manner to keep an eye open for any strange insects, crop mutations, et cetera, for the US authorities feared that the Japanese would use the balloons for biological warfare. USAAF records show that nine balloons were shot down on 13 April 1945 by Grumman F6F Hellcats over Attu Island, Aleutians. Although the air force had Chance Vought F4U Corsairs and Lockheed P–38 Lightnings on standby, only two balloons were shot down anywhere near the North American coast (one was brought down in Oregon by a Bell P–63 Kingcobra).

Records further show that of the 9,300 estimated balloon launches, only 285 arrivals in America were logged by the authorities in an area stretching from the Aleutians to Michigan and from Alaska to Mexico.

Strategically the balloons were a failure although Japanese propaganda told of 'thousands killed' by them. Writing in 1974, *Shosa* Kiyoshi Tanaka observed that Operation *FUGO* had been abandoned for two reasons:

'1. A-Type balloon cannot reach United States in spring and summer. [One of the failure areas for the incendiary bombs was that they were landing on wet forests and plains where conflagrations could not be started.]

2. B-Type balloon might be able to reach and cause forest fire in spring and summer. However, most of them were destroyed by B–29 bombardment. [And as US bombing of the railway system had been so effective, transportation of hydrogen was disrupted.]'

Just after the war *Shosho* Kuraba made this comment in a private paper:

'To my great regret, the progress of the war was faster than we imagined. Soon after the campaign began the air raids against our mainland were intensified. Many factories which manufactured various parts were destroyed. Moreover, we were not informed about the effect of *FUGO* during the war. Because of the combination of hardships we were compelled to cease operations.'

Taking into consideration the number of balloons launched, it is more than likely that many more relics of them remain scattered over America's west coast states. Some of the payloads may still be intact to explode if disturbed as a violent memory of the will of the *Kami* in WWII.

CHAPTER TWENTY

THE WHOLE NATION ARE KAMIKAZE

Suga suga shi / Bofu no ato ni / Tsuki kiyo shi. (Refreshingly / After
the violent storm / The moon rises radiant.) — Testament *'haiku'* of *Chujo*
Takijiro Onishi for his friend Rin Masutani, just before the suicide of
'The Father of the Kamikaze'.

On 29 May 1945 *Chujo* Takijiro Onishi had been appointed Vice-Chief of
Naval General Staff to *Chujo* Soemu Toyoda, and for the remainder of the
war his opinions were treated with coolness by the *Kaigun Sho*. Onishi firmly
opposed surrender and believed that every able-bodied Japanese should
assume a kamikaze role. Indeed he ruffled many feathers in the Naval
General Staff by his forthright opinions, particularly in his rebukes of, for
example, Operations Bureau First Chief *Shosho Danshaku* Sadatochi Tomioka.
The closer the bitter end of the war approached, the more ascerbic Onishi
became and it was common knowledge that if Japan were to surrender
(under any circumstances) he would commit *seppuku*.

Japan, of course, was to put in place *KETSU-GO*, the Operational Defence
Plan, which was designed to obstruct the invasion of Japanese soil. It would
go into effect as soon as the enemy landed on any of the main islands of
homeland Japan. It called for the all-out employment of every available
weapon and person. It was to be the final nation-wide kamikaze action.

At 0600 hrs on 26 July 1945, the overseas radio bureau of NHK monitored
a broadcast from San Francisco. It announced details of the Potsdam Declaration agreed by the Allies, demanding the surrender of Japan. A transcript
was rushed to the *Gaimusho*:

'The time has come for Japan to decide whether she will continue to be
controlled by those self-willed militaristic advisers whose unintelligent
calculations have brought the Empire of Japan to the threshold of annihila-
tion, or whether she will follow the path of reason.

'Following are our terms. We will not deviate from them. There are no
alternatives. We shall brook no delay.

'There must be eliminated for all time the authority and influence of those
who have deceived and misled the people of Japan into embarking on world

conquest, for we insist that a new order of peace, security, and justice will be impossible until irresponsible militarism is driven from the world ...

'We do not intend that the Japanese shall be enslaved as a race or destroyed as a nation, but stern justice shall be meted out to all war criminals, including those who have visited cruelties upon our prisoners. The Japanese government shall remove all obstacles to the revival and strengthening of democratic tendencies among the Japanese people. Freedom of speech, of religion, and of thought, as well as respect for the fundamental human rights shall be established ...

'We call upon the government of Japan to proclaim now the unconditional surrender of all Japanese armed forces, and to provide proper and adequate assurances of their good faith in such action. The alternative for Japan is prompt and utter destruction.'

Although the Japanese Government officially intended to *mokusatsu* (ignore by silence) the Declaration, the fact that it would have been heard throughout Japan urged them to issue a censored version nation-wide at the behest of the *Rikugun Daijin* Korechika Anami.

The Japanese were playing for time. A Neutrality Pact between the USSR and Japan had been signed by Vyacheslav Molotov and *Gaimu Daijin* Yosuka Matsuoka and the Japanese Ambassador Yoshitsugu Tatekawa on 13 April 1941. There was no suggestion in it that the Soviets would act as honest broker, but the Japanese believed naïvely that the Soviets would help them sue for peace with the Allies. In the event the USSR declared war on Japan on 8 August 1945.

On Monday, 6 August, an Allied response to the Japanese *mokusatsu* came about. A USAAF aircraft, named *Enola Gay*, after the mother of its pilot Colonel Paul Tibbets, dropped an atomic bomb on Hiroshima. Sixty per cent of the city was destroyed by the blast, the equivalent of 20,000 tons of TNT. Despite the fact that the Emperor and the *Jushin* were pressing members of the Supreme Council for the Direction of the War to sue for peace, the anti-surrender cadre was influential among the decision makers.

Rikugun Daijin Anami was fiercely opposed to outright surrender and *Chujo* Onishi decided to add his weight against capitulation. He made an approach to a younger brother of the Emperor's, *Takamatsu no Miya Denka* (His Imperial Highness) Prince Takamatsu, to pressurise the pro-surrender group members of the General Staff, such as *Kaigun Daijin* Mitsumasa Yonai, to continue the fight. Onishi met the Prince finally on 13 August but to no avail, and was to say this on returning from the Imperial interview:

'*Shibai wa owarimashita* (The show is over). The prince will not try to influence the admirals unless there is a concrete and realistic plan to strike the enemy a telling blow. Knowing the Navy view, I went to see the Army Chief of Staff. He offered no encouragement because the Army had no plan either.'

A few hours after the USSR had declared war on Japan and launched an offensive in Manchuria, at 1100 hrs on Thursday, 9 August the US Air Force dropped its second bomb – a plutonium device – on Nagasaki, annihilating of 40,000 Japanese. Thus were Japanese civilians treated to another wave of *genshibakudansho* (radiation sickness).

Sori Daijin Danshaku Kantaro Suzuki now recommended to the Supreme Council that Japan should surrender, but the Council was equally divided on the yes or no to surrender. And even those who were for surrender were anxious about the future status and sovereignty of the Emperor in the surrender terms. *Rokugun Daijin* Anami was adamant against surrender and hinted that the whole Japanese nation be recruited as kamikaze. He said:

'We cannot pretend to claim that victory is certain, but it is far too early to say that the war is lost. That we will inflict severe losses on the enemy when he invades Japan is certain, and it is by no means impossible that we may be able to reverse the situation in our favour, pulling victory out of defeat.

'Further, our army will not submit to demobilisation. Our men simply will not lay down their arms. And since they know they are not permitted to surrender, since they know that a fighting man who surrenders is liable to extremely heavy punishment, there is really no alternative for us but to continue the fight.'

Japan's war assets, after all, were great. In the homeland there were 100,000 troops, all well armed; there was a *Kaiten* in almost every creek and there were some 10,000 aircraft left.

The *Naimu Daijin* Genki Abe added his weight to Anami's rhetoric by noting that he 'could not promise civil obedience' if the nation capitulated. And, it could be added, there were thousands of combatants and non-combatants who would be willing kamikaze. In the event the *Sori Daijin* and the *Gaimu Daijin* Shigenori Togo decided that the deadlock could only be broken by the Emperor himself, even though for cabinet ministers to approach the Emperor without a clear cut policy for His August Mind to agree to was unheard of.

As rumours of the probable surrender policy spread among the high command, *Chujo* Onishi was furious and he blustered that his kamikaze had given their lives for nothing. He castigated the *Kaigun Daijin, Taisho* Mitsumasa Yonai, implying cowardice. Onishi's anger had caused him to break protocol by insulting a superior; he was summoned to an interview with Yonai and was reduced to tears of shame, humiliation and frustration in Yonai's office. However it fuelled the Father of the Kamikaze's resolve not to give up.

The Emperor had a meeting with the Supreme Councillors, his Chief Cabinet Secretary Hisatsure Sakomizu and the President of the Privy Council, *Danshaku* Keichiro Hiranuma at midnight on 9/10 August 1945 in his underground shelter at the *Kyujo*. No written record was taken so future reconstructions of what took place were based on the memoirs of those who were there.

Each side put forward its arguments and the *Sori Daijin* invited His Majesty to make a decision. The Emperor told them 'the time has come to bear the unbearable', and at 0200 hrs recommended surrender. Three hours later cables declaring the decision were sent to the US Secretary of State, James F. Byrness, through the Swiss *chargé d'affaires* M. Max Grassli, and via Japanese Ministers at Berne and Stockholm for transmission to the European Allies.

While the Allies were perusing the cable, Tokyo and other Japanese cities were heavily bombed. That night NHK broadcast two conflicting statements. The first was announced with the authority of *Rikugun Daijin* Anami:

'We have but one choice: we must fight on until we win the sacred war to preserve our national polity. We must fight on, even if we have to chew grass and eat earth and live in the fields, for in our death there is a chance of our country's survival. The hero Kunusoki [Masashige] pledged to live and die seven times in order to save Japan from disaster. We can do no less.'

The statement has been taken as being a coded call for kamikaze action at all levels. The second statement came from the Cabinet. Its preamble mentioned the enemy's launching of bombs of great devastation and went on:

'Our fighting forces will no doubt be able to repulse the enemy's attack, but we must recognise that we are facing a situation that is as bad as it can be. The government will do all it can to defend the homeland and preserve the honour of the country but it expects that Japan's hundred million will also rise to the occasion, overcoming whatever obstacles may lie in the path of the preservation of our national polity.'

The Japanese *Gaimusho* also authorised the Domei News Agency to broadcast (in Morse Code) to the world that Japan now accepted the surrender terms just received from the Allies. It was still feared that a rumoured third atomic bomb might be dropped on Japan if the country were seen to be dragging its feet over the acceptance. Indeed the *Gaimusho* also feared that the army would censor all outgoing messages and he wanted the widest possible dissemination of the news. The bombing of Japan continued for the time being.

As the reality of the surrender began to sink in, reactions among nationalists, military and civilians were confused and contradictory. The ordinary folk were much perturbed. Over the years Japanese military propaganda had urged the populace to struggle against the Allies to the death, or be taken as slaves. The average Japanese feared being reduced to *hinin* ('non-persons') as the Imperial Japanese Army had treated the victims of war, by loss of face in relation to the enemy. The Lord Keeper of the Privy Seal, *Koshaku* Kolchi Kido, was afraid that military and nationalist factions would stir up assassination (of the 'pro-peace ministers') and suicide groups. Indeed as the *Kaigun Daijin* Toyoda had pointed out at the final Supreme Council meeting with the Emperor, there was no guarantee that the Navy would co-operate in surrender, and as the Navy was the foundation of the kamikaze all remaining maritime combatants were potential suicide *samurai*.

Already in a bomb-shelter at the *Rikugunsho* on Ichigaya Hill, Tokyo, a group of officers under Army *Chujo* Masahiko Takeshita – brother-in-law of the *Rikugun Daijin* – was meeting to discuss assassinations of such as Kido. To avoid this the call to surrender would have to come from the highest level. To Kido's mind, the *Koe no Tsuru* ('The Voice of the Crane'), i.e., the Emperor's sacred voice, would have to be heard throughout the land.

The conspirators to assassination at Ichigaya took their plans to the *Jikan Rikugun Daijin*, Army *Chujo* Tadaichi Wakamatsu. He treated them with what they regarded as coolness, so they then sought an interview with the *Rikugun Daijin* himself. Anami succeeded in calming them down and recommended caution until the full text of the Allies' surrender proposals had been studied. Elsewhere, though, youth movements such as the *Hissho Gakuto Renmei* (Students' Federation for Victory) were being stirred up by such as Army *Tai-i* Takeo Sasaki. And in the wings *Chujo* Onishi was encouraging all who would listen to him to make the whole nation kamikaze.

By now the Americans were dropping leaflets setting out Japan's acceptance of surrender. The 'pro-peace' faction were dismayed as the leaflets might stir such as the young officers from Ichigaya to carry out their proposed *coup d'état*, with the help of the troops deemed 'humiliated' by the leaflets' contents. Another meeting with the Emperor was considered necessary.

At this second meeting with the twenty-four members of the Supreme Council, the Emperor re-emphasised his wish to see the nation surrender without further great loss of life; the last thing he wanted was for his people to become kamikaze. By a strange set of circumstances he was now able to express his own preferences as a 'cabinet decision'. Despite the wording of Japan's Constitution the Emperor's role lay in the fact that he was the tool of the 'influence of the Throne'. In effect he was never able personally to influence the declaring of or cessation of war. There were those in the Supreme Council now who recalled the Emperor's words in the Imperial Rescript declaring war: 'It has been truly unavoidable and far from Our Wishes that Our Empire has now been brought to cross swords with America and Britain.' So he now agreed that an Imperial Rescript announcing the end of the war be prepared, noting that as such a surrender would be a hard thing for Army, Navy and Nation to come to terms with, he was willing to broadcast to the people the reasons for capitulation. The Japanese cabinet approved the Emperor's 'decision' to surrender the nation, as their acceptance (or otherwise) was a constitutional requirement before further steps could be taken.

The Chairman of NHK, Hachiro Ohashi, was aghast when told that the Emperor would himself read the Imperial Rescript ending the war. Such a thing had never been contemplated in any rational Japanese mind, although the voice of the Emperor had been broadcast by a 'strange acoustical phenomenon' in 1928 while he was reviewing troops. Then Director of the Domestic Bureau, Kenjoro Yabe, was set on the road to slitting his belly open in shame, but was saved by *Ayako no Miya Hidenka* (HRH Princess Ayako, aunt of the Emperor), saying that she had enjoyed the unofficial broadcast. It was decided that the Emperor's voice would be recorded at the *Goseimu-shitsu* (Imperial Administration Office).

Meanwhile those who were considering a *coup d'état* before the Emperor could broadcast, the Ichigaya officers and such as Army *Shosa* Kenji Hatanaka, an influential officer of the Military Affairs Section, were joined in their contemplated kamikaze action by the corps commander of the Air Defence Unit, the 302nd Air Corps at Atsugi Air Base, Navy *Taisa* Yosuna Kozono. From a makeshift dais on the main runway Kozono harangued his men as to how the order to surrender meant an end to Japanese civilisation after a thousand years of development. 'Join me [as kamikaze] and destroy the enemy', he shouted, to be answered by choruses of *Banzai!* from the pilots. Kozono now led a flight over Tokyo dropping leaflets accusing the *Jushin* and the *Sori Daijin* of misleading the Emperor into surrender. Hearing of all this disaffection the Emperor indicated that he would personally appeal to the troubled officers to stop any kind of kamikaze action.

On 14 August at 1140 hrs, at the *Rikugunsho*, a statement was signed by the Chiefs of Staff: 'THE IMPERIAL FORCES WILL ACT STRICTLY IN ACCORDANCE WITH THE DECISION OF HIS IMPERIAL MAJESTY THE EMPEROR.' A little while later it was signed on behalf of the United Air Force by Commander-in-Chief Masakazu Kawabe. With this document the Imperial Japanese Army had made any future kamikaze action (or any other deviation or insubordination) treasonous. After several hours of contention between Cabinet ministers a final wording of the Imperial Rescript for surrender was agreed, and Emperor Hirohito signed it; the document was sealed and dated 'The Fourteenth Day of the Eighth Month of the Twentieth Year of *Showa*' (i.e., 14 August 1945; *Showa*, 'Enlightened Peace' being the reign name chosen by Hirohito on his accession).

The *Rikugun Daijin* Anami now summoned the Chief of Military Affairs Section of the *Rikugunsho*, Army *Taisa* Okitsugu Arao. He told his section chief that he wanted no kamikaze acts by junior officers and no *seppuku*. The *Rikugun Daijin*'s expectations were to be lost on Navy *Taisa* Yasuna Kozono, Commander of 302nd Air Corps. Alhough wracked by an attack of malaria, he sat in his office at Atsugi Airbase and reached his final decision. He alone would lead what was left of the Imperial Japanese Navy personnel in a series of kamikaze attacks. To this end he composed – between bouts of malarial chills, fever and sweating – a call to all naval officers. In the records of the Pacific War Research Society is to be found Kozono's cable:

'The order to cease fire, and the order to disarm that will follow, must inevitably mean the end of our national structure and of the Emperor. To obey such orders would be equal to committing high treason. Japan is sacred and indestructible. If we unite for action, we will destroy the enemy. Of that there can be no doubt whatsoever. I hope that you will agree with me.'

The Emperor recorded the Imperial Rescript of Surrender at the *Goseimu-shitsu* on 14 August 1945. The language he used was the formal (and unfamiliar to most people) parlance of the Imperial Court, but the gist was only too clear. Meanwhile various groups of conspirators to assassination (of the *Sori Daijin* and others) and kamikaze action were making their final preparations. The Ichigaya officers met again as did *Taisa* Kozono and *Tai-i* Takeo

Sasaki, of the 3rd Brigade of the Tokyo Guards (on which the Yokohama Guards were dependent) to discuss the elimination of the 'traitors' in the Cabinet.

At his headquarters at Surugadai Army *Chusa* Masahiko Takashima of the Military Affairs Section of the *Rikugunsho* was informed by Army *Shosa* Kenji Hatanaka (representing the Ichigaya officers) that 2nd Regiment, Imperial Guards were inside the *Kyujo* and would be ready to seize power. All depended upon the decision of Army *Chujo* Takeshi Mori, Commander of the Imperial Guards Division. Mori, however, proved adamant in supporting the Emperor's stance – no rebellion, no nation as kamikaze. In a scenario that remains somewhat mysterious as to who did what, Army *Shosa* Hatanaka shot Mori, while *Taisa* Shigetaro Uehara of the Air Academy decapitated the staff officer Army *Chusa* Michinori Shiraishi.

Army *Chusa* Masataka Ida of the Military Affairs Section and Army *Taisa* Kazuo Mizutani, Chief of Staff, Imperial Guards, now set off to persuade the Eastern District Army (defenders of Tokyo's environs and the surrounding Kanto Plain) to join the *coup d'état*.

Meanwhile Army *Shosa* Hatanaka forged (using Mori's personal seal) what is known as 'Strategic Order No 584' formulating plans for the coup. Within the hour, using the fake order, the *Kyujo* was secured and the Guards took up positions, sworn to protect the Emperor against the 'traitors' who had brought the country to surrender, and to defend his sacred life with their own bodies in suicide charges if necessary.

As soon as *Taisho* Shizuichi Tanaka, commander of the Eastern District Army, heard details of the proposed coup, he made it clear that he would have nothing to do with it and that the Eastern District Army would not join in. Orders were issued by his office stating that Strategic Order No 584 was false and that the troops surrounding the *Kyujo* should disperse.

Army *Tai-i* Takeo Sasaki, Commander of the Yokohama Guards, had now formed his own kamikaze group and was making his way with them to Tokyo. They numbered thirty-seven men; thirty were soldiers of the Imperial Japanese Army, five were students from the Yokohama Engineering College and two were recruits from the Yokohama Youth Corps. They called themselves *Kokumin Kamikaze Tai* (National Divine Wind Corps) and all were eager to die for Japan and the Emperor and to continue the war by doing so. Step one of their plan – for they believed that their deaths would ignite Japan into being a nation of kamikaze – was to assassinate the *Sori Daijin*.

As these keen kamikaze were driving to Tokyo the *Rikugun Daijin* was preparing for his own suicide in the presence of his brother-in-law Army *Chusa* Masahiko Takeshita. As they drank *sake* together Anami issued the order to kill the *Kaigun Daijin Taisho* Mitsumasa Yonai. Anami believed that his own death would prevent the Army from continuing the fight.

At dawn the *Kokumin Kamikaze Tai* devotees arrived at the Tokyo residence of the *Sori Daijin*. They immediately opened fire on the house with the two machine-guns they had brought from Yokohama. On seeing the soldiers the *Sori Daijin*'s staff had fled, and the kamikazes discovered that their prey, *Danshaku* Kantaro Suzuki was at his private residence at Maruyama. At the same time a group of maverick *Tokubetsu Koto Keisatsu* (*TOKKO* = Thought Police) were attacking the residence of *Koshaku* Koichi Kido, Keeper of the Privy Seal, again to no avail because he was in hiding at the *Kyujo*.

In accordance with the fake Strategic Order No 584, troops of 1st Regiment, Imperial Guards were now occupying the offices of NHK. Their intention was to stop the Emperor's broadcast from being made. Soon after they had taken up position Army *Shosa* Hatanaka arrived with the idea of broadcasting himself the Army's case for continuing the war. All the while, and for many hours before, soldiers were searching for the recorded discs which the Emperor had made, but which were safely hidden.

Meanwhile, during the early hours of the morning, Army *Taisho* Tanaka, Commander of the Eastern District Army, had arrived at the Imperial Guards headquarters to arrest rebellious officers. After personally apprehending Staff Officer *Shosa* Sadakichi Ishihara, Tanaka went to the *Kyujo*.

Rikugun Daijin Anami's preparations for suicide were well under way. He had dressed himself in a white shirt given to him by the Emperor when he was his aide-de-camp, and pinned his medals on his dress uniform jacket which he laid aside with instructions to *Chusas* Takeshita and Ida that he be covered with it in death. On the uniform, now set before the room's *tokonoma* (alcove), he placed a photograph of his dead soldier son. Nearby were his resignation as *Rikugun Daijin* and his short will prefaced with this comment of true *samurai* sentiment: '*Isshi motte daizai wo shashi-tatematsuru, shinshu fumetsu wo shinji tsutsu*' ('Believing firmly that our sacred land will never perish, I – with my death – humbly apologise to the Emperor for the great crime). His apologies were for Japan's defeat. With this he placed a specially written poem: '*Ogimi no fukaki megumi ni amishi mi wa iinokosubeki katakono mo nashi*' ('Basking in the Emperor's great favour in life; I have not a syllable or word, to leave behind').

Anami chose the place for his *seppuku* carefully. He had ruled out committing suicide in the garden; to die on the bare earth would be to admit guilt for his personal actions in the Great East Asia War; to die in his living quarters would be to show that he felt no guilt at all; he compromised by kneeling cross-legged in the corridor outside his living quarters. With his torso facing the *Kyujo*, he slit his belly with the excruciatingly painful *kappuku* strokes (a slash to the right then straight up); he then drew the blade of his dagger across where he believed his carotid artery to be. He knelt upright awaiting death. *Chusa* Takeshita offered to dispatch him by decapitation; Anami refused. Two hours later when he fell unconscious, Takeshita stabbed him to death in the neck.

By now *Tai-i* Sasaki and the *Kokumin Kamikaze Tai* soldiers had arrived at the house of the *Sori Daijin*; tipped off, the Prime Minister had fled. The house was put to the torch and the kamikaze band set off in pursuit of their next target, *Danshaku* Kiichiro Hiranuma, President of the Privy Council.

Taisho Tanaka had now reached the *Kyujo* and secured the palace and the Imperial Family's safety. All this time the Emperor and Empress had been sheltering in the *Gobunko* (Imperial Library) awaiting the hour that the broadcast was to be heard. At NHK *Shosa* Hatanaka continued his belligerent threats to the staff until he was informed of Tanaka's success in putting down the coup; he then withdrew. And just before most Japanese began breakfast *Tai-i* Sasaki and his *Kokumin Kamikaze Tai* arrived at *Danshaku* Hiranuma's house and set fire to it, not bothering to see if there were anyone inside. In fact Hiranuma had escaped to a neighbour's house. Sasaki returned to Yokohama, and it was his *samurai* students of the *Kokumin Kamikaze Tai* who caused the disintegration of his group; they gave themselves up to the *Kempeitai* and were charged and imprisoned. Sasaki himself was to go into hiding until 1959.

A group of kamikaze-style fanatics – in touch with such as *Shosa* Hatanaka – now appeared to target the life of Privy Seal Kido. Known as the *Sonjo Doshikai* (they took their name from the phrase '*Sonno Jo-i*' – 'Revere the Emperor and Expel the Barbarians'), some of them surrounded Kido's Tokyo residence at Akasaka, but were repelled by police guards. Next day they made another attempt to find Kido (who had been in the *Kyujo* all the time) at his brother Dr Konoku Wada's house; again failing in their assassins' mission they left without fuss.

The conspirators Ida, Hatanaka and *Chusa* Shiizaki joined forces and stood outside the *Kyujo* handing out leaflets in one last vain attempt to exhort passers-by to rise up as kamikaze and protect nation and Emperor. The leaflets were met with apathy. Shortly afterwards Hatanaka and Shiizaki shot themselves.

The recorded discs of the Emperor's address to the nation were now taken from their safe place and delivered to NHK's Studio 8. The life of the capital city of Tokyo ground to a halt as noon on 15 August 1945 approached. At 1200 hrs the broadcast was begun with the playing of the *Kimigayo* and the sacred 'Voice of the Crane' was heard.

One who remembered the Emperor's broadcast was writer Kazuo Kawai. In his *Japan's American Interlude* (1960), he recalled:

'First came a squawk and a splutter, then a band playing [the *Kimigayo*], then the hoarse, strained voice of aged [*Sori Daijin*] Kantaro Suzuki in a few words of introduction. In a moment followed the voice of the Emperor. It was a surprisingly musical voice; somewhat high-pitched but gentle, liquid and mellow, a little tired and pathetic, not very clear and sincere. The measured cadences of the classically phrased rescript which the Emperor read were not easy to follow, but there was no doubt about their general import. It meant surrender; but the call was not to arms but to restraint and fortitude in enduring the pangs of defeat.'

Hidden by flowery euphemisms and avoiding the taboo words of 'defeat', 'surrender', and 'capitulation' throughout, the final paragraph of the Imperial Rescript exhorted all to forswear any kamikaze retribution for the surrender. The Emperor's words were:

'Beware most strictly of any outbursts of emotion which may engender needless complications, or any fraternal contention and strife which may create confusion, lead ye astray and cause ye to lose the confidence of the world.'

All attempts at kamikaze action now came to an end. Although an aborted attempt by the Mito Army Air Division on 17 August may be recorded. In reality the vows of Japan's nationalists to become kamikaze for the Emperor were diluted in the confusion of surrender. The spirit of the kamikaze, with its basis in *Bushido* and *samurai* militarism, suddenly vanished. But what happened to the major supporters of the kamikaze action, Onishi and Ugaki?

Early in the morning of 15 August 1945, *Taisa* Takashi Miyazaki, senior officer of 5th Air Fleet, was ordered to *Shosho* Ugaki's new headquarters at Oita, north-eastern Kyushu. The admiral was using a hillside cave for his office, and Miyazaki was directed to it by duty officer *Shosa* Takekatsu Tanaka.

Tanaka briefed Miyazaki that the admiral had ordered the preparation of bombers for a special suicide sortie to Okinawa. Tanaka was of the belief that Ugaki intended to lead the sortie himself; so Miyazaki's first question for his chief concerned the truth of such an intention. Ugaki confirmed that this was his intention. Miyazaki protested strongly. The admiral was adamant, and although Miyazaki withdrew to consult Ugaki's chief of staff, the ailing *Shosho* Toshiyuki Yokoi, neither of them could dissuade the seaman. Persisting, with the assent of *Shosho* Chikao Yamamoto, they approached Ugaki's old and close friend *Shosho* Takatsugu Jojima to join the protesters. The admiral heard out his old friend, then commented: 'This is my chance to die like a *samurai*. I must be permitted this chance. My successor has already been chosen [*Chujo* Ryunosuke Kusaka] and he can take care of things after I have gone.'

Rapidly an order was formulated, and read: 'Oita Detachment of 701st Air Group will attack the enemy fleet at Okinawa with three dive-bombers. This attack will be led by the commanding admiral.' Notice of the order was sent to *Tai-i* Tatsuo Nakatsuru, dive-bomber commander of the 701st, to prepare the aircraft for sortie.

Given that the Emperor had broadcast the surrender, historians have mused over Ugaki's decision to lead a suicide attack, in defiance of the Emperor and violating an Imperial Command. Ugaki must have realised that should his mission be successful, the war might continue with worse consequences to the homeland. Yet in *Record of Sea Battles: Diary of the late Vice-Admiral Matome Ugaki* (1952–3) he writes:

'There are many causes which have brought Japan to this situation. I must assume responsibility. However, to take a broad view, the main cause was the difference in strength between the two nations (Japan and America). I hope that not only military men but the whole Japanese people will endure hardships, stir up the *Yamato* spirit and do their utmost to rebuild the nation so that Japan can have her revenge in the future. I, too, have made up my mind to serve our country forever with the spirit of Masashige Kusunoki.'

So, a small farewell group assembled to hear Ugaki's last commands. He drank a last cup of *sake* with his staff at 5th Air Fleet HQ and voiced his sorrow that his efforts had not been successful in defending his country. With this, accompanied by his staff, his rank insignia removed from his uniform, he headed for Oita airfield. He carried only binoculars and the *samurai*-type sword given to him by Commander-in-Chief of the Combined Fleet *Gensui* Yamamoto; the sword was one of ten that Yamamoto had had made for his chiefs of staff.

Instead of the three aircraft ordered for the sortie, Ugaki saw eleven *Suisei* dive-bombers with twenty-two crewmen lined up with *Hinomaru hachimaki*. Every pilot of *Tai-i* Nakatsuru's command had volunteered for what was to be the last kamikaze trip of the war. Ugaki's last public words have become a part of kamikaze legend. The dialogue went like this:

Ugaki: Commander [Nakatsuru] the order must be given for three aircraft.

Nakatsuru: Although our Commander-in-Chief is going to launch a special attack by himself, we can't stand by and see only three aircraft dispatched. My unit is going to accompany him with full strength.

Ugaki: Will all of you go with me?

Crew: [With acclamation]. Yes, sir.

Ugaki: My thanks to you all.

Admiral Ugaki bade farewell to each of his staff and boarded the *Suisei* to be piloted by Nakatsuru. To his surprise *Hiko Heisocho* Akiyoshi Endo squeezed himself in beside the admiral; he was refusing to be left behind. En route four of the aircraft developed engine trouble and dropped out; seven went on to Okinawa. Back at Oita Air Base Ugaki's last message was received at 1924 hrs and logged from the command aircraft's radio transmission:

'I alone am to blame for our failure to defend the homeland and destroy the arrogant enemy. The valiant efforts of all officers and men of my command during the past six months have been greatly appreciated.

'I am going to make an attack at Okinawa where my men have fallen like cherry blossoms. There I will crash into and destroy the conceited enemy in the true spirit of *Bushido*, with firm conviction and faith in the eternity of Imperial Japan.'

'I trust that the members of all units under my command will understand my motives, will overcome all hardships of the future, and will strive for the reconstruction of our great homeland that it may survive forever. *Tenno Heika Banzai!*'

The transmission ended with the comment that Ugaki's aircraft was crashing into an enemy target. There followed a similar testimony from the other aircraft. In reality no US vessel was recorded as having received a kamikaze attack on 15 August 1945.

But in his book *The Fall of Japan, World War II* (1983), Keith Wheeler records how US seaman Danny Rosewall told a Japanese historian that he had sighted several kamikaze off Iheyaushiro-jima, to the north of Okinawa on 15 August 1945. He reported that next day he examined the wreckage of an aircraft on the beach 'and found three bodies, one of which had an "ornate samurai sword"'. Was this Ugaki? The report is inconclusive. The following quote was found in Ugaki's belongings: 'Having a dream, I will go up into the sky'.

On the evening of 15 August, Takijiro Onishi – 'Father of the Kamikaze' – who had just been appointed Vice-Chief of the Naval General Staff, committed ritual *seppuku* in the second-floor study of his residence. For four days he had endeavoured to persuade members of the government that surrender was unthinkable. It is clear that he was humiliated by the thought that Japan's leaders were not going to sacrifice their lives for their country. So he had borrowed the sword of his aide, Yoshio Kodama, who now found him dying. Onishi refused the traditional *coup de grâce* and died twelve hours after he had plunged the sword into his vitals in the crosswise cuts known as *jumonji*. On his desk was a farewell letter to his wife, framed in the style of a kamikaze pilot saying farewell to loved ones. Before he died Onishi ordered Kodama to take his last suicide declaration (in the form of a letter) to be read out at Atsugi Air Base. It was a plea for the stubborn young men who had held opinions like his own to make the best of the peace:

'I wish to express my deep appreciation to the spirits of the brave Special Attackers. They fought and died valiantly with faith in our ultimate victory. In death I wish to atone for my part in the failure to achieve that victory and I apologise to the spirits of these dead flyers and their bereaved families.

'I wish the young people of Japan to find a moral in my death. To be reckless is only to aid the enemy. You must abide by the spirit of the Emperor's decision with utmost perseverance. Do not forget your rightful pride in being Japanese.

'You are the treasure of the nation. With all the fervour of spirit of the Special Attackers, strive for the welfare of Japan and for peace throughout the world. [Signed] *Chujo* Takijiro Onishi, [died] at the age of fifty-four.'

Yoshio Kodama stayed with Onishi until he died at 1800 hrs on 15 August. In his book *I Was Defeated* (1951), Kodama remembered the funeral of the 'Father of the Kamikaze':

'The casket to contain the remains of *Chujo* Onishi was made by soldiers, but because of a shortage of planks, the casket was five inches too small for the body of the admiral. The naval authorities, who had lost all their dignity and presence of mind as a result of the defeat, did not have the sincerity to provide a casket for one of their own comrades who had committed suicide out of a realisation of his responsibilities. Neither did they have the magnanimity to provide him with a funeral hearse.

'On the way to the crematorium in a truck carrying his body, I saw one naval aircraft flying towards Tokyo from the direction of Atsugi Air Base. It circled slowly over our heads dipping its wings. This was the last tribute being paid by one of *Chujo* Onishi's men. Incidentally, this was the last time that I was to look upon a Japanese aircraft.'

At Atsugi Air Base *Taisa* Yasuna Kozono, the self-appointed recruiter of the last-ditch kamikaze, continued to rant to anyone who would listen to his agitation and was finally restrained, injected with morphine and taken to the Yokosuka Naval Hospital in a strait-jacket.

In his book *Tojo and the Coming War* (1961), writer Robert J. C. Butow avers that army *Taisho* Hideki Tojo (erstwhile Chief of Staff, and Class A war criminal; executed at Sagamo prison, 1948) also delayed a suicide attempt in order to lead a group of kamikaze who had decided to dive on the first American to land on Japanese homeland soil.

As to the later history of other kamikaze supporters, hardly anything is to be found in the public domain on Army *Chujo* Takeo Yasuda, *Shosho* Kenji Yamamoto, *Chujo* Michio Sugawara or *Chujo* Masakazu Kawaba. Little is known of Army *Chujo* Kyoji Tominaga, except that he was captured by the Soviet Army, imprisoned in a Siberian labour camp and released in 1955. Navy *Chujo* Soemu Toyoda was arrested as a war criminal. He was found not guilty and died, aged 72, of a heart attack in 1957. *Choju* Koshiro Oikawa gave evidence at the International War Crimes Trials, Tokyo, 1946–8; *Shosho* Shigeru Fukudome signed the Japanese surrender at Singapore.

The *Nihon Kofuku Bunsho* (Instrument of Surrender) was signed by the *Gaimu Daijin* Mamoru Shigemitsu and Chief of Staff Army *Taisho* Yoshijiro Umezu aboard the USS *Missouri* in Tokyo Bay on 2 September 1945. And some who had survived the kamikaze corps service joined the new Japanese Self-Defence Force (the pre-war military services were disbanded) formed by the New Constitution (1946) or merged into the echelons of Japan's post-war industry. Two such were Army *Shosho* Akira Hirano who joined the Air Self-Defence Force, and Army *Taisa* Morimasa Yunokawa, a founder of the *Hagoromo-kai*.

THE RECKONING

'Correspondents have been prohibited for the past six months from reporting on Japanese kamikaze attacks. This meant that we were forced to pass up reporting on the fiercest assault in this or any other war in history.'
— Robert Charlotte, US War Correspondent in 'News Report'.

Today the last room the visitor walks through in the museum at the *Yasukuni-jinja* is devoted to the artefacts of the kamikaze. Here are swords, flags, leather helmets, *hachimaki*, diaries and calligraphic banners, all offering poignant memories; and, in the last museum case of all is a montage that tugs at the emotions. In the case is a photograph of *Tai-i* Hajime Fujii. Repeatedly he had been refused permission to fly as a kamikaze because he was a family man. Knowing his sadness at this, his wife drowned herself and their three daughters so that he could be free to fulfil his destiny as a kamikaze; his soul took up residence at the *Yasukuni* on 28 March 1945 as the US forces forged into Okinawa. The kamikazes' sacrifice was soon forgotten.

After the surrender Japanese public opinion swung decidedly against the suicide ethic. Even former members of the proud Cherry Blossom Squadrons openly criticised the strategy. Their public thoughts were mixed with the humiliating remarks of the US forces, the *baka* bombers (*Ohka*) were now a public scorn that had once been national pride.

Bereft parents of kamikaze were outspoken in public as never before. The kamikaze missions had 'violated the basic tenets of humanity' they said. The missions had etched the Japanese in history as 'savages in a barbarous country'. 'Kamikaze' became a derogatory term, and articles critical of wartime political leaders and 'fanatic generals' appeared in the popular press. Toadying to the Army of Occupation became rife and for the general Japanese public the once vaunted kamikaze 'gods' were soon forgotten ghosts of war.

What might an overview of the kamikaze tactics reveal for the Allies and for the Japanese? What could be said is that the Allies never really resolved the defence problems raised by the kamikaze attacks. Despite warnings from the radar picket destroyers, the heavy air cover in target areas and intensive anti-aircraft cover from the ships, the Okinawa campaign alone showed that the kamikaze had a 20 per cent success rate in hitting ships, with 25 per cent of the fleet (i.e., 402 ships hit) either sunk or stricken as inoperable.

Kamikaze missions were a constantly dwindling asset because of aircraft and crew losses. It was during the Okinawa campaign that the Japanese High Command saw that the ideological spirit of an élite corps of kamikaze giving their lives for an effective destruction of the enemy had to be abandoned and that all available air units should take part in suicide missions. This self-destruction made the Japanese position even more dire. There is evidence too that pilots were resisting self-sacrifice by returning to base saying they had not encountered a suitable target.

There is more to it than that in the final reckoning for the Japanese. Despite the initial camaraderie among the kamikaze one could not really say that it was a 'team effort' of the 'Dambusters' variety. At best the kamikaze missions were always individual efforts at random targets. Again, pilots (many of them still under instruction) at Okinawa, for instance, hurled themselves at the first Allied vessel encountered. This could mean that they were wasting effort on minor vessels some fifty miles from the main core of the enemy fleet. The Japanese also found it difficult to keep a running survey of what was happening with a view to co-ordinating best efforts, though kamikaze missions against carrier fleets were more effective because of their relative isolation from core fleet formations and their bulk.

Because of these defects the Allied defences, although themselves imperfect, prevailed over the kamikaze and with the fall of Okinawa time was on the Allied side.

GLOSSARY

AND BACKGROUND NOTES OF JAPANESE TERMS AND 'KAMIKAZE' VOCABULARY USED IN THE TEXT

Pronunciation stress-marks have been omitted and the *romaji* (romanisation) of Japanese terms and vocabulary follows the Modified James C. Hepburn System. Where Japanese persons are mentioned, given name then surname are set out in Western style.

Akatombo: 'Red Dragonfly'; Nakajima Model 95 Ki–9 training aircraft.

Amatake: 'Heaven Peak'; name of a *Kaiten* suicide unit.

Baik(w)a: 'Plum Blossom'; name of a Kawanishi-designed aircraft.

Baka: Fool; Allied term for the *Ohka* suicide aircraft.

Bakushi: Traditionally death by the accidental explosion of a bomb. A term used in kamikaze history if a death occurred through premature bomb explosion before hitting a target.

Banzai!: '[May the Emperor live for] 10,000 years.' battle cry; salute; exclamation of joy.

Buntai: [air] division.

Buntaicho: divisional officer, air attack force.

Bushido: 'The Way of the Warrior'. A code of honour on which every warrior was expected to base his conduct.

Chibaya: a castle near the ancient Japanese capital of Nara; name given to a *Kaiten* suicide unit.

Chiji: governor.

Chohi bakugeki: skip bombing.

Chosen: Japanese name for Korea: Japan annexed the country in 1910.

Chu: loyalty to one's feudal lord.

Chu-i: lieutenant (junior grade).

Chujo: vice-admiral: lieutenant-general.

Chusa: commander.

Chutai: air division.

Daimyo: feudal lord; the descendants of this class of aristocrat proved to be a prolific source for the first kamikaze volunteers.

Dai Nippon Teikoku: Empire of Great Japan.

Dai Nippon Teikoku Kaigun: Imperial Japanese Navy.

Dai Nippon Teikoku Rikugun: Imperial Japanese Army.

Daitai: squadron.

Dai Toa Ryozonken: Great East Asian Co-Existence Sphere; commercial scheme for Japanese-occupied countries.

Dai Toa Sen: Japanese name for WWII ('Great East Asia War')

Danshaku: baron.

Domei: official Japanese News Agency.

Eikoku Taishikan: British embassy. (Sir Rutherford Alcock (1809–97), arrived in Japan in 1889 as the first British Consul-General.

Eiyu: man of great deeds.

Fugo: 'Windship Weapon'; balloon carrying incendiary bombs.

Fujujun: disobedience.

Fukuryu: suicide frogman.

Gaijin: foreigner.

Gaimu Daijin: Foreign Minister.

Gaimusho: Foreign Office.

Geisha: 'art person'; a skilled entertainer, witty conversationalist, and skilled in the arts of music, flower arranging and the tea ceremony. Allied personnel mistook them for prostitutes.

Genshibakudansho: radiation sickness.

Gensui: field marshal.

Ginga: 'Milky Way'; Yokosuka PiYi aircraft.

Gobunko: Imperial Library at the Imperial Palace.

Gocho: corporal.

Goi shinju: a family suicide by mutual consent.

Goseimu-shitsu: Imperial Administration Office.

Gozen Kaigi: Imperial War Council.

Gunjin Chokuyu: Imperial Rescript to service personnel.

Gunreibu: naval general staff office.

Gunshin: war gods.

Gunso: flight sergeant; army sergeant.

Gunto: groups.

Gusho: 'Foolish Admiral'; nickname of Admiral Onishi.

Gyokusai: Armageddon; the act of seeking death rather than dishonour.

Hachimaki: headband, being a replica of those worn by medieval *samurai*; it became a uniform accessory of the kamikaze.

Hagoromo-kai: 'Feather-Robe Society' (the name is taken from a traditional story of the magic robe worn by the fairy attendant of the lunar deity). Formed in 1951 to commemorate their dead comrades, this was an association of surviving *Ohka* pilots of 721st Naval Air Corps. By 1972 membership had expanded to include escort crews, bomber pilots and any associates (survivors or families) of kamikaze. They meet tri-annually at the *Yasukuni-jinja*, usually on the day marking the vernal equinox. Prayers are said in the inner sanctum where an altar covered with memorabilia is erected, after which the gathering adjourns to a local restaurant for *sake* toasts, orations, and the re-telling of tall stories.

Hai: 'flies'; nickname for the two-man midget submarines.

Haiku: short Japanese poems of seventeen syllables (three lines of 5-7-5 syllables respectively). Many kamikaze composed *haiku* as part of their final farewell to their families. *Chujo* Takijiro Onishi wrote this in the style of the kamikaze to his wife as a last memento before his suicide:
'Now all is done
And I can doze
For a million years.'

Hakko Ichiu: 'The Whole World Under One Rule'; Japanese national sentiment for occupied territories.

Hakushaku: count.

Hayabusa: 'Peregrine Falcon'; Nakajima Ki–43 aircraft.

Hayate: 'Tempest'; Nakajima Ki–84 aircraft.

Hiko Heisocki: Flight Warrant Officer.

Hikobuntai: air attack force .

Hikodan: air brigades.

Hikojo chutai: air companies.

Hikojo daitai: air battalion.

Hikoki: aircraft.

Hikokitai: carrier air groups.

Hikosentai: air regiments.

Hikoshidan: air divisions.

Hikotai: air group.

Hikotaicho: air group leader.

Hiryu: 'Flying Dragon'; Mitsubishi Ki–67 aircraft.

Hissho Gakuto Renmei: Students' Federation for Victory.

Hito Shogo Sakusen: Operation 'Victory'.

Hitsuji-kai: 'shepherds'; name given to experienced kamikaze pilots of the Okinawa campaign.

Ika: cuttlefish; one of the dishes usually included in kamikazes' last ceremonial meal.

Jibaku: suicide of a kamikaze by aircraft or torpedo.

Jikan Rikugun Daijin: vice-war minister.

Jiketsu: to commit suicide.

Jinrai Butai: 'divine/heavenly thunder'; hence Divine Thunderbolt Corps of kamikaze.

Jisatsu: to commit suicide (modern expression).

Johohei: military intelligence.

Jumonji: crosswise incisions in ritual *seppuku*, as used for example by *Chujo* Onishi.

Junshikan/Jun-i: warrant officer.

Jushin: elder statesman.

Kaigun: Navy. Also used to distinguish a naval as opposed to army (*Rikugun*) rank. Thus *Taisho* (meaning 'admiral' or 'general') can be expressed as *Kaigun Taisho* or *Rikugun Taisho*.

Kaigun Daijin: Navy minister.

Kaigun Heigako: Naval Academy, at Etajima, Hiroshima Bay.

Kaigun Koku Gijutsu-cho: Naval Aeronautical Technology Arsenal.

Kaigun Sho: Navy Ministry.

Kairyu: suicide submarines.

Kaiten: 'Heaven Shaker'; 'dare-to-die' manned torpedo.

Kamanori-kami: 'Thunder God'; respectful nickname for a kamikaze pilot.

Kami: general term for Japanese pantheon of gods.

Kamikaze: 'divine wind'; nickname for suicide pilots.

Kamikaze Tokubetsu Kogekitai: see *Tokkotai*.

Kamisori: razor; nickname of Prime Minister Hideki Tojo.

Kanto Dai Shinsai: great earthquake disaster in the Kanto Plain.

Kashikan: flying petty officer 1st class.

Kembu: 'building up *samurai* spirit'; name given to Zero fighter.

Kempeitai: military police.

Kendo / Kenjutsu: the art of sword fighting; an element of *Bushido* skills highly regarded by kamikaze.

Kesshi: 'dare-to-die' tactics.

Ketan-Go: operational defence plan for Japanese homeland.

Kichikai: 'madmen'; pejorative term for those who behaved suicidally in heat of battle.

Kiku: chrysanthemum; imperial symbol; flower honoured by kamikaze.

Kikumisu: 'chrysanthemum water'; name given to first *Kaiten* unit.

Kikusui: 'floating chrysanthemum'; euphemism for kamikaze attacks in Okinawa campaign.

Kimigayo: Japanese national anthem.

Koe no Tsuru: 'Voice of the Crane'; euphemism for the sacred voice of the Emperor. The Japanese crane is the symbol of the Emperor or The Imperial Throne (cf. *Takamikura*), much as 'The Crown' is synonymous with the British sovereign. An old Japanese saying held that although the crane was hidden from sight its call could always be heard.

Koku: aviation.

Koku Heiss: Petty Officer.

Kokugun: air army.

Koku Hombu: naval aviation HQ.

Kokuki: aircraft.

Kokusentai: air flotilla.

Kokutai: striving for fame and honour for one's country.

Koku Tsushin Rentai: air signal regiment.

Koryu: '[the nation] rises up'; suicide submarine.

Koshaku: marquis.

Kunaicho: Imperial Household Agency.

Kyoku: bureau.

Kyujo: Imperial Palace.

Kyukoko Heiki: national salvation weapon; name given to *Kaiten*.

Manchuquo: Japanese name for Manchuria; today Dongbei, China. From 1931 to 1945 the provinces of modern Heilongjiang, Jilin and Liaoning were a Japanese puppet state. Many kamikaze acquired their combat experience in the Manchurian campaigns.

Maru Roku Heike: 'Circle Six Mountain'; *Kaiten* production project.

Mokusatsu: typical Japanese reaction to a situation by silently ignoring it (from *moku* 'to be silent' and *satsu* 'to kill').

Mombusho: Ministry of Education.

Mure: 'herds'; name given to flight groups of kamikaze in the Okinawa campaign.

Naifu: knife.

Nansei Shoto: main island of Okinawa Gunto.

Nihon Hoso Kyokai (NHK): Japanese Radio Service.

Nihon Isokukai: Bereaved Families' Association.

Nihon Kofuku Bunsho: Japanese Instrument of Surrender.

Nihon Koku Kempo: New Constitution, 3 May 1947.

Nikudan: 'flesh bullets'; suicide soldiers.

Niniroku Jiken: 26 February [1936] Incident – army revolt.

Nishi Kaze: the West Wind.

Nosatsu: votive cards; sent to kamikaze by friends and relatives.

Ohka: suicide aircraft.

Okii sensho: 'Great Victory'.

Okuja: *geisha*-house.

On: gratitude (to one's superiors / mentors / betters).

Otosama no Kamikaze: 'Father of the Divine Wind', i.e., *Chujo* Onishi.

Renzan: 'Mountain Range'; Nakajima bomber.

Rikugun Daijin: War Minister.

Rikugun Koku Sokambu: Inspector-General of Aviation.

Rikugunsho: War Ministry.

Ronin: independent *samurai* (without a master).

Saiun: 'Painted Cloud'; Nakajima long-range reconnaissance aircraft, operational 1944–5.

Sakae: engine produced by Nakajima.

Sake: Japanese rice wine.

Sakura: cherry blossom; much-loved kamikaze symbol.

Sambo: staff officer.

Sambo Hombu: army general staff officer.

Samurai: medieval Japanese warrior; third level of Japanese social class.

Samurai no Kami: 'warriors of the gods'; nickname for *Kaiten* operatives.

Samurai no Umi: 'warriors of the sea'; nickname for *Kaiten* operatives.

Sanzu-no-kawa: the Buddhist Styx.

Sayonara: 'little good-bye'.

Seishin: national spirit.

Sen: Japanese coin.

Senji-kun: ethics in battle; a soldier's code of ethics.

Sennin-bari: 'A thousand stiches worked by a thousand people'; cloth / silk band offering occult protection to the wearer.

Senshi: death in battle.

Sensui Butai: the submarine arm.

Sentotsu: death in battle.

Seppuku: ritualistic disembowelment; the polite version of the vulgar *hara-kiri*. Japan's aristocracy were unique in evolving a highly ritualised method of committing suicide. It underlined the *Bushido* code of 'Victory or Death'. In a general sense it also lauded 'Supreme Honour' (to die fighting for a noble cause) or, 'Supreme Infamy' (to die because of having survived a shameful defeat).

Seto Naikai: the 'Inland Sea'; that part of the Pacific Ocean between the Japanese main island of Honshu to the north and east and the southerly main islands of Shikoku and Kyushu. The scene of much naval training in WWII.

Shiden: 'Violet Lightning'; Kawanishi N1K2–J fighter and fighter-bomber, operational 1944–5.

Shikkan: regent.

Shimbu: 'Gods' warriors'; name of a *Kaiten* suicide group.

Shimpu Tokubetsu Kogekitai: Divine Wind Special Attack Force (cf. *Tokkotai*). Here *toku* (special) is used as a euphemism for *jisatsu* (the committing of suicide).

Shinto: 'The Way of the Gods'; Japan's ancestor-worship religion that was a state institution pre-WWII.

Shinyo: 'ocean shaker'; motor-boats crammed with explosives.

Shinjuwan Kogeki: the attack on Pearl Harbor.

Shishi: lion; name given to 341st Air Group.

Shogun: generalissimos who exerted almost unlimited power in medieval Japan in the name of puppet emperors.

Sho-i: naval rank of ensign.

Shojushi: pilot.

Shokan: general; flag officer.

Shokonsha: shrine where Spirits are invoked.

Shonen hikohei: schoolboy trainees for military duties during WWII.

Shosa: lieutenant-commander.

Shosho: rear-admiral; major-general.

Shotai: platoons/air sections.

Shugo: constable (medieval).

Shutsujei meirei: to fly to certain death.

Sonjo Doshikai: group of 'fight-to-the-death' fanatics who tried to assassinate Privy Seal Koichi Kido. They based their name on the four-character phrase *Sonno Jo-i* used during the *Meiji* Restoration 1867–8 to signify 'Revere the Emperor: Exile the Barbarians'.

Sori Daijin: prime minister.

Suisei: 'Comet'; Yokosuka D4Y dive-bomber and reconnaissance aircraft designed at Yokosuka Naval Air Depot and operational 1942–5.

Sukeibei: 'letchers'; derogatory nickname for those pilots who did not become kamikaze; it was presumed that they preferred the tea-house to active service.

Sumeagi: 'His Majesty'.

Sumo: traditional Japanese wrestling, dating from 23 BC.

Tai-atari: 'body-crashing'; aerial suicide tactic.

Taifu: typhoon.

Tai-i: first-lieutenant.

Taikan-kyoho-shugi: naval strategy devoted to development of 'big warships and big guns'.

Taisa: naval captain; army colonel.

Taisho: admiral; general.

Takamikura: Imperial Throne of Japan.

Tanka: traditional poetic form of 31-syllable verses.

Tatara: the beach in Northern Kyushu where the Mongol fleet was destroyed by the *Kami Kaze* of antiquity; name of *Kaiten* suicide group.

Teikoku Kaigun Ringo Kantai: IJN Combined Fleet.

Teishin Butai: volunteer corps formed to fight to the death.

Tenno: the Emperor.

Tenno Banzai!: 'Long Live the Emperor' (colloquial).

Tenteki kogeki: 'constant dribble'; tactic adopted for *Ohka* suicide bombers, as opposed to massed attacks.

Tenzan: 'Heavenly Mountain'; Nakajima B6N2 aircraft.

Tokko Gunjin: special attack troops.

Tokkotai: special attack units.

Tokonoma: alcove in traditional Japanese home where relics of a kamikaze son would be displayed by proud parents.

Tokubetsu Koto Keisatsu: known as *TOKKO*, these were the 'Thought Police' who sought out and arrested anyone who expressed disagreement with the war policy or questioned the use of kamikaze.

Tokuso: cadet pilots.

Toryu: 'Dragon Slayer'; Kawasaki Ki–45 night-fighter.

Tsurugi: 'Sword/Sabre"; a Nakajima aircraft.

Unubore: (naval) self-conceit/pride.

Washi-kami: 'eagle god'; respectful nickname for a kamikaze pilot.

Yamato-damashii: Japanese *esprit*.

Yasukuni-jinja: shrine at Yasukuni.

Yushukan: museum pavilion at the Yasukuni shrine.

Zeroshiki Kanjo Sentoki: the 'Zero' fighter.

Zuin: 'Auspicious Cloud'; Aichi E1641 collapsible reconnaissance aircraft.

APPENDIX

RELICS

A number of museums in the US and Japan contain relics of the kamikaze. The US relics are too widely scattered to be listed here. The main sources for relic research in Japan are: The Yushukan, The Yasukuni Jinja, 3-1-1 Kudankita, Chiyoda-Ku, Tokyo; The Peace Museum for Kamikaze Pilots, 17881 Chiranthou, Kawabe-gun, Kagoshima 897–03; and the Kaigun Heigakko, Etajima-cho, Aki-Gun, Hiroshima-ken.

WAR GRAVES

The American Battle Monuments Commission (Washington, DC, 20314–03300, confirm that there are no specific war graves for Allied service personnel killed by kamikaze. Those who were not lost (or buried) at sea were interred at the nearest landfall graveyard. For instance, the thirty-one dead from the destroyer USS *Laffey* were taken (17 April 1945) for burial at the 6th US Marine Division Cemetery at Okinawa.

GENERALLY ACCEPTED TOTALS OF KAMIKAZE SORTIES
OCTOBER 1944 – AUGUST 1945

1944	**1945**		
October 55	January 230	April 1,162	August 59
November 143	February 196	May 596	
December 232	March 37	June 210	
		July 20	Total 2,940

THE STATE OF THE WAR IN THE PACIFIC
IMMEDIATELY BEFORE THE BIRTH OF THE KAMIKAZE

1944

2 Jan. Japanese bypassed at Sio; US occupation of Saidor.

31 Jan–23 Feb. US forces invade Marshall Islands; Allies gain control. This is the first pre-war Japanese territory to be captured. Japanese lose Sio, Madang, Green Island; US forces occupy Emirau, Admiralties.

1 Feb. Japanese lose Roi-Namur, Marshalls.

5 Feb. Japanese lose Kwajalein, Marshalls.

10 Feb. Japanese abandon Truk, Caroline Islands as main naval base.

17–18 Feb. Massive US carrier-borne aircraft and ship attack destroys Truk naval base.

15–20 Feb. Solomon Islands cut off by Allies.

19 Feb. US forces land on Eniwetok Atoll and Engebi Island, Marshalls.

31 Mar. *Taisho* Mineichi Koga disappears on flight to Palau; *Chujo* Soemu Toyoda becomes new C-in-C.

3 April. Japanese lose Manus, Admiralties.

22 April. Allies launch major invasion at Hollandia, Dutch New Guinea; Japanese caught off guard and 84,000 US troops establish themselves. Japanese lose Aitapi, New Guinea.

18 May. US forces clear Japanese from Admiralty Islands.

21 May. Japanese lose Wake and Sarmi.

27 May. US troops invade Biak Island, off New Guinea.

31 May. Japanese make first attempts to reinforce Biak.

16 June. Saipan, Mariana Islands invaded by US Marines, Japanese Navy shifts emphasis to this theatre.

19–20 June. Battle of the Marianas. Second 'decisive battle' lost by Japanese Navy.

18 July. *Taisho* Tojo resigns as Prime Minister and Chief of Staff. Cabinet changes reflect escalating desire to end war. Hard-liners talk of 'stronger measures'.

11 Aug. US forces occupy Guam.

12 Aug. US forces occupy Tinian.

20 Aug. US forces take Biak.

15 Sept. US Marines invade Peleliu Island, Palau Group.

22 Sept. Ulithi Atoll in West Carolinas occupied by US Pacific Fleet and used as premier anchorage.

12–14 Oct. Allies organise series of attacks against Formosa from off-shore carriers.

17 Oct. US forces begin landings on islands in Leyte Gulf, Philippines.

The countdown to the birth of the kamikaze begins ...

SEQUENCE HISTORY OF THE AIR AND SEA KAMIKAZE

1931

18 Sept. Japanese troops attack Chinese in Manchuria, South Manchuria Railway cut. RAF foresee possibility of Japanese suicide tactics.

1941

7 Dec. Midget submarines active at Pearl Harbor in unspecified kamikaze missions before the suicide concept evolved in all its horror.

18 Dec. Early use of term *Tokkotai*.

1942

April. Imperial Japanese Navy High Command decide to use mini-submarines for *jibaku* coastal defence.

31 May. Attack day fixed for mini-submarine unspecified kamikaze missions against British forces at Diego-Suarez, Madagascar.

Aug. Escalation of *banzai* attacks at Guadalcanal and the Solomon Islands.

October. *Kesshi* tactics escalate.

1943

Jan. *Shosho* Chumi Takama draws up plan for kamikaze (i.e., human) torpedoes.

Mar. Inspector-General of Army Aviation, *Chujo* Takeo Yasuda commends clandestine *Tokkotai* training programme.

July. *Shosho* Kameto Kuroshima, Chief of 2nd Division of Naval General Staff, advocates suicide attacks at War Preparation Examination Conference.

1944

Feb. Senior Deputy Chief of Army General Staff, *Taisho* Jun Ushiroku advocates use of *nikudan* tactics.

April. *Shosho* Sueo Obayashi, Commander of 3rd Division, 1st Mobile Fleet, and *Taisa* Eiichiro Iyo suggest *Tokkotai* tactics to 1st Mobile Fleet Commander *Taisho* Jisaburo Ozawa.

25 May. 'First officially planned suicide attack on *Submarine-Chaser 699* off the coast of West New Guinea' as recorded by *Tai-i* Hatsuho Naito.

June. Work started on prototypes of suicide submarines *koryu* and *kairyu*.

Sept. The ramming of enemy bombers by Japanese pilots becomes more common.

15 Sept. *Tai-i* Naoshi Kanno, 306th Fighter Squadron, devises version of 'suicide mission', Palau Islands campaign.

October. Plans formulated for employment of *Shin Yo* (suicide torpedo-boats) and *fukuryu* (suicide frogmen).

15 Oct. Personal suicide crash-dive on USS *Franklin* by *Shosho* Masafumi Arima, Commander of 26th Air Flotilla. *Chujo* Soemu Toyoda, C-in-C Imperial Combined Fleet, consents to formation of kamikaze corps.

17 Oct. *Chujo* Takijiro Onishi becomes 'Father of the Kamikaze' and moves to Manila to set up kamikaze corps.

19 Oct. *Taisa* Rikihei Inoguchi suggests that the traditional name 'kamikaze' be used for Onishi's suicide pilots.

20 Oct. *Tai-i* Yukio Seki appointed leader of 201st Air Group Tokkotai. In Leyte Gulf campaign fundamental errors begin to appear in Japanese suicide tactics:
Japanese under-estimate US combat powers.
Failure to develop radar.
Complete waste of pilots/strategists/leaders caused by *Bushido* doctrine's blind insistence on self-destruction in the face of failure
Priorities given by *Chujo* Shigeru Fukudome to air attack against US carriers instead of land defence of battle fleet. *Chujo* Takeo Kurita's failure, through dithering, to exploit Admiral Halsey's fundamental error in not exploiting intelligence reports.

21 Oct. Kamikaze sorties when US Task Force sighted east of Leyte.

23 Oct. *Chujo* Onishi encourages *Chujo* Fukudome, Commander of 2nd Air Fleet, to join kamikaze missions. After initial refusal, Fukudome agrees.

24 Oct. Imperial Japanese Army's 1st Air Group launches kamikaze attacks.

25 Oct. Kamikaze units score first strikes as an official entity. US censor news reports on kamikaze; British Admiralty also recommends silence.

28 Oct. NHK radio station begins to broadcast kamikaze 'successes' (false) as propaganda tool.

29 Oct. USS *Intrepid* first Allied capital ship to be struck by an officially planned kamikaze.

Nov. Plans formulated for every Japanese man, woman and child to form *teishin butai* (suicide waves) to repulse US invaders. Kamikaze attacks become more effective in Philippines campaign.

8 Nov. First sortie of *kaiten* (suicide torpedoes) makes for Ulithi Atoll, Carolinas.

December. Kamikaze successes in Sulu Sea.

23 Dec. Kamikaze units pulled out of Formosa. Kamikaze unable to delay US reconquest of Luzon.

1945

Jan. *Chujo* Onishi assures ground staff that they too are kamikaze. US Intelligence reports number of kamikaze 'miscalculations' by suicide divers because of poor/inadequate pilot training.

6 Jan. Rear Admiral Theodore E. Chandler mortally wounded in kamikaze attack on USS *Louisville*.

9 Jan. *Shinyo* suicide boats attack US Forces in Lingayen Gulf.

10 Jan. West coast of USA 'attacked' by Operation *FUGO* 'divine wind' balloons.

15 Jan. US estimate 1,198 kamikaze pilots lost in endeavour to halt Allied forces.

18 Jan. New kamikaze units inaugurated at Formosa by *Chujo* Onishi.

22–3 Feb. *Kaiten* suicide units active at Iwo Jima.

Mar. A definite pattern established of pilots of crippled aircraft trying to become 'unofficial' kamikaze.

21 Mar. First *Ohka* bomb attack fails.

26 Mar. *Kaiten* suicide units active at Okinawa, as are *Koryu* by April.

6 April–7 May. HMSs *Victorious, Indefatigable, Indomitable, Formidable*, all attacked by kamikaze. First massed *Kikusui* attacks.

12 April. US Naval forces record first encounter with *Ohka* suicide bombers when US destroyer *Mannert L. Abele* is sunk in attack by *Jinrai Butai* Squadron. Release of official statements about kamikaze in US press evoke little public interest because they coincide with news of President Roosevelt's death. Dossier on kamikaze prepared by Lieutenant Commander Ellery Sedgwick, intelligence officer to Admiral Ingolf N. Kiland, who ordered its suppression. Information did reach Chief of Naval Operations, Admiral Ernest King.

26 July. British SE Asia Command ships *Sussex, Ameer* and *Vestal* attacked by kamikaze.

29 July. US heavy cruiser *Indianapolis* (CA-35), Fifth Fleet flagship, after kamikaze attack, sunk (controversial) by suicide *kaiten* in Leyte Gulf; the last major US warship loss of the war.

15 Aug. Emperor Hirohito makes 'Surrender' broadcast. Official end of kamikaze sorties. *Shosho* Matome Ugaki leads last *kamikaze* mission. *Chujo* Takijiro Onishi, 'Father of the Kamikaze' commits suicide.

30 Aug. Last-gasp attack by suicide *Shinyo* on British Pacific Fleet entering Hong Kong harbour.

BIBLIOGRAPHY

PRIMARY SOURCES

Adams, Andrew (ed.). *The Hagoromo Society of Kamikaze Divine Thunderbolt Corps Survivors: The Cherry Blossom Squadrons Born to Die*. Ohara Publications, 1973. (Based on memories of the families and survivors of the suicide pilots.)

Barker, A. J. *Suicide Weapon*. Pan/Ballantine, 1972. (A popular-style illustrated book on Japanese suicide tactics on land, sea and air, within a series *History of World War II*.)

Ebina, Kashiko. *Saigo no Tokko Ki*. Yamashita Mitsuo Tosho Shuppangaisha, 1975. (English trans. *The Last Suicide Plane*, this is the biography of *Shosho* Matome Ugaki).

Hoyt, Edwin Palmer. *The Kamikazes*, Arbor House, New York, 1983. (A history of the kamikaze that includes data on the Army Air Services).

Inoguchi, Rikihei; Nakajima, Tadashi; and Pineau, Roger. *The Divine Wind*. Hutchinson, London, 1959. Copyright data from the US Naval Institute, Annapolis, Maryland, USA. Original Japanese edition: *Shimpu Tokubetsu Kogekitai no Kiroku*, 1951. (A seminal examination of kamikaze history from personal testimony. Contains extracts from the last letters sent to loved ones by kamikaze pilots, collected by Ichiro Ohmi.

Kusanayagi, Daizo. *Tokko no Shizo*. Bungei Horu Aki, Tokyo, 1972. (Trans. as *The Kamikaze Idea*, this is the biography of *Chujo* Takejiro Onishi.)

Larteguy, Jean. *The Sun Goes Down*: Last letters from Japanese Suicide Pilots and Soldiers. William Kimber, 1956. Published in Japan as *Voices from the Sea*. (An anthology of letters collected by a committee of students at Tokyo University.)

Millot, Bernard. *L'Epopée Kamikaze*. 1970. English trans. *Divine Thunder: The Life and Death of the Kamikazes*. McCall Publishing Co, NY, 1971: Macdonald, London, 1971. (A good overall assessment of the kamikaze with a slant towards the US point of view. Relies heavily on Inoguchi, *et al.*)

Nagatsuka, Ryuji. *I was a Kamikaze*. Abelard-Schumann, 1973. (Autobiograpy from enrolment in the Army Air Fleet, through cadet training and air battle experience to the development of the kamikaze tactics)

Naito, Hatsuho. *Ohka Hijo no Tokko Heiki*. (English trans. *Thunder Gods: The Kamikaze Pilots Tell their Story*. Kodansha Int., 1989. (Good descriptive background to the *Ohka* bombers).

Ugaki, Matomi. *Sensoroku*. English trans. *Fading Victory*. University of Pittsburg, Penn., 1991. (Diary of *Shosho* Matomi Ugaki).

Warner, Denis Ashton, and Warner, Peggy. *The Sacred Warriors: Japan's Suicide Legions*. Van Nostrand Reinhold Co, 1982. (A wordy overview of the kamikaze, interlarded with the lives of civilians at home; a little on suicide seagoing vessels).

GENERAL SOURCES

Buton, R. J. C. *Japan's Decision to Surrender*. Stanford University Press, 1954.

Clostermann, Pierre. *Feux du Ciel* (English trans. *Flames in the Sky*), Chatto & Windus, 1952.

Hana, Tameichi. *Japanese Destroyer Captain*. Ballantine, 1961.

Makoto, Ikuta. *Kaigun Koku Tobetsu Kogekitai Shi*. Tokyo. (History of the Army Aviation Special Attack Force)

Morison, Samuel Eliot. *History of US Naval Operations in World War II*. Little, Brown and Co, Boston, Mass., OUP, London, 1958.

Munson, Kenneth G. *Aircraft of WWII*. Ian Allan, 1969.

Roskill, Captain S. W. *The Navy at War, 1939–45*. Collins, 1960.

Spurr, Russell. *A Glorious Way to Die: The Kamikaze Mission of the Battleship Yamamoto, April 1945*. Sidgwick & Jackson, 1982.

Yokota, Y., and Harrington, Joseph. *Kamikaze Submarine*, Leisure Books, New York, 1962.

Boei Cho Bogyo Kenshujo Senshi Shitsu Cho. Tokyo, 1955–6. (Self-Defence Agency War History).

Handbook on Japanese Military Forces. US War Dept., Louisiana State University Press, 1995.

Nihon Rikukaigun no Seido, Soshiki Jinji (System, Organisation and Personnel of Japan's Army and Navy).

Japan's Longest Day. (The Pacific War Research Society). Souvenir Press, London, 1968.

DOCUMENTARY SOURCES

Army General Staff documents of Army kamikaze attacks were destroyed at the end of the war.

NB. Preliminary Narrative: *The War at Sea*, vol VI. Pt II. Jan–Sept 1945, Imperial War Museum, London, 1946.

Other documents mentioned in text.

INDEX